MOTIGRAPHICS

The Analysis and Measurement of Human Motivations in Marketing

Richard C. Maddock

Q

QUORUM BOOKS
Westport, Connecticut · London

Library of Congress Cataloging-in-Publication Data

Maddock, Richard C.
   Motigraphics : the analysis and measurement of human
motivations in marketing / Richard C. Maddock.
      p.   cm.
   Includes bibliographical references and index.
   ISBN 1–56720–284–5 (alk. paper)
   1. Motivation research (Marketing)   I. Title.
HF5415.34 .M33   2000
658.8—dc21   99–27546

British Library Cataloguing in Publication Data is available.

Library of Congress Catalog Card Number: 99–27546
ISBN: 1–56720–284–5

First published in 2000

Quorum Books, 88 Post Road West, Westport, CT 06881
An imprint of Greenwood Publishing Group, Inc.
www.quorumbooks.com

Printed in the United States of America

The paper used in this book complies with the
Permanent Paper Standard issued by the National
Information Standards Organization (Z39.48–1984).

10 9 8 7 6 5 4 3 2

Motigraphics and Silent Side Research are sales marks of Silent Side research.

Copyright Acknowledgments

The author and publisher gratefully acknowledge permission for use of the following material:

Copy reference only to Federal Express Corporation television commercials entitled: (i) FAST PACED WORLD © 1982 Federal Express Corporation. All Rights Reserved; (ii) PICK UP © 1982 Federal Express Corporation. All Rights Reserved; (iii) THE PAPER BLOB © 1981 Federal Express Corporation. All Rights Reserved; (iv) PICK UP THE PHONE © 1982 Federal Express Corporation. All Rights Reserved; (v) NEVER HEAR THE END OF IT © 1982 Federal Express Corporation. All Rights Reserved; (vi) YOU GOT IT © 1983 Federal Express Corporation. All Rights Reserved; (vii) EASY TO USE © 1980 Federal Express Corporation. All Rights Reserved; (viii) OUT OF BUSINESS © 1980 Federal Express Corporation. All Rights Reserved.

This book is dedicated to
the Maddock men,
Jeff, Max, and Ned
Jerry and Biff
Andrew and Matthew
and to the Maddock woman, Elizabeth

Contents

Acknowledgments ix

Introduction: Methods and Methodologies 1

PART I Subliminal Cues

1 Motives, Emotions, and Marketing:
The Silent Side of Human Behavior 9

2 A Eulogy for Professional Psychology 23

3 Subliminal Cues as Discrete Units of Mental
Measurements 37

4 The Right and Left Sides of the Brain 51

5 Consumer Resistance 61

6 Absurdities 73

7 Paradigms and Personalizations 85

Part II Human Motivation

8 The Structure of Human Motivation 103

9 The Orientation Motives 121

10 The Survival Motives 139

11 The Adaptation Motive 167
Diana Gonsalves

12 The Expectation/Resolution Motive 183

13 The Play Motive and Laughter 197

Part III Silent Side Methodology and Measurement of Motives and Desires

14 The Basic Building Blocks of Human Behavior   205

15 Interviewing on the Right Side of the Brain   211

16 Motigraphics   239

Part IV Applications to Advertising and Marketing

17 Specialized Applications   261

18 A Blueprint for Human Motivation   273

Appendix: Motivation Is the Missing Link   281

Name Index   293

Subject Index   297

Acknowledgments

Becky Adair, Bridget Austiguy-Preschel, John Beck, Diana Gonsalves, Bob Gulovsen, Jim Hunt, Jeff Maddock, Max Maddock, Taylor Maddock, John Malmo, Steve Puckett, Rick Robinson, Dave Swearingen, Eric Valentine, and Dick Vineyard.

MOTIGRAPHICS

Introduction:
Methods and Methodologies

> All animals are created equal, but some animals are more equal than others.
>
> —George Orwell, *Animal Farm*

A BETTER BEAR TRAP

I was a Park Ranger in Grand Teton National Park in Jackson Hole, Wyoming, the first year that the park opened as one of our nation's officially recognized national parks. One of my jobs was to keep the bears out of the campground. Since this was an impossible task, my job description was rewritten and stated that my duties were actually to *get* the bears out of the campground, not to keep them out. Since they usually came at night, that's when I worked. The bears' objective, of course, was to get to the bacon and other goodies that were safely sealed away in the Coleman ice chests that everyone had at that time and were quite easily opened. Bears are rather intelligent creatures and had learned where the ice chests were kept (in tents) and had discovered that it only took one swipe of a bear paw to tear open a tent. Subsequently they had learned to open the ice chest, which at that time was sealed with a tiny stainless steel hasp. Following that sequence of events, they took over the campground, moving from campsite to campsite in a kind of "movable feast."

The National Park Service has a policy of preservation, whereas the Forest Service's policy is conservation. Under a policy of preservation, pesky bears are not shot or destroyed no matter how pesky they become, and that's the way it should be. So my job was to trap them in a steel trap which consisted of two fifty-five gallon barrels welded together with a trigger at the end. The trigger held a ham bone, some bacon or some dead fish. The bear would smell the bait, hop up inside the barrels and pull on the trigger, and this would drop a heavy steel gate over the entrance. At that point the bear would raise all kinds of commotion and create an enormous disturbance which awakened all of the campers in the campground who in turn would call me at the ranger station. My job was to haul the bear thirty miles out into a wilderness area, open the gate and set him free.

The only problem with this whole methodology was that the bear trap was hooked by a trailer hitch to a 1956 six-cylinder Chevrolet pickup. This was a rather slow and cumbersome combination, and most of the time the bear would beat me back to the campground. So this scenario was repeated over and over again; enough so that I actually began to recognize the various bear offenders by sight and call them by names that I would give them.

This all occurred forty years ago, during the first three years that Grand Teton National Park was open to the public. Fialka (1999) reports on this same species of bear in Yosemite and Yellowstone National Parks. However, today, instead of opening ice chests, they have created over $11 million worth of damage to auto-mobiles by forcing open the doors and opening the trunks. Fialka says that the bears have developed a very specific methodology or frame-work for getting into the cars. Not only do they prefer certain models (Hondas and Toyota Tercels), but they have learned to insert their claws into the upper part of the door (or windows on vans) and pull downward. They stop halfway down, and the destroyed door pro-vides them with a stepladder into the car. They then proceed to the back seat, where they tear through the upholstered seat back and into the trunk, where the goodies are stored.

Fialka presented this scenario as if it is a deplorable situation, which I am certain that it was to the various car owners who were visited by the bears. But to me it represented some real progress. In only forty years, these same bears had progressed from opening Coleman ice chests to opening the doors to Toyota Tercels, Ford Windstars, and late model Hondas and Buicks. Isn't this progress? Isn't this, in a way, what evolution is all about? Who knows? In another forty years they may be driving off in the latest model se-dans (they seem to prefer red), with the goodies in the trunk, thumb-ing their noses at the indignant and terrorized tourists! In fact, some park officials predict that it will only be a few years before they find the Yosemite grocery store and discover the numerous and abundant vending machines that are stationed around the park. What is important here is that the bears have a methodology or a framework which they are systematically teaching to their cubs. With a system in place, there's no telling how far a person (or a bear) can go. Some animals are smarter than others.

IF IT DON'T WORK, FIX IT

A few years ago I met my oldest son on a college campus, a few hundred miles from our home, to be with him for Thanksgiving. He was a graduate student in a university, working on his Ph.D. in psychology. He took me on a tour of the facilities, including the psychology laboratories where they were running experiments with rats, monkeys, and pigeons. What was eye opening and at the same time appalling to me was that it was clear that in these laboratories they were doing the same thing that we had done in graduate school twenty years before that. I couldn't believe it. It looked to me as if the "science" of psychology had made no progress in twenty years, and it appeared as if it was standing still. It was possible that it had even regressed. And as I continued to read the professional journals that I subscribed to, it became even more clear that the same wheels were being spun and the same songs were being sung. And that's true even today. Fortunately, my son soon realized this, dropped out of school, and finished an MBA. Today he is a successful director in a large corporation and is looking forward to a bright future. I am very proud of him because he has, since that time, made a whole series of good decisions that have put him on the right track.

As an adjunct professor I have worked with teachers who are pursuing master's degrees in education and in management. It is quite clear that the psychological methods that they are familiar with in the classroom are not working or, if they do work, are too cumbersome and unwieldy to apply. Behavior-modification methodologies that require an observer to record every response that a child makes are unworkable. Kohn (1993) had indicated that these methodologies are not only quite unworkable in educational, managerial, sales, and other settings but often have an effect that is the opposite of what is intended.

Much of what professional psychology offers to people today clearly does not work. Managed care has all but stopped paying for psychotherapy, which has not demonstrated efficacious results. Behavior-modification methods have very limited applications because of their hopeless oversimplification of human behavior. These methods have all but been abandoned by educators and others who welcomed them in the past. And "cognitive psychology," which is now promoted as the wave of the future in psychology (Abra, 1993; Bornstein & Masling, 1998), is nothing more than behavior modification reintroduced in a new disguise. It is becoming clearer and clearer to managed care gurus, psychologists, and their patients that indeed the emperor does not have any clothes.

THE FIX

Although it will become clear in Chapter 2 that the methodologies developed by psychologists over the last 100 years have yielded very little in terms of results, it is already quite clear that the methodologies developed in medicine during the same time span have had considerable success and have helped millions of people. Shorter (1998), in an article entitled "How Prozac Slew Freud," indicates that "Thorazine's obvious effectiveness in 1952 gave it the same persuasive punch as Penicillin and initiated the search for other kinds of psychiatric drugs."

The difference in what psychology has done and what medicine has done is commonly referred to as the *medical model*. In psychology, therapists and experimenters trained in the model of behaviorism or cognitive psychology look at and address symptoms and signs, not at underlying causes. On the other hand, the medical practitioner looks at underlying causes and explanations. Although symptoms are certainly considered in medicine, the real issue in medicine is always the underlying cause. A person who has a temperature is not placed in an ice bath; instead, they are effectively treated with antibiotics which attack the underlying causes of the problem until the person gets well.

I worked closely and effectively with a psychiatrist in his practice for a number of years. We not only worked together with patients, but we authored many articles together on new methodologies and techniques. Although I was subjected to some criticism by colleagues in psychology for some of the things that we wrote about, we continued to treat patients in this manner and write articles, eventually initiating our own journal. I was able to observe a pattern of looking at underlying causes and using an effective combination of psychotherapy and medication to treat these underlying causes effectively. We carried out research and patient-satisfaction surveys and were able to measure our results. As I look back and try to explain some of the effective results that we obtained, the only explanation that makes sense is the medical model. The fact is that we did look at underlying causes, and not just behavior. We addressed the underlying causes of the patients' problems, and this method was effective.

Many of the principles that have been applied in this and another marketing book written by us (Maddock & Fulton, 1996) have their roots in the medical model. They deal with underlying causes. As a result, when we do a marketing project, marketers learn things about their product or service that they never knew before. They get explanations and not just descriptions. They do not get the same information over and over again, year after year. They don't hear about the symptoms of their problem(s), they hear about the causes and how to address and correct them. They are not taught how to live with their problems, they are taught how to cure them.

METHODS

This book is about methods. First, we have developed building blocks of human motivation which make sense, and which have been tested in the real world with research. We have looked at over 5,000 people and where they spend their money. We have examined over 250 product and service areas, such as theme parks, casinos, grocery stores, on-line services, restaurants, and so on. We have asked people questions about why they do what they do, and when they couldn't answer that question (since most people can't respond to the question "why"), we asked the same question over again, in different ways. This is similar to the way that an attorney conducts a deposition or courtroom examination and gets to the bottom line and to the truth. We asked people obvious questions, and ones that were not so obvious. The complete description of this methodology and the way that it was carried out is found in Chapter 15.

After developing the building blocks of motives, fully described in Chapter 8 and the other chapters in Part II, we found the elements of motives and how these elements fit together to make an individual motive, and then how the motives fit together in an entire structure which describes human behavior in the marketplace as well as in the workplace.

The next step was finding out how to measure the motives. This is the method that we call *Motigraphics*. It is elementary, but it forms the basis and the foundation for further statistical analysis and ways of looking at motives through more advanced techniques, such as cluster analysis, factor analysis, and multidimensional scaling. These methods are beyond the scope of this book, but they are mentioned for purposes of further developing this approach.

Motigraphics also gives us the ability to graphically represent customer motives and desires, which has not been done before. Hence, this is truly a breakthrough. Also, we are capable of presenting Motigraphics as the third dimension in consumer behavior; that is, to take its rightful position alongside demographics and psychographics. Without Motigraphics, the marketer knows only two-thirds of what he or she needs to know about his or her customer. With Motigraphics, the marketer knows almost all of what he or she needs to know about his or her customer. With Motigraphics, demographics, and psychographics, the marketer knows it all.

Our research has spanned a period of twenty-five years. Most of the factors that are found in the building blocks of human motivation have been derived by empirical methods; most notably, factor analysis. Factor analytic studies were carried out on nonconsumer (mostly adult student and production worker) populations.

TO BUILD A BETTER BEAR TRAP

To put this book on a more scientific and technical basis, we started off with a longitudinal "study" of the progress of the North American black bear over a period of forty years. This is a very respectable time frame for a longitudinal study, even if our research methods may have been somewhat casual and informal. We also looked at and included (or will examine later) some methodologies that have been very effective (medicine and advertising) and some that have not been effective (psychology). The results are seen in the ensuing chapters. The bottom line is that we define, measure, and formulate an approach to motivation that has been all but ignored by those who are supposed to define it: psychologists, marketers, and other social scientists who study people.

In comparing our situation in the study of motives and motivation with that of the North American black bear, we believe that we have made a breakthrough, just as the bear has made a breakthrough in moving from the ice chest to the automobile. Now that we know about motives and motivation, and now that we can measure motives, who knows what the next forty years might bring.

REFERENCES

Abra, J. (1993). *Should psychology be a science?* Westport, CT: Praeger.

Bornstein, R. F., & Masling, J. M. (1998). *Empirical perspectives in the psychoanalytic unconscious.* Washington, DC: American Psychological Association.

Fialka, J. (1999, January 13). Toyotas and Hondas for late night snacks. *Wall Street Journal.*

Kohn, A. (1993). *Punished by rewards.* New York: Houghton-Mifflin.

Maddock, R. C., & Fulton, R. L. (1996). *Marketing to the mind: Right brain strategies in advertising and marketing.* Westport, CT: Quorum Books.

Shorter, E. (1998, September). How Prozac slew Freud. *American Heritage,* pp. 43–53.

PART **I**

SUBLIMINAL CUES

1

Motives, Emotions, and Marketing: The Silent Side of Human Behavior

Demographics and psychographics have long been the key to the analysis of consumer behavior. No marketer would attempt to write a marketing plan without using these two "tools of the trade." Just as a physician or a dentist relies upon x-rays and physical examinations, marketers have made giant strides since these two methodologies became available to them.

What has been missing, however, is a third dimension. That dimension is customer motivation. Every marketer has asked, at one time or another, "What motivates my customer to do what they do?" It would seem like the most likely approach to getting an answer to this question would be to ask the customer directly: "Why do you do what you do?" But unfortunately, most people can't tell you why they do what they do. And the reason is that much of the variation in human behavior has its origins in the unconscious mind.

For example, why would a customer pay $35,000 for a car when she could buy one for $12,000? Why would she purchase a boat for $200,000 that she only visits once or twice a year? Or why would she drive past three or four banks to get to "her bank," and then tell the researcher that her most important consideration in choosing a bank is convenience? These examples defy rational explanations, and without knowing what really motivates customers we will never know the "real" answers.

Motigraphics is the third dimension of consumer behavior, ranking with demographics and psychographics. Motigraphics is the measurement of motives, and it allows us to take qualitative data that arise from focus groups and other discussion-type settings and turn them into quantitative data that can be ranked, compared, covaried, and normalized. Motigraphics allows the empirical investigation of that third dimension of consumer behavior. That third dimension, motives, has been considered by many marketers and advertisers to be the most important factor in customer behavior, even before it could be measured.

The fact that motives can now be described quantitatively and not just qualitatively allows for a more effective and efficient prediction of what people will do and when they will do it. As McClelland (1987) has stated, "The key to progress in science lies not only in theoretical clarification, but also in adequate measurement" (p. 588). Trend lines become more stable and more predictive of future trends. Clusters become easier to interpret. Research becomes more reality oriented and less academic. New insights come to the surface and recommendations are much more abundant and bountiful.

SUBLIMINAL CUES

The key to motivation lies in the subliminal cues that consumers act upon, often without knowing why they do what they do. These subliminal cues come from many sources, but a large number of them come from television and other entertainment mediums. Although we don't like to admit it, subliminal cues are entering our minds in large numbers every day. And the reason that we don't like to admit it is because if we do, we also have to admit that we don't have complete control over what goes into our minds and into our brains.

An example of how subliminal cues enter our minds is best illustrated by the way that television works. Television shows entertain. But one of the most effective ways that subliminal cues can be implanted is when the "recipient" of the cues is relaxed, with all his or her defenses down, which is almost always the case in a scenario involving entertainment. This is why Procter & Gamble, Chrysler, and others will pay big dollars to get their products "sneaked" into one or more of the scenes, a television revenue producer called *promotional consideration.*

In the 1950s, a theater in Fort Lee, New Jersey ran a message across the screen at one-sixtieth of a second. The message said, "Eat popcorn." Popcorn sales went up. But the FCC decided that this was deceitful and misleading, and so laws were enacted that prohibited messages that could not be seen and deciphered at the conscious or rational level. Whether or not the message was really responsible for an increase in popcorn sales was never firmly decided.

In the 1970s, a television sitcom called "All in the Family" entertained record numbers of viewers, using some of the finest actors of the decade. This sitcom, produced and directed by Norman Lear, had a double message. One message was entertainment, pure and simple; watching Archie Bunker (Carrol O'Connor) make a fool of himself. But the other message, which was the subliminal one, was to change people's attitudes about racism and segregation in America. This was a tall order, but it worked, probably better than any show on television or any other attempt to reduce segregation in America has ever worked. The message that the viewing audience got was that racism is narrowminded, dogmatic, and stupid. And no one wanted to be branded with that profile. Slowly but surely, many viewers moved away from that profile in an attempt to be less and less like Archie Bunker and more and more like Gloria and Edith, who were more liberal and broadminded, and less race conscious. The subliminal message was that younger, better educated, and forward-looking people are tolerant, progressive, and unbiased, and that was the direction in which the world seemed to be moving.

One subliminal message that television delivers today is a message of conformity to social norms. Sitcoms as well as sixty- and ninety-minute dramas deliver the message of political correctness to families, particularly during prime-time television. This message includes racial harmony, as blacks and whites are often seen working and living together and occasionally in romantic involvements and intrigues with each other. Women are seen in commanding executive and professional positions, where they wield authority that they have not had in the past. Unfortunately, white males are often shown as buffoons who not only use bad judgment but are clumsy and have no social skills. A new twist is seeing women punching men and laying them out on the floor. What a beautiful example of a subliminal cue. On television, not only are women smarter than men, since they command the key management positions, but they are tougher and end up competing at all levels.

Subliminal cues emanate from other sources and not just from television; particularly from childhood experiences, intense medical procedures, traumatic and emotional events that occur during a lifetime, and "flashbulb memories." As expected, the strongest and most prominent cues are from life experiences, and not from television or from the movies.

MOTIVATION

Subliminal cues are the DNA of motivation. Subliminal cues tend to group themselves together and "fold" themselves into motives.

Motives are what make customers and potential customers (or ex-customers) do what they do, when they do it. Almost any businessperson, politician, professional, or anyone else needs to know what motivates their customers/constituents/patients in order to service them properly. However, until recently, it has not been possible to know what motivates customers since there was little if any direction on this, either in the literature or any place else. We might put forward the statement that the only businessperson who really knew the motivation behind his or her customers' behavior was the professional paramour or prostitute!

In 1996, we introduced a structure of motives and motivation that was based upon three major sources. The first source was advertising. We looked closely at advertising and ad persons, because they work closely every day with human motives and motivation. If an ad agency is about to spend $3 or $4 million of its client's money on advertising, then they need to know what motivates the viewers.

A second source for motivation was the research that was done on the brain and the central nervous system which took place during the "Decade of the Brain," which ran from about 1987 to 1997. During this period, major expenditures were made by our government in sponsoring brain research, and particularly research into the areas which control and regulate the expression of emotion. From this research, all kinds of new antidepressant and antipsychotic medications appeared on the market, most of which worked directly on the neurotransmitters and synapses of the brain. The names Xanax, Prozac, and Paxil, among others, have now become household terms. One of the major sources that we used to uncover these findings and report them was MacLean (1990).

The third source that we relied upon was empirical investigation, using statistics to validate our findings. The empirical investigation has always been the hallmark of psychological research. However, during the twentieth century, as psychology has struggled to be a "science," empirical methods have assumed the position of the tail wagging the dog. Therefore, our first attempt at describing motivation was to conduct over 5,000 individual interviews in both clinical and consumer settings. It was only after these one-hour, in-depth individual interviews took place that we could begin using multivariate techniques and statistics to lend support to our beliefs about what really motivates people to do what they do.

After combining the insights of the professions of advertising, neuroscience, and empirical investigations, we feel that we have a reliable three-point platform that allows us to describe motives and motivation in some detail. In addition to that, we have conducted over 2,500 consumer interviews in over 250 product areas. From these in-depth, one-hour interviews we have examined a plethora of products that range from termites to tissue paper, from automobiles to zebras (i.e., from a to z). From all these investigations and techniques we have evolved the building blocks of human motivation that are seen in Figure 1.1.

MOTIVES, MARKETERS, AND MOTIVATION

Marketers have gone on so long without a handle or an understanding of motives that they now find it very difficult to try to integrate motives and motivation into their plans. What will motives tell us that other schemes have not told us? What will motives do that positioning won't do? Why are motives more important than demographics? Psychographics? Cluster analysis? Behavior modification? Rewards? We could go on and on.

Motives are important and motives are unique because they tell us why consumers do what they do. We already know what they do, how they do it, when they do it, and where they do it. Motives give us the why. Why is why important? Why is important for two reasons:

1. because consumers can't tell you why they do what they do.
2. because most consumer decisions are based on emotion and not reason.

Figure 1.1
Building Blocks of Human Motivation

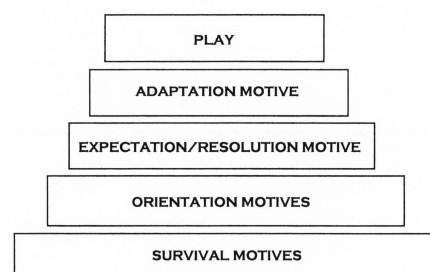

The first reason is generally accepted. We are free to ask people anything that we want to ask them in surveys and in focus groups, but we can't ask them why. Why is off limits for several reasons, but the most important reason is that consumers can't answer that question. They can tell you that they did not like your hotel or your automobile, but they can't give you the real reasons why they won't come back or won't buy another one of your cars. This is generally accepted by most marketers.

The second assertion, that most consumer decisions are based upon emotion and not reason, is more debatable. It is debatable because it takes us into the realm of emotion, which in psychology, marketing, and other fields is considered an abyss. In business, we are told to ignore emotion, or at least to cover it up when it rears its ugly head. But this at best creates a schizophrenic situation, where we may be in the business of selling emotion and passion to our customers (theme parks, sports, videos, screenplays, etc.), but at the same time trying to screen it out of our own lives and our own day-to-day interactions with other people.

Also, emotion is an integral part of motivation. Ashforth and Humphrey (1995) have indicated that the traditional approaches to motivation in the workplace have overlooked the connection between the individual and his or her work. We refer to this as *intrinsic motivation*. Theories of reward and reinforcement cannot explain why some individuals literally live for (and are willing to die for) their work. These writers refer to Kahn (1990, 1992) and his assessment of three levels of motivation:

The lowest investment is solely physical (i.e., devoid of cognitive or emotional involvement); the next level is cognitive, the traditional focus of rational theories of motivation; and the highest level is emotional, typified by the individual who forgets to have dinner and works late into the night, isolated in the thrill of her work. Individuals experiencing high "personal engagement" (Kahn, 1990, 1992) and "flow" (Csikszentmihalyi, 1990), become physically, cognitively and emotionally immersed in the experience of the activity, in the pursuit of a goal. In a real sense they may forget themselves and their context, and rational calculations of inducements and contributions cease to be salient. Fine (1988) quotes a cook discussing the "high" that characterizes smooth performance: "I just love the activity . . . I concentrate totally, so I don't know how I feel. . . . It's like another sense takes over." (p. 125)

It is clear that these various theorists are talking about the whole phenomenon of losing oneself in one's work. This is often seen in computer software developers, who forget to go home at night and eventually fall asleep at their desks from fatigue, not even noticing where they are or the fact that they need rest. This phenomenon is covered in the emotional structure that we have presented and which is further detailed in this book. Specifically, what we refer to as the *Orientation Motives* (orientation to person, place, time, and circumstances) completely cover the contingencies that have just been described. These motives, individually and separately, explain how and why an individual becomes intrinsically motivated and, in Ashforth and Humphrey's (1995) terminology, this only happens at the highest of the three levels of emotional involvement. Hence, the integral and essential link between emotions and motives. All consumer choices involve some degree of emotion, and this is seen in Chapter 5, where the relationship between reason, resistance, and emotion is presented graphically.

Up to now, the only choice available to marketers has been what Ashforth and Humphrey (1995) refer to as levels one and two, the purely physical and the cognitive. Now, with Motigraphics, we add the third level, and that is the emotional and intrinsic level of motivation. One reason that it has not been addressed in the past is that it was not measurable, but Motigraphics now ensures that it can be measured and calibrated, which is what this book is about.

According to Ashforth and Humphrey (1995), all the literature to date holds what they call an overrationalized view of individuals. This point of view holds that individuals are basically motivated by outcomes, such as grades, money, bonuses, bribes, and so on. Ashforth and Humphrey say that this is an "image of rational exchange," and that what is missing is the emotional connection between the individual and his or her work. Motigraphics supplies that connection and measures the strength of that connection.

Strong motivation and psychological involvement are not possible without an emotional connection between oneself and one's work. The boss would like everyone to feel the same way that he or she does about their work, but at the same time rules out the expression of emotion in the workplace. This is the most flagrant example of a double standard that we know of. Without emotion there can be no motivation. Again, the boss wants everyone to feel the same way he or she does about his or her work, but is the boss not emotional about the company that he or she is heading?

The assertion that most consumer decisions are based upon emotion and not reason may be unpopular. People in general do not want to believe that their decisions are based upon emotions. They offer formidable resistance to this notion, and this resistance is detailed in Chapter 5. They also offer justifications and rationalizations, so that their behavior will not be construed as irrational or emotional. This is particularly important when an individual is spending hard-earned money. They offer these rationalizations not only to others but also to themselves.

MOTIVES AND MOTIGRAPHICS

Motives and emotions operate upon what we refer to as the *Silent Side* of the mind. It is silent because many if not most of its operations take place in the unconscious, which implies that we are not conscious of the operations during the time that they are taking place. For example, we don't actively "think" about walking down a flight a stairs when we do it. The motor skills involved in doing this are automatic and unconscious.

This unconscious part of the mind is also silent because it does not use words or language to express itself. It "thinks" in pictures or graphics, not in words. This is why a student, when studying for an important examination, will try to construct what he or she needs to remember in terms of a picture. If successful, the student finds that the data that he or she needs to know for the test are much more memorable when they are saved in a visual format. These visual formats are referred to as *mnemonics*.

The most well-known mnemonic that is used in medical school is, "On Old Olympus towering top and fat, again Greek poured some hops." This mnemonic, which paints a rather unusual or even absurd picture in the mind, serves as a reminder of the twelve cranial nerves: olfactory, optic, oculi, trochear, trifacial, abducent, facial, auditory, glosso-pharyngeal, pneumogastric, spinal accessory, and hypoglossal. The chances that this will be recalled at the crucial time—on a test—improves 200 percent with the mnemonic picture of the fat, old Greek drinking beer on top of Mount Olympus.

Motives and emotions are on the Silent Side. This makes them much more inaccessible than words and language. Since researchers like the convenience of getting data over the telephone or on a five- or seven-point scale, they are limited to looking at rational responses rather than irrational and emotional ones. This means that most research typically overlooks emotion and, by default, overlooks motivation. It is quite clear that in order to study these aspects of the mind, the researcher has to bypass words and language. Typically, this has not been done. Even very recent studies of motivation (e.g., Reiss & Havercamp, 1998) rely upon written profiles and verbal responses in order to assess motivation.

For this reason, as well as for several others, motivation has not been studied and, to date, has never been measured. Initially, using the methodology that we will be covering in this book, we were able to describe and define motivation but could not measure it, simply because of the Silent Side factor. However, Motigraphics allows us not only to describe and define emotions and motives but also to put numbers to these most important and powerful causes of human behavior.

METHODOLOGY

The method of defining motives and then measuring them that we will introduce in this book involves the following steps.

First, subliminal cues will be defined. A subliminal cue is a word, a phrase, or a graphic that we either give ourselves or is given to us by others (notably television or movies), often (but not always) under conditions of stress and trauma. These subliminal cues tend to stay with us for a long time, even for an entire lifetime. We have arrived at this definition by transcribing every word that a respondent says in one-on-one interviews, and then inserting these phrases into the motives that we have outlined in Figure 1.1.

Second, motives are defined in terms of the building blocks of human motivation that are found in Figure 1.1. These building blocks express the order of the importance of things.

Third, one-on-one interviews, which are defined and described in detail in Chapter 15, are conducted in which *visualization* is promoted and preferred over *verbalization*. In order to ensure this visualization respondents are blindfolded and then taught simple visualization skills.

Fourth, we recognize that our statistical universe or population is subliminal cues and not people. Therefore, we can carry out this part of the process with small numbers of people (ten to fifteen), since ten people yield 120 to 150 subliminal cues. Similarly, twenty people will yield 240 to 300 cues, but there will be many duplicates and the process quickly reaches a point of diminishing returns.

Fifth, the subliminal cues fold into motives and are counted.

Sixth, the frequency count of subliminal cues determines the strength of each motive in the study. Most products do not involve all of the motives that we have defined. An exception is automobiles, which do involve and appeal to all eleven motives.

Seventh, the motives are *normalized*, or placed on a normal distribution or bell curve, so that they may be compared with one another and compared with motives of other products. This is a statistical process and is described in Chapter 15.

Eighth, motives are converted into T-scores so that they may be graphed and diagrammed, and so that they may be entered into other studies and regressed or covaried with demographics, psychographics, zip codes, or any other quantitative measure of consumer behavior. T-scores are preferable since they have a mean of fifty and a standard deviation of ten, and are therefore easy to work with.

Ninth, motives are grouped together for purposes of presentation. For example, a marketer may want to know which motives form his or her loyal customer groups, or which motives cause a customer to change to another provider (negative motivation). Motives, being closely associated with emotion, also allow us to measure the equity that is in a brand, and combine this with sales, expenses, and the like. Brand equity is the emotion that is associated with a product.

Tenth, the motives that have been uncovered and which define Motigraphics can be used to construct a questionnaire that may then be used in telephone or intercept interviews to include a much larger sample (150 to 300 people or more) in what we refer to as *Extended Motigraphics*. While we have said that written questionnaires cannot be used effectively to assess emotions and motivations, Extended Motigraphics is not a contradiction, since the motives have already been defined in the Motigraphics or in the visualization stage of the interview. By the time we enter the stage of Extended Motigraphics, we know what the motives and emotions are. We are merely asking the respondent to agree or disagree to the various motivational categories, and consumers do recognize their own motives once they are pointed out to them.

A second apparent contradiction is that we said that we reach a point of diminishing returns when we go beyond twelve or fifteen people. This is only because some marketers don't like to make their decisions on the basis of twelve or fifteen people. They prefer larger numbers. Hence, Extended Motigraphics is really a validation of what we found in Motigraphics. Many of the marketers that we have dealt with are very comfortable with the idea that the statistical universe or population is subliminal cues, and not people. When they do a study with fifteen people that yields 150 subliminal cues, this is enough for them. Others feel that there is safety in numbers.

The combination of Motigraphics and Extended Motigraphics not only provides access into most of the unconscious processes of the consumer, but also will work with any size sample that the marketer requires.

WHAT ABOUT MASLOW?

Whenever motives are mentioned, the name of Maslow comes up. This is because Maslow (1970) put his motives into a neat little pyramid, which is very easy to remember. When cramming for a test in graduate school, it's always nice to have a graphic which serves as a mnemonic device.

In *Marketing to the Mind* (Maddock & Fulton, 1996), we introduced the reader to the possibility that Maslow's hierarchy of motives may not be a workable solution to the whole issue of motivation. It is unscientific, unworkable, and has no basis in fact. For example, we showed that if physical survival was really the bottom-line motive, then people would not commit suicide and they would not experiment with dangerous substances like cocaine and heroin. They would not use alcohol and would not smoke cigarettes.

Then why is Maslow still the industry standard for describing what motivates people? The answer is that it is a graphic, and therefore easily remembered. Nevertheless, Maslow's explanations of motivation don't help teachers to understand why school children do what they do, or marketers to create exciting and motivating advertising campaigns, or salespersons to understand what makes people buy. Soper, Milford, and Rosenthal (1995) summarized this problem in the abstract to their landmark article: "Maslow's hierarchy of needs is frequently cited in texts, even though most of the evidence has failed to support its validity. Science requires that theory be supported by empirical facts. . . . Reasons are given and empirically supported for the continued popularity of Maslow's theory in marketing despite lack of scientific support" (p. 415). These investigators conclude their review by citing Rothman (1989) in cautioning marketers: "The option is not the decades-old debate whether to have either a science or an art of marketing but, instead, whether to have a science or a parascience of marketing" (p. 34).

SILENT SIDE

The history of psychology, at least in the twentieth century, seems to have been to present a scientific procedure that is as close as possible to what physical science has done, and in order to do this, emotion has had to be excluded. This is because emotion is so hard to control and therefore to research. This is not unusual. We are told, whenever we go into business and professional situations, that emotion is unwelcome and unacceptable in a business setting. It is off limits. And yet, as Ashforth and Humphrey (1995) have noted, Freud, Jung, and others have suggested that emotions that are covered up and swept under the carpet will have a way of breaking through the thin veneer of rational thinking and causing destructive and disruptive results. Ashforth and Humphrey also raise some very practical questions related to how organizations that sell emotional arousal in the form of books, music, videotapes, sporting events, or other emotionally laden issues tend to function when on a day-to-day basis they are involved in hiding and suppressing emotion within their organization.

Our own approach, which we consider more innovative and applicable, is to abandon the misleading theories of behaviorism, humanism, and cognitive psychology in favor of our three-phase approach. We begin with subliminal cues, which are described in Chapter 3, and then fold these cues into motives, which are described in Chapters 8 through 13. These motives can then be measured in terms of their relative strength and contribution to the overall appeal of the products being investigated (Chapters 15 and 16).

Since we work closely with consumers, we are always in contact with the products that they use. With this in mind, we have found that motives change with products. Unlike most psychologists, who measure traits that are stable across time, the motives that we measure change from product to product. Motives involved in health care are not the same as the motives involved in banking or in attendance at sporting events. Nevertheless, the structure of human motivation that is shown in Figure 1.1 contains what we believe to be the human motives which account for all human behavior at one time or another. These motives also assume a particular structure when at rest. This structure, which is supported in factor analysis and fully elaborated upon in Chapter 9, accounts for the strength of these motives, with the strongest at the base and the weakest at the top. Unlike Maslow's pyramid, we have found the Spiritual Survival Motive to be more essential than the Physical Survival Motive, which is why people commit suicide, eat and drink too much, and in general place their own physical survival lower on the scale than their spiritual survival. From an altruistic point of view, it is also why they will run into a burning house in order to save someone that they love, even if the chances of coming out are 50–50 or less.

REFERENCES

Ashforth, B., & Humphrey, R. (1995). Emotion in the workplace: A reappraisal. *Human Relations, 48,* 97–118.

Fine, G. A. (1988). Letting off steam: Redefining a restaurant's work environment. In M. D. Moore & R. C. Snyder (Eds.) *Inside organizations: Understanding the human dimension.* Newbury Park, CA: Sage, pp. 119–28.

Kahn, W. A. (1992). To be fully there: Psychological presence at work. *Human Relations, 45,* 331–49.

Kahn, W. A. (1990). Psychological conditions of personal engagement and disengagement at work. *Academy of Management Journal, 33,* 692–724.

MacLean, P. D. (1990). *The triune brain in evolution: Role in paleocerebral functions.* New York: Plenum Press.

Maddock, R. C., & Fulton, R. L. (1996). *Marketing to the mind: Right brain strategies in advertising and marketing.* Westport, CT: Quorum Books.

Maslow, A. H. (1970). Motivation and personality (2d ed.). New York: Harper & Row.

McClelland, D. C. (1987). *Human motivation.* Cambridge: Cambridge University Press.

Reiss, S., & Havercamp, S. (1998). Toward a comprehensive assessment of fundamental motivation. *Psychological Assessment, 10,* 97–106.

Rothman, M. (1989). Mythis about science . . . and belief in the paranormal. *The Skeptical Inquirer, 1,* (14): 25–34.

Soper, B., Milford, G., & Rosenthal, G. (1995, September). Belief when evidence does not support the theory. *Psychology and Marketing,* pp. 415–22.

2

A Eulogy for Professional Psychology

Psychology and the law are two professions that are totally dedicated to the generation of paperwork.

—Woody Allen, 1993

THE PSYCHOLOGY OF MOTIVATION

When a parent brings a child to a psychologist's office for treatment, they generally ask on the first visit *why* the child does what he or she does. Why does he or she all of a sudden exhibit failing grades? Why does he or she suddenly become oppositional and defiant at home and at school? Why does he or she suddenly become sullen and noncommunicative? The emphasis, and what they want to know, is why.

When a marketer or advertising executive senses a trend among consumers, whether positive or negative, the question asked is usually why such a trend exists and why did it get started. When a manager sees a decrease in productivity among a group of workers in a particular division, or perhaps in only one worker, the natural question asked is why?

Marketers, advertising executives, educators, and even law enforcement personnel look to psychologists in the same way that engineers and architects look to physicists for direction and authority when they are building a bridge or any other structure. But psychologists have not provided that direction. They have not directed their research, their interests, or their insights to the question of why people do the things that they do. When a heinous crime is committed and the local law enforcement facility does not have a clue as to what has occurred, or why, they often call in psychics rather than specialists in the behavioral sciences: psychologists or psychiatrists. Experience has told them that psychics, although sometimes incorrect in their intuitions and leads, can offer more useful information than behavioral scientists can.

Asking the question why inevitably leads to a discussion of motivation and, particularly, what motivates people to do the things they do. To respond to that question, psychologists and business leaders have always deferred to Abraham Maslow (1970), who has become the pundit and the virtuoso of what motivates people.

MORE ON MASLOW

Watson (1996) addresses this issue of automatically assigning authority to Maslow in the field of motivation. He says that it is a function of graduate education today, particularly in the field of management. Watson compares graduate education today to a word-association test, where students learn to respond to teachers in a knee-jerk, stimulus-response fashion. When asked about motivation, they automatically respond "Maslow." When asked about management, the knee-jerk response is "Drucker." When asked about quality, the knee-jerk response is "Tom Peters." Obviously, this sequence, and much of what goes on in graduate education today, is aimed at passing tests and getting acceptable grades. For this reason, when students are asked to defend Maslow's theory they have no knowledge with which to mount a defense. When the theory is exposed to them in more depth and detail, according to Watson, they are forced to agree that it does not really explain why people do what they do, and it leaves more questions unanswered than it leaves answered. Watson uses the example of Maslow to demonstrate the implications of superficial learning in management training and in the social sciences in general.

A more critical approach to Maslow's theory has been taken by Soper, Milford, and Rosenthal (1995) in an article that shows that Maslow's approach to motivation has never received any kind of empirical validation and that it in no way qualifies as a scientific explanation for why people do what they do. As such, these authors feel that Maslow's approach to motivation qualifies more as a "belief system" or a "religion" than it does as a scientific explanation of motivation. What is unusual is that disciplines such as psychology, marketing, and management, which consider themselves to be taking a scientific approach to the facts of their respective fields, still hold unswervingly and with fierce loyalty to Maslow's theory. The reason that they do will become clear shortly.

According to Watson (1996), the reason that students in management hold so tightly to Maslow's theory, even though it does not explain anything, is because of the graphic implications of the theory. Maslow has constructed a little pyramid with physical needs at the bottom of the structure and "self-actualization" at the top. We noted in Chapter 1 the problems inherent in this structure, but Watson stated that when the students were asked about their loyalty to Maslow, they always cited the little pyramid as a mnemonic device which, when all else failed, would be available to them on a final examination, which was all that was really important to them.

Psychologists hold to Maslow's theory for different reasons. In psychology, there are two very dominant approaches which prevail over all other theoretical approaches: humanism and behaviorism. It is estimated that about 90 percent of all psychologists represent these two approaches on a mutually exclusive basis. A third approach, cognitive psychology, is growing and becoming more prevalent.

Maslow was a humanistic psychologist who felt that everyone had an innate or inborn capacity to fully blossom and exercise their unique capacity for inherent goodness and excellence, given the proper environment in which to do so. Out of this approach grew the school of nondirective counseling, in which the therapist merely provided the opportunity for the patient to "grow" psychologically and it was said that the patient would then seize the opportunity. The therapeutic environment was more like a greenhouse. Many psychologists today who practice therapy are nondirective, hence supporting the humanistic trend. But it is these same psychologists who hold to the notion that psychology is a science, even though the school of humanism has provided very little data or empirical support for their beliefs and practices. The humanistic approach as a whole, and not just Maslow, has more of a status as a belief system or a religion than it does as a scientific structure. It is amazing to read articles that are written in the rigid, precise, and meticulous style of APA format under the guise of being scientific, and yet they end up justifying their approach because it is consistent with Maslow's hierarchy (Williams, 1992; Shapiro, Schwartz, & Astin, 1996; Bass, 1997; Carstensen, Isaacowitz, & Charles, 1999).

PSYCHOLOGY AS A SCIENCE

Psychologists have led the race between all of the social sciences to identify themselves as a science. They have, in this effort, managed to leave others behind in the dust. But in the race to achieve scientific status they have lost considerable credibility. This is because the client—the person who is being served—could not care less about whether or not psychology masquerades as a science or as an art. The client, whoever that is, is concerned only with getting results. Therefore, the race to achieve scientific status by psychology is a self-serving one at best, and one which serves the profession but may overlook the needs of the client.

Most psychologists feel that they have found the holy grail which allows them to masquerade as scientists; if not pure, then at least hybrid. That holy grail is behaviorism. Behaviorism looks at discrete behaviors and focuses only on what can be seen and measured. Therefore, not only does psychological science lack insight into and explanation of human behaviors, but it is characteristically nonproductive. As Deese (1969) has pointed out, "The characteristic emphasis of the psychological laboratory is the measurable response and this is responsible for the sterility of the study of thought (in psychology). The model of experimenting taken from the physical sciences no longer belongs to the center of psychology" (p. 522).

Because of this very narrow focus, psychology has been nonproductive. Abra (1998) has observed

Many committed scientists answer and say that psychology is a young science of extraordinary difficulty, so to ask for quick miracles is unfair. While this answer has some validity, and real contributions have been made, it sounds increasingly like an excuse. Seventy-five years is a long time, especially given the massive investments of resources and talent involved. The natural sciences after equal opportunities to show their wares have more to offer. (p. 36)

It was mentioned that when law enforcement agencies need to solve a difficult problem involving crime that they will often call upon a psychic instead of a behavioral scientist (*Paradise Lost*, 1995). This is testimony to the fact that psychology as a profession has produced very little. Further testimony resides in the fact that managed care companies, who are responsible for managing health care resources, have become more and more reluctant to pay for psychotherapy.

What seems strange and unusual is that so many psychologists adhere to behaviorism in spite of the fact that the party ended in 1959 with Chomsky's review of Skinner's *Verbal Behavior* (Chomsky, 1959). In this landmark and classic article, Chomsky showed that there was no way that language could be an "acquired behavior" (Skinner's definition), since there were various language universals that are known to all cultures and, furthermore, language is acquired very quickly at a certain age (between two and three years of age). Chomsky compared language in humans with flight in birds, saying that just as birds fly, people talk. The obvious implication is that no one teaches them and learning is not involved. The fact that Chomsky showed that certain behaviors occurred without learning undermined the whole operant paradigm in behaviorism. But the fact that psychologists continue to support, promote, and advocate behaviorism forty years after its death is even more incredible and astonishing.

From a practical point of view, behaviorism, which consists primarily of generalizations from animal to human behavior, has never worked. For educators, the whole concept of rewards and punishments (consisting of "time out") has been too costly and burdensome to administer. Furthermore, most teachers who have tried to use behavioral techniques in the classroom will testify to the fact that it does not accomplish anything. For managers, it has also been a wash, since the practice of rewarding people for what they do does not produce results and does not promote or nurture intrinsic motivation (Kohn, 1993). Kohn provides a mountain of evidence to show that not only do rewards not work but that they often have a paradoxical effect; one of punishing the rewardee rather than rewarding. A simple example given by him is the second-grade child who is rewarded with gold stars by the teacher because she is the only one in the entire class who did her homework assignment correctly, and then is harassed by other students during recess on the playground because she made them look bad.

Our own research with consumers and with patients in a clinical setting not only supports Kohn's findings but goes even further. Not only are people punished by rewards but we have found that some people are rewarded by punishment. The wife who is beaten and bruised by a jealous husband returns not once but many times, asserting her "love" for him in spite of his brutality and beatings. There is also the career criminal who is punished with confinement and brutal treatment for the crimes that he commits, only to return over and over again to the same correctional facility that he asperses. Or clinicians regularly report the abused housewife whose husband finally leaves her and who sits at home smoking and watching television while burning herself under the forearm with the lit cigarettes that she is smoking (i.e., administering her own punishment now that her husband is gone). Why? In Silent Side motivational terms it is simply because physical pain is less painful and more bearable than spiritual pain. Can behaviorism come up with an explanation for this? Is a cigarette burn rewarding? Remember, if a theory cannot describe all human behavior it can't describe any human behavior.

Much of our research has been in casinos, which is the fastest growing industry in America. Behavioristic psychologists would say that this phenomenon is related to the fact that slot machines in particular are programmed in accordance with schedules of reinforcement, derived from the principles of operant conditioning. But our experience and research has shown that this has little if anything to do with casino visitation, and casino management knows this intuitively. We have been told over and over again by management that "if they win, they bring it back again; and even if they lose, they come back for more." We will show that casino visitation is motivated primarily by the need to disorient and "disconnect" from the real world and only secondarily by a notion of reward or reinforcement. You will never see a clock in a casino, and the most successful casinos do not have windows in them. Frequent visitors to casinos are looking for escape, disconnection and disorientation from the real world, more than they are looking for reward.

Organized psychology, in its exuberance and burning desire to become a science, has sold short some of the critical issues in human development and human behavior. Behaviorism had its day because, like Maslow's approach to human motivation, it was incredibly simple and unembellished. It explained a lot of behavior that was seen in monkeys, birds, and other laboratory animals, and it also served the primary interest of making psychology a science. So behaviorism is in the service of the psychologist but has had very little benefit to the individual client or patient, whether they be in education, management, or marketing. Why? Simply because it does not provide answers. This is why we say that psychology has been self-serving rather than client serving. Neither humanism or behaviorism, which are of considerable interest to psychologists, have very much to say to the potential user, nor have they been able to produce much in the way of lasting benefits. Maslow's theory may be easily remembered, but it has little if any application and, like behaviorism, it is descriptive but not explanatory. No prescriptions can be written since there are few if any applications for the theory. Would you go to a physician who had memorized many theories but never had applied any of them?

Why Psychology Has Failed as a Science

Psychologists have tried to model the study of psychology after physics, making the assertion that behavior is motivated by the immutable laws of physics. But what they have overlooked is the issue of free will. Human beings are self-motivated, because they have free will. Machines and mechanisms (such as automobiles) do not have free will, and so the classical scientific terms of cause and effect can never be applied to creatures as it has been applied to the physical universe. The whole assumption that the two are governed by the same set of laws is absurd.

Psychologists, researchers, and marketers may predict what consumers might do, but they will never be able to predict what they will do. Marketers talk about motivating customers, but in fact customers motivate themselves. Researchers and marketers may be fairly accurate, using scientific sampling techniques in predicting what a particular demographic or other large group of consumers might do, but they will never be able to predict what a single individual will do. All that a marketer can do is expose consumers to a product or concept that may activate the mechanisms of motivation, but it will not assure them.

I cannot predict what kind of an automobile, deodorant, hair spray, cereal, or refrigerator you will buy because you are not, as psychologists might have you, a cause-and-effect robot driven by naturalistic forces. I may be able to predict with some certainty what kind of products you might buy, but never with 100-percent accuracy. To improve prediction, I need to know something about you. But I can only know what you tell me, and what you tell me is always going to be distorted by the rational, logical, and reasonable answers that you think you ought to give me, because you think that's what I want to hear.

Here is exactly where Motigraphics comes in. Because it provides me with dependable benchmarks to assess the meanings of what you tell me, Motigraphics provides categories which can be used to assess the meanings of what you tell me and what you say. It helps me to modify the overt descriptions that you give me of your circumstances with the subliminal influences that underlie them. It provides the building blocks that underlie what you might do and where you might spend your money.

Psychology and marketing will never succeed as a science until they come head to head with the issue of free will.

NO AMOUNT OF GOOD ADVERTISING
CAN SELL A BAD PRODUCT

In advertising, we have found over and over again that no amount of marketing, advertising, or lobbying can succeed in selling a bad product. If there is no benefit to the consumer, the product or service will eventually meet a well-deserved death. The marketplace serves as the judge and jury. In the early 1950s, Bob and Ray did an ad for Piel's Beer. The ad was probably the best remembered of the decade, but the product lasted only about a year after the advertising was introduced. The advertising was great, but the product wasn't. No amount of good advertising will sell or revive a bad product. The same thing needs to be said for psychotherapy and for other procedures that have been introduced by psychologists into business, education, and marketing, but which have very limited success.

COGNITIVE PSYCHOLOGY

Abra (1998) concludes his discourse on psychology as a science by admitting that, just as we said that the police turn to psychics to help them with solutions to perplexing crimes, many people turn not to psychologists but to literature and movies to find out how grief and jealousy are handled or how power does or does not corrupt. Where has psychology failed to provide direction? Most of those who read this book have probably had at least an introductory course in psychology, and can remember a voluminous and rather foreboding looking textbook called *Psychology* (Santrock, 1997). This title could refer to any one of a number of textbooks that were used, each of which started out by defining the field of psychology. The following definition is quite typical: "Psychology is the scientific study of behavior and mental processes. There are three aspects to this definition: science, behavior and mental processes. Let's examine behavior first. Behavior is everything that we do that can be directly observed—two people kissing, a baby crying, a college student riding a motorcycle" (p. 4). Although this definition includes "feelings" under mental processes, they get very little attention and are grouped with thoughts and thinking, which appear to dominate this category. The emphasis, of course, is on science.

Abra (1998) sees a positive change on the horizon, and that change is in the discipline of cognitive psychology. He says, "In the past few years it has been my experience to see a larger and larger number of psychologists flee from the dogma of behaviorism and enter the folds of cognitive psychology." For Abra, this is a positive and intelligent move, for he feels that cognitive psychology alone provides a new and productive direction for professional psychology. In his words, this is the "last frontier" in psychology and "makes psychology an exciting discipline." However, in my opinion, and in the opinion of others (LeDoux, 1996), cognitive psychology is nothing but another form of behaviorism and represents nothing unique or new.

I was a cognitive psychologist twenty-five years ago when I wrote my dissertation in the area of Kohlberg's moral development theory. I was impressed by the way that Piaget and Kohlberg did their research, breaking away from traditional research paradigms and looking in depth at individuals rather than at crowds and big numbers. Furthermore, they presented their results in readable and understandable formats, not in the rigid, monolithic, and behavioristic style and tradition which is so characteristic of the traditional APA format (Vipond, 1996).

However, since most of today's cognitive psychologists are ex-behaviorists, the same tradition prevails. McClelland (1987), who has written more on motivation than anyone, defines, describes, and measures motivation. His method of measuring motivation is by "coding operant thought content and helping people to 'shape' their thoughts" (p. 521). McClelland's theory of motivation is completely disconnected from values. It is very difficult to understand how someone could be motivated to do something that they don't value.

Bornstein and Masling (1998) present a cognitive approach to the study of the unconscious, but it is quite clear that their book actually represents an attempt at presenting a disguised behavioristic approach to the unconscious, which is unworkable. For one thing, this 312-page book devotes only about two and a half pages to sex, which Freud showed us was a very significant part of the unconscious that had to be reckoned with. Briefly, the book does not deal at all with primary process but rather with a secondary processing system which parallels the primary (rational) processing system. For Bornstein, Masling, Epstein, and others, the psychoanalytic unconscious is made up of learned behaviors, such as the ability to ride a bicycle, swim, or do keyboarding on a computer. There is little if any reference to emotion and if there is no study of emotion, there can be no study of motivation.

Epstein (1994) recognizes the need to update Freud's theory, which does not take into account any of the basic principles of Darwinian evolutionary theory, probably because Freud was not very familiar with it at the time. It is another sad commentary on organized psychology that it represents itself as a scientific endeavor and yet does not consider basic evolutionary theory in its approach to human behavior and human motivation. On the other hand, Epstein presents his Cognitive–Experiential Self Theory (CEST) as a dual information processing device. In this scheme, there is both a rational and an irrational system which, according to Epstein, lies somewhere between the primary process of Freud and rational thinking. However, the way in which Epstein describes this experiential system sounds like a description of the operations of the right hemisphere rather than a separate cognitive system (see Chapter 4). Second, it appears that what Epstein is trying to do is to elevate emotions to the level of thoughts, which is the same process that LeDoux (1996) has described as ineffective and inadequate. Third, the primary process activities which involve passion are not seen in Epstein's CEST approach in the experiential system, where one would expect to find them. These activities would include sex, jealousy, hatred, love, possessiveness, and other passionate emotions. What Epstein has recognized, however, is the fact that every culture and society on record, from the time that history was first recorded, has included religion, and it is foolish and absurd to rule it out as most psychological approaches have done in order to establish themselves as a science.

LeDoux (1996), who is a psychologist, has addressed this issue. He has stated that professional psychologists have overlooked the "mysterious underpinnings of emotional life." As a result, they have overlooked emotion entirely and are given to studying "thoughts about emotions":

In fact, psychologists interested in emotion, seduced by the intellectual excitement and appeal of cognitive science, have for some time been preoccupied with attempts to explain emotions in terms of cognitive thought processes. By this way of thinking, an emotion is no different from a cognition—emotions are just thoughts about situations that we find ourselves in. Although this approach has had its share of successes, these have come at a high price. In trading in the passion of an emotion for thoughts about it, cognitive theories have turned emotions into cold, lifeless states of mind. Lacking sound and fury, emotions as cognitions signify nothing, or at least nothing very emotional. Our emotions are full of blood, sweat and tears, but you wouldn't know this from examining modern cognitive research on emotion. Emotion research wasn't always this way, so let's see how and why the transformation occurred. (p. 43)

LeDoux goes on to quote Allen Newell, who noted that "no satisfactory integration yet exists between these phenomena [emotions] and cognitive science. But the mammalian system is clearly constructed as an emotional system." LeDoux says that the problem is, instead of heating up cognition, the efforts to integrate cognition and affect has turned emotion cold in the cognitive models: "Emotions, filled with and explained by thoughts, have been stripped of passion" (p. 38).

PSYCHOLOGY AS RELIGION RATHER THAN AS SCIENCE

In holding onto outmoded procedures that have no predictive value (the goal of science is prediction), professional and academic psychology would be more accurately characterized as a religion rather than a scientific pursuit. This is more consistent with what Soper et al. (1995) said about Maslow in particular and humanism in general: It is a belief system that is not supported by research or by any set of facts. Keep in mind that an organization can function as a religion without having a deity as the centerpiece. The major characteristic of a religion is that it is an *enduring institution governed by a set of rules.* In this case, the enduring institution is the profession, which has endured in spite of itself, and the set of rules, or the bible, is the *Ethical Standards of Psychologists.*

Chidester (1996) shows how organized baseball meets all of the criteria for a religion, which include, in addition to the set of rules, the following:

- Baseball ensures a sense of community in the midst of a constantly changing America through the forces of tradition, heritage, and collective memory.
- Baseball supports a sense of uniformity or a sense of belonging to a larger family that attends the same church (and goes by the same rules).
- The religion of baseball represents the sacred space of home. In psychology, the sacred space is either the laboratory or the place where psychotherapy is carried out.
- The religion of baseball represents the sacred time of ritual when (quoting Boswell, 1994) "everything is high-polish ritual and full-dress procession."

The word psychology or many other substitutions could be made for the word baseball, and it would be clear that there are many more religions than there are churches. Psychologists themselves are becoming more and more aware that professional psychology functions more as a religion than it does as a science. In reply to a controversial article by Brown (1997) in *American Psychologist,* Dineen (1998) states, "In recent years, a shift has been occurring in which psychology is coming to be seen less and less as a science and to be presented as a religion replete with dogma and liturgical hierarchy. The principles of objectivity, rationality, reliability and validity are being replaced with the values of subjectivity, emotionality, peer consensus and client satisfaction" (p. 487).

SUMMARY

This eulogy for professional psychology has been written in this chapter because of the failure of psychology to respond to the real needs of clients, students, marketers, teachers, and others. This is because psychologists have been, to some extent, more interested in furthering the welfare of their own services, rather than the welfare of the consumer of psychological services. There are several reasons for this.

First, psychology and psychologists have adopted a theoretical approach, behaviorism, which works well with animals but does not work well with people. Its popularity is based upon its simplicity. There are, of course, some rare exceptions where behavior modification does work, and one exception is in speech therapy. In general, however, behavior modification does not work and the evidence for this is overwhelming and is found in the work carried out by Kohn (1993).

Second, and even more damaging, psychology continues to hold on to this methodology even though it has been shown to be ineffective and it does not explain most behavior. The example that was cited was Chomsky's (1959) review of Skinner's *Verbal Behavior,* which signaled the end of the party for behaviorism.

Third, most of the psychologists who do practice could not by any stretch of the imagination be seen as doing something scientific. I refer to the clinical psychologists, who are the largest group within the American Psychological Association and who routinely make diagnoses from a book (*DSM-IV,* 1994), using a procedure that has very little reliability and no concept of inter-rater agreement. Inter-rater agreement is when two or more individuals agree upon a diagnosis, and this concept of reliability needs to be built into any procedure that considers itself scientific.

Fourth, the APA is bitterly divided between scientists on the one hand and practitioners on the other. Scientists attempt to adhere to scientific procedures and publish and broadcast their work, whereas practitioners practice an art, not a science, and desire to keep their methods and procedures secretive and proprietary. An example is seen in the bifurcation that first occurs in graduate programs in psychology. There are a number of "tracks" in psychological training, giving the impression that the profession has been carved up into many different little pieces. There is little if any crossover between the tracks. For example, graduate students who want to become social psychologists are not admitted to courses for clinical psychologists. This means that in their research in social psychology they will not have access to some of the assessment instruments and tests that are typically reserved for use only by clinicians. The profession as a whole is deeply divided in several areas such as this, and is an excellent example of "a house divided against itself."

REFERENCES

Abra, J. (1998). *Should psychology be a science?* Westport, CT: Praeger.
American Psychiatric Association. (1994). *Diagnostic and statistical manual of mental disorders* (4th ed.). Washington, DC: Author.
Bass, B. M. (1997). Does the transactional-transformational leadership paradigm transcend organizational and national boundaries? *American Psychologist, 52,* 130–39.
Bornstein, R. F., & Masling, J. M. (1998). *Empirical perspectives in the psychoanalytic unconscious.* Washington, DC: American Psychological Association.

Boswell, T. (1994). The church of baseball. In G. C. Ward & K. Burns (Eds.), *Baseball: An illustrated history.* New York: Alfred A. Knopf.

Brown, A. L. (1997, April). Transforming schools into communities of thinking and learning about serious matters. *American Psychologist, 52,* 399–413.

Carstensen, L. L., Isaacowitz, D. M., & Charles, S. T. (1999). Taking time seriously: A theory of socioemotional selectivity. *American Psychologist, 54,* 165–81.

Chidester, D. (1996). The church of baseball, the fetish of Coca-Cola and the potlatch of rock n' roll: Theoretical models for the study of religion in American popular culture. *Journal of the American Academy of Religion, 64,* 743–64.

Chomsky, N. (1959). Review of Skinner's *Verbal Behavior. Language, 35,* 26–58.

Deese, J. (1969). Behavior and fact. *American Psychologist, 24,* 515–22.

Dineen, T. (1998). Sacred cows and straw men. *American Psychologist, 54,* 487–88.

Epstein, S. (1994). Integration of the cognitive and the psychodynamic unconscious. *American Psychologist, 49,* 709–24.

Ethical Standards of Psychologists. (1992). Washington, DC: American Psychological Association.

Kohn, A. (1993). *Punished by rewards.* Boston: Houghton-Mifflin.

LeDoux, J. (1996). *The emotional brain: The mysterious underpinnings of emotional life.* New York: Simon & Schuster.

Maslow, A. H. (1970). *Motivation and personality* (2d ed.). New York: Harper & Row.

McClelland, D. C. (1987). *Human motivation.* Cambridge: Cambridge University Press.

Newell, A., Rosenbloom, P. S., & Laird, J. E. (1989). Symbolic architecture for cognition. In M. Posner (Ed.), *Foundations of cognitive science.* Cambridge: MIT Press.

Paradise Lost. (1995). Documentary on triple murder in West Memphis, Arkansas. New York: HBO, Division of Time-Warner Entertainment.

Santrock, J. (1997). *Psychology* (5th ed.). Madison, WI: Brown and Benchmark.

Shapiro, D. H., Schwartz, C. E., & Astin, J. A. (1996). Controlling ourselves, controlling our world: Psychology's role in understanding positive and negative consequences of seeking and gaining control. *American Psychologist, 51,* 1213–30.

Soper, B., Milford, G. E., & Rosenthal, G. T. (1995). Belief when evidence does not support the theory. *Psychology and Marketing, 12,* 415–22.

Vipond, D. (1996). Problems with monolithic APA style. *American Psychologist, 51,* 653.

Watson, T. J. (1996). Motivation: That's Maslow, isn't it? *Management Learning, 27,* 447.

Williams, R. N. (1992). The human context of agency. *American Psychologist, 47,* 752–60.

3

Subliminal Cues as Discrete Units of Mental Measurements

BACKGROUND

Subliminal cues are like beliefs, and in fact they often start out that way; strictly as beliefs. But they differ from beliefs in that, according to the dictionary definition, "they propel people to action." A cue, such as a cue in theatrical operations, propels or incites an actor to start acting his or her part or to begin with his or her assigned lines. A cue is "a signal, such as a word or action, used to prompt another event in a performance, such as an actor's speech or performance." Cues are quite different from facts, thoughts, or beliefs, because "cues incite people to act" (*American Heritage Dictionary*, 1996). Beliefs do not necessarily lead to action.

Subliminal cues are different from opinions because opinions are usually based on facts, and, of course, opinions, like beliefs, don't always incite people to act. People will go for a lifetime holding an opinion or a belief system and never do anything about it. Church leaders, political leaders, and leaders of other organizations continually complain that 10 percent of the membership accounts for 90 percent of the activity and funding. This is a solid testimonial to the fact that beliefs and opinions have little if anything to do with action.

Subliminal cues don't always cause action, but if action is forthcoming it is the cue that is responsible for it. Subliminal cues are not conscious, meaning that they are below the level or threshold of consciousness. However subliminal cues exist at different levels of consciousness, from quickly recalled on an as-needed basis to repressed or suppressed and never recalled. Few of us can remember our first, second, or third birthday parties, whereas most of us can recall information such as the number of floors in the Empire State Building or the schedule of eruptions for Old Faithful in Yellowstone Park.

The critical importance of subliminal cues for marketing and advertising will become more and more obvious in this book. People in general and consumers in particular have subliminal cues in their minds about products and services and they act on these subliminal cues daily. Hence, the astute marketer or advertiser needs to become familiar with these cues, since they are the sum and substance of consumer decision making and behavior.

WHERE SUBLIMINAL CUES COME FROM

Subliminal cues come from two sources. They are either from outside sources or from the self, in which case they are referred to as *auto-cues*. Similarly, they are delivered under two sets of conditions. One condition is repetition. The other is on a one-time basis, but under extremely emotional or traumatic conditions. It will be shown that when cues occur under extremely traumatic conditions there is an increased flow of adrenaline across the synapse which results in the cue having more impact and more importance in terms of clarity and control. Figure 3.1 illustrates the relationship between the two different kinds of cues and where they come from.

Subliminal Cues Delivered by Others

Subliminal cues were first discovered by us in a clinical psychiatric setting. When detailed histories were taken on patients it was found that they had significant events in their life from which they would give themselves cues, which later became subliminal but continued to have a decided effect over their behavior. In psychological practice, we found that the most critical subliminal cues enter the mind in childhood. This is hard for a lot of people to accept, and the notion that things that we can't see and can't remember govern and guide our behavior is foreign. It is hard to accept because it lessens the control that we feel that we have over our own lives. We like to believe that we know it all, and the notion that there are memories that are long forgotten that guide and direct our behavior is completely foreign and alien us. So the notion that we do not have subliminal cues is a much more popular one, albeit false, than the notion that we have them, and this is because most people don't want to accept the notion that they don't have total and absolute control over their thoughts and decisions.

Figure 3.1
Source of Subliminal Cues

		Type of Cue	
		One Time	**Repetitive**
Subliminal Cue Delivery System	**Self-Delivered (Internal)**	"I'll never get it again at this price."	"I want it, I need it. I want it, I need it. I want it, I need it."
	Delivered by Others (External)	"When these are gone, there will be no more."	"Two all-beef patties, special sauce, lettuce, cheese, pickles, onions, on a sesame seed bun."

In the investigation of any product or service history, we always look at the impact that the product had on children by taking them back to their first experience with the product. There are several reasons for this. There is overwhelming evidence now that the brain is not fully developed until a child reaches the age of ten. During the first ten years of life the brain is "under construction" (Nash, 1997). During this time, children accept cues from others uncritically and on a wholesale basis. Belief in Santa Claus and the Easter Bunny is an example of this. Children assimilate what adults have to say. This is one of the reasons why children act and behave, in many ways, just like their parents do. Another reason is genetic inheritance. The notion of imitation, learning, and copying is covered in Chapter 11 on adaptation. We have found in our own research that since children do not reason in terms of intention or hidden motivation before the age of eight they are more accepting and uncritical of cues before the age of eight than they are afterward.

Bettleheim (1975) elaborated on this in his investigations into fairy tales. According to Bettleheim, the importance of fairy tales is that they give children a clear and very distinct choice between the two ways that they can go in life. There are always two options.

Like the three pigs, you can build a house out of straw or you can build it out of brick. Cinderella experienced the worst part of life when she was under the domination of a cruel and hateful step-mother, and the best part when the prince of the whole kingdom proposed marriage. There was Sinbad the porter, who resented his mundane way of life and the fact that no one really appreciated him, and Sinbad the sailor, who after traveling the world and having some hair-raising experiences was glad to get back to his safe and mundane way of life as a porter. And, as Little Red Riding Hood found out, her granny was a sweet, loving, and kind grand-mother and she always looked forward to the idyllic existence that she found in going to her home, but she also found out that there were inherent dangers in going there. Bettleheim contrasts these and other fairy tales, which are read to children very early in their lives, to the Bible. The Bible, he says, shows children that there is only one way to live, whereas fairy tales present the child with the notion of a clear and ever-present choice in life (p. 52).

Also with reference to subliminal cues, Bettleheim (1975) shows that in at least one fairy tale, Cinderella, powerful cues can be in-stilled in children's minds that last a lifetime, controlling and di-recting behavior. The example that he gives is the lost slipper. The phallic implications here of the foot sliding into the slipper have had a substantial impact on cultures all over the world in terms of foot and shoe fetishes, which are some of the most widespread and most highly subscribed male fetishes, next to breast fetishes. This sexual fetish was seen for years in ancient China in foot binding, and more recently on an international basis on the World Wide Web, on which the number of foot, shoe, slipper, and boot fetish pages are very prominent. Bettleheim has noted that the Cinderella myth has been read to many generations of children over at least 900 years, and that those who feel that it needs to be changed be-cause it degrades women's roles in life are sadly mistaken. This is because, according to him, the story has nothing to do with a woman's role or plight, but instead is about the real choices that exist between good and evil and also about the slipper-vagina, which represents the sexual choices that one may make in life (p. 270).

Bettleheim (1975) denigrates those who would change fairy tales after they have been read to children in their current form for many centuries. This is because those who change them want to remove children from the violence, sexual implications, and gender prob-lems that are inherent in fairy tales. Rather than remove them, he says that children should be exposed to the conflicts in life, which is the major issue involved in fairy tales. The issue is that life does have its conflicts, and because of these conflicts there will be many forks in the road and choices will need to be made. According to Bettleheim, the child who is exposed to fairy tales when very young is much better prepared to consider the various options that life presents and make these confusing and difficult choices (pp. 17–18). This conclusion is undoubtedly a reference to the subliminal cues that are inherent in fairy tales.

What is most interesting about Bettleheim's (1975) treatment of fairy tales is that it underscores the importance of cues. In both Cinderella and Snow White, the young girls are saved. In Snow White, the stepmother is cold and distant, leaving the child lost and in despair. But Snow White is saved, first by the dwarves and later by the prince. Cinderella is also delivered from a wicked step-mother situation by a prince. In both cases, the five- or six-year-old child who is exposed to these stories is encouraged and inspired by the hope, resolution, revenge, and sense of justice that these stories convey. These positive cues that are received by the child are far more important than the issue of gender, and this is the point that is made by Bettleheim. Even though many up-to-date feminists would change these stories so that females do not believe that they have to be rescued from life's troubles by males, this is not the point. The point is that children who are in despair, who are lonely, and who are lost in any number of situations receive subliminal cues from fairy tales that give them hope, trust, and expectation for the future. This is why children who have been exposed to fairy tales exhibit qualitative differences from children who have not been exposed.

Bettleheim (1975) gives an excellent example of this. He is writing about Hans Christian Andersen's *The Little Match Girl*, which is "a deeply moving story, but hardly one suitable for identification." He continues, "The child in his misery may indeed identify with this heroine, but if so, this leads only to utter pessimism and defeatism. 'The Little Match Girl' is a moralistic tale about the cruelty of the world; it arouses compassion for the downtrodden. But what the child who feels downtrodden needs is not compassion for others who are in the same predicament, but rather the conviction that he can *escape this fate* [italics added]" (p. 105).

Subliminal Cues Delivered by the Self

A second source of subliminal cues is the self. These self-given and self-received cues are referred to as *auto-cues*. Since there are so many cues delivered over a lifetime, there must be many that have little or no impact. But all cues will lead to behavior, no matter how minute or small. For example, people may have cues which lead them to buy a certain kind of detergent or baking flour. The cue, "If grandmother used it, it must be good because her biscuits were so good," is an auto-cue which is self-delivered and instilled and will lead to purchasing decisions about flour that is used for baking. It also leads to brand loyalty. Auto-cues about mother using a certain laundry detergent instead of the myriad of others is a cue that will also lead to detergent-purchasing decisions and at the same time eliminate time-consuming decision-making processes and confusion.

But some cues are much more important than others, and when we speak of importance, what we are talking about is the amount of control that subliminal cues exert over behavior later in a person's life. We have found in our own research that the earlier cues are delivered, the more effective they are. But even so, a child by the age of eight must have received thousands of cues, and so how are they sorted? Which ones will control and direct behavior? There are several answers to this question.

First, age is important. The younger the person when the cue is delivered, the more likely the cue will be influential in that person's life. It has already been noted that in our own ongoing research we have found that children under the age of eight, when giving themselves an auto-cue, cannot deal with the issue of intent or motivation. They are unable to reason in this direction (i.e., from the physical event toward the intent or motive that explains the reason for the event). Other research (Piaget, 1932; Kohlberg, 1984) substantiates this observation.

Second, some cues are delivered under extremely traumatic or emotional conditions. Examples are when an individual is sick and is running a very high temperature, is unconscious, or is comatose. Surgery is often a source of cues, especially for children, since there is no way that anyone can explain to them what is happening at the time. We have seen examples of individuals who were in motor vehicle accidents (MVAs) who were pronounced dead or near dead by an EMT or ambulance attendant, only to recover later on through surgery or life support. The problem was they still had the subliminal cue that they were dead or almost dead. Acting upon these cues, they became "walking zombies" (Sexton & Maddock, 1979). The result is that they have symptoms that are typical of depression, but do not respond to the typical treatment that is offered to depressed patients. This is because the cue, which was subliminal, continually reminds them that they were dead or close to death, whereas their conscious and rational minds continue to assure them that they are among the living. Medication is usually not effective in treating this form of "depression."

Auto-cues are often, but not always, associated with incidents that are traumatic or at least memorable. For example, most of us who were alive at the time can recall in vivid detail where we were and who we were with when it was announced that President Kennedy was shot in Dallas, when President Reagan was shot by John Hinckley, or when the Challenger spacecraft exploded. These are often referred to as *flashbulb memories.* Cues that are given under conditions of flashbulb memories are more powerful and more motivating than cues that are given under ordinary conditions, and LeDoux (1996) explains why. Referring to the work of McGaugh et al. (1995), he shows that when rats were given shots of adrenaline right after they had learned something, it would enhance their memory for what they had just learned. This implies that if adrenaline is released naturally from the adrenal gland during a special situation which involves emotional arousal, the auto-cue that is associated with that situation, as well as all of the external cues, will be more powerful and explicit than memories of nonemotional situations. McGaugh and his associates have tested the effects of adrenaline in human subjects who were read emotional stories. Some were given an adrenaline blocker and others were given a placebo. Those who were given the placebo remembered more of the details of the emotional story than those who were given the adrenaline blocker (LeDoux, 1996, p. 207).

A third contingency, which is seen in the upper right-hand quadrant of Figure 3.1, is when cues are delivered under conditions of repetition. Advertisers and politicians know this better than anyone. The more often a product or a politician can deliver their name to the public, the better chance they have of being purchased or elected. Similarly, in clinical situations, a child who is given the repetitive suggestion by his or her parent that "you have great potential" is likely to maximize that potential, particularly when compared to the child who receives the repetitive suggestion that "you are no good and will grow up to be a drunk, just like your father." These cues are quite different, and they have the opposite effects if they are delivered under conditions of repetition.

PLOT POINTS

According to Field (1994), every dramatic presentation or screenplay must have at least one and preferably more *plot points* and must also have a *paradigm.* The paradigm is the framework around which the plot rotates, and the plot points are major occurrences in the paradigm which change the direction or the headings of the plot and turn the whole destination of the plot. In our own experience, people also have plot points in their lives. Plot points and paradigms and their relationship to people's lives are more fully discussed in Chapter 7, where we review what people personalize.

Plot points consist of definitive times in people's lives in which subliminal cues are delivered, just as there are plot points in drama where people's lives are changed. Often these plot points will occur under stress or under duress. When it is understood that plot points are critical junctions in a person's lifetime, and that the subliminal cues that occur during these times are crucial to the understanding of human behavior, then it will also become clear why people do what they do, and not just how they do it. Plot points and subliminal cues allow us to explain behavior, and not just to describe it. Since neither academic nor professional psychologists deal with plot points or subliminal cues in their overall interpretations of behavior, what they end up with is sterile, flat, and colorless descriptions of human behavior that do not allow for explanations or solutions to human problems. Every drama has plot points. Imagine a drama without them, and you understand what is meant by sterile, flat, and colorless.

NEUROLOGICAL SUPPORT FOR SUBLIMINAL CUES

We have already offered some solid neuroanatomical support for the existence of subliminal cues from the work of LeDoux (1996) and McGaugh et al. (1995) which explains why one neurotransmitter, which is seen to be present in abundance during certain emotional experiences, is responsible for that particular experience being stored in long-term memory. There is not enough room in the brain to store all the subliminal cues that are received during a lifetime or even half a lifetime (Damasio, 1994). This explains why many subliminal cues, such as the ones that we get from advertising, have little if any effect upon behavior. Damasio has indicated that if these cues were held in the brain as facsimiles there would be an insurmountable problem with storage. Therefore, Damasio proposes that what we are calling subliminal cues are actually neural firings made up of momentary constrictions which are attempts at replicating patterns that were experienced at one time. He says that they may actually be good replicas, or they may be incomplete and inaccurate. He goes on to say, "I suspect that explicit recalled mental images arise from the transient synchronous activation of neural firing patterns largely in the same early sensory cortices where the firing patterns corresponding to perceptual representations once occurred. The activation results in a topographically organized representation" (pp. 100–101).

It is that "topographically organized representation" that we are referring to as subliminal cues. The idea of a "neural firing pattern" relieves us of the difficulty of explaining storage space for past memories, since they are not stored in a "hard drive" as a facsimile but instead are stored as "read only memory" and recalled on an as-needed basis.

In fact, we all receive so many different and varied subliminal cues from ourselves and from others that storage of these cues would be inconceivable. However, everyone has experienced the déjà vu phenomenon where there is a certain familiarity with a face, a scene, or an event. The familiarity is such that the individual would "swear that I have been here before." That experience seems to illustrate, in a primitive way, the way that these cortical and subcortical neural firings take place.

Subliminal Cues from Television

Any discussion of the origin of subliminal cues would be incomplete without considering the role of television. For the most part, this is where most subliminal cues originate today, and have for twenty years or more. Television plays a unique and unparalleled role in the implanting and interjection of subliminal cues.

The ordinary prime-time television viewer is, during the viewing process, split into two parts. At one level he or she is being entertained. Entertainment involves a lot of positive emotions, including enjoyment, laughter, fun, and so on. Entertainment also involves relaxation. Furthermore, the viewer believes that he or she is being entertained and pays very little attention to anything else that is going on, since he or she is completely focused on the entertainment segment of TV. But there is another side to this.

We don't wish to imply, at this point, that this is a right brain–left brain dichotomy. This is too simplistic. However, there is a dichotomy, and it would appear that the most appropriate way to describe this would be in terms of the viewer's ego. The ego, which Freud characterized as the executive part of the psyche, processes and assimilates information. This information consists of irrational and rational, and it is assumed that there is a "sorting" task going on, where the information is placed into different levels. So at one level the viewer is being entertained, while at another level he or she is receiving subliminal cues from the drama or entertainment medium that is being viewed.

How does television implant subliminal cues? Very simply. During the 1970s, in the aftermath of the turbulent 1960s, there was a fallout in the American culture. In spite of the implementation of the Civil Rights Law of 1964, there was still racism and racial strife in our country. But during that time one television program, as noted in Chapter 1, "All in the Family" might be said to have done more to combat racial strife than any other single medium, television or otherwise. It was done by attacking the viewer's mind when and where he or she was the most vulnerable: at home, relaxed, casual, unconstrained, laid back, and disconnected from the events of the day. In other words, the viewer's mind was in a highly suggestible state. One side of the viewer was entertained while the other side was receiving subliminal cues about racism, about the kind of people who engage in racial hatred, and about how nobody wants to be like those people.

Television continues today to put subliminal suggestions into viewers' minds, against which they have very few defenses. Consider a practice called product placement. It is one thing to watch a paid advertisement for the Dodge Durango where a voice-over begs you to buy one, but it is quite another thing to watch the Dodge Durango in a major chase scene which is part of the drama. This is especially true if the good guys are driving the Durango and the bad guys are driving something else. Product placement is a way of getting your product written into the script and paying for it, but entering the viewer's mind through the back door instead of through the front.

Television has many other ways of implanting and interjecting subliminal suggestions. Perhaps the most fruitful way is to write the cues into the script. Today, television continues to address racism since it is still a problem. However, on a much larger scale, television addresses the issue of gender roles. Consider the following set of subliminal cues:

Can men do no right these days? Cowed by women critical of their behavior, they increasingly find themselves portrayed as insensitive, bad in bed, a danger to children, incapable of expressing emotion or intimacy and unable to contribute to family life. Concerned at the growing chasm between the sexes, Tettina Arndt urges more men to speak up for themselves.

A recent episode of the American television series "Roseanne" makes the point rather nicely. Roseanne's husband, Dan, is shown making an insensitive remark to one of his daughters, causing her to run off in tears. "Oh, Dan, you're such a . . . a man," exclaims Roseanne as she goes to comfort her daughter.

Dan Junior is puzzled. "Dad, why did Mom call you a man?" he asks. "Because she's mad at me," Dan replies. "I thought it was good to be a man," puzzles the boy. "Oh no son," comes the reply, "not since the late sixties." (Arndt, 1993)

Another example of subliminal cues of this nature was briefly encountered by this author while channel "surfing." A black woman was talking to a white woman and said, "You talk about crime! The real crime is the number of incompetent white men who are holding down jobs today!" In fact, there are incompetent people of both sexes and several races that are holding down jobs in which they cannot perform. This dubious distinction is not limited to white men.

Television has many other ways of implanting subliminal cues in viewers' minds, as viewers are preoccupied with the entertainment aspect of TV. Television screenplay writers are masters at it but, on the other hand, it is the nature of the beast and of communication today.

INTRINSIC VERSUS EXTRINSIC MOTIVATION

This discussion of cues is important, and it is also novel and unprecedented. As shown in Chapter 2 with the help of LeDoux, Kohn, and others, learning and rewards have only a very small effect upon motivation and do not effect intrinsic motivation at all. They have an effect on extrinsic motivation, as when consumers are given a coupon for a discount on a grocery product. The problem with extrinsic motivation is that it is short lived, temporary, and does not build loyal customers. And everyone wants loyal and dedicated customers who keep coming back, over and over again.

In contrast, we are dealing with intrinsic motives. These intrinsic motives are permanent rather than temporary and have a long-term effect upon behavior and motivation. More important, they explain why people do what they do, whether or not they are rewarded for what they do.

When we restrict our investigations to behavior, we get descriptions of what people do. Also, if we are lucky, we may get a description of how they do what they do. Conversely, when we start with subliminal cues we get explanations and not just descriptions. At this point, we begin to understand why people do what they do.

VISUAL CUES VERSUS VERBAL CUES

Up to this point we have dealt only with verbal subliminal cues. Visual subliminal cues can be even more powerful, since the right hemisphere of the brain tends to "think" in pictures. Language and logic are generally on the left side of the brain, in what is referred to as Broca's area. In 1863, Paul Broca, a Parisian neurologist, described eight cases of aphasia, all of which had damage to the left hemisphere.

The right hemisphere, whose role we shall describe more fully in Chapter 4, also has a role in language, but it seems to consist more of stringing the words together and putting words into phrases and sentences.

The Michelin "Baby in the Tire" is a visual subliminal cue. It has been in use for many years, and it consistently conveys the subliminal cue, "You care about what is riding on your tires." Michelin sells love and family values, not tires. Even though Michelin invented the radial tire in 1948, very few people know this important fact. Ask almost anyone what comes to mind when they hear the word "Michelin" and they will tell you "the baby."

The Marlboro man is a subliminal cue. Smoking is not natural; it is an imitated behavior. Usually, it is picked up by adolescents before they reach the age of twenty and is basically an imitation of what their peers are doing. Adolescent girls are much more likely to pick up smoking than boys because of weight consciousness. Hence the Marlboro man, who appeals especially to boys with the subliminal cue, "Be your own person."

The Nike swoosh is a subliminal cue. In the nineteenth century, the Native Americans used fetishes. A fetish was a statue or representation of some kind that embodied power or dominance. It was often an eagle or some powerful animal. Warriors would sniff it before going into battle and it supposedly imputed power and strength for the battle. Today we no longer have fetishes, but we do have representations like the Nike logo. The swoosh carries with it the subliminal cue of performance.

When advertising reaches the point of the Michelin baby in the tire or the Marlboro man it has gone beyond words. Through repetition, these symbols penetrate the right hemisphere and are stored in long-term memory. Generally, words are superfluous when these symbols achieve the power and status that those described have achieved. And when a product can be represented and described without words, the audience expands exponentially.

REFERENCES

American Heritage Dictionary of the English Language (3d ed). (1996). A. Soukhanov (Ed.). Boston: Houghton Mifflin.

Arndt, B. (1993, 22–23 May). Men under siege. *NSW, The Weekend Australia*, Internet edition.

Bettleheim, B. (1975). *The uses of enchantment.* New York: Random House.

Damasio, A. R. (1994). *Descartes' error: Emotion, reason and the human brain.* New York: Avon Books.

Field, S. (1994). *Screenplay: The foundations of script writing* (3d ed.). New York: Dell.

Kohlberg, L. (1984). *Psychology of moral development: The nature and va-lidity of moral states.* San Francisco: Harper & Row.

LeDoux, J. (1996). *The emotional brain: The mysterious underpinnings of emotional life.* New York: Simon & Schuster.

McGaugh, J. L., Cahill, L., Parent, M. B., Mesches, M. H., Coleman-Mesches, K., & Salnias, J. A. (1995). Involvement of the amygdala in the regulation of memory storage. In J. L. McGaugh, F. Bermudez-Rattoni, & R. A. Prado-Alcala (Eds.), *Plasticity in the central nervous system: Learning and memory.* Hillsdale, NJ: Erlbaum.

Nash, J. M. (1997, February). Special report: Fertile minds. *Time, 149,* 48–56.

Piaget, J. (1932). *The moral development of the child.* New York: Harcourt Brace.

Sexton, R. O., & Maddock, R. C. (1979, December). The walking zombie syndrome in depressive disorders. *Journal of the Tennessee Medical Association, 72,* 886–89.

4

The Right and Left Sides of the Brain

RESPECTIVE ROLES OF THE HEMISPHERES

There are a lot of subliminal cues going around about the right and left hemispheres of the brain and their respective roles. In other words, people have certain beliefs that have been promulgated by the press and others about the different roles of the different sides of the brain, but not very much has been said about the way that they work together. Ornstein (1997) represents an exception to this rule. In his book, *The Right Mind: Making Sense of the Hemispheres*, he presents an integrated and wholistic theory as to how the two hemispheres complement each other in what they do together, rather than separately and on their own.

Clearly, the left side of the brain is involved in language. Specifically, this is located in the left prefrontal lobe. With language comes rational thinking, analysis, logic, and logical functions. Since academic psychology has had a considerable impact upon the measurement of intelligence, we might also say that most intellectual functions that are measured in IQ testing are in the left prefrontal lobe. As a result, schools and educational institutions are set up to favor people who are left brain dominant. That is, people who are logical, analytical, and have high verbal and math skills are at a considerable advantage in schools today. Not only are they more likely to get admitted to competitive academic programs, but they are also more likely to succeed. Tests that are designed to determine who will succeed and who will not succeed in schools, colleges, and universities are designed to measure these left brain functions almost entirely.

The left (and the right) prefrontal lobe in lower animals is dedicated almost entirely to the olfactory functions. It is interesting that in humans this function has been relegated almost entirely to the main olfactory bulb, which is in the area of the right and left inferior temporal gyrii of the brain. Obviously, this is a function of evolution and has occurred over a period of millions of years.

The right prefrontal lobe of the brain, as opposed to the left frontal lobe, is more specialized in creative endeavors, including planning, intuition, emotional, spatial, and artistic ventures. Few tests measure these functions. If there are tests that are designed to measure right brain functions, they are fewer in number than those that measure left brain functions, and part of the reason for this is that it is more difficult to measure these capacities. According to LeDoux (1996), organized psychology has ignored emotions and dealt with them by turning the emotions into thoughts. Therefore, since psychology and psychologists usually take the lead in activities involving measurement, these functions have just not been measured. A major purpose of this book is to introduce a system of measurement that deals directly with motivation and indirectly with the emotions that are such an important part of motivation.

There is also a lot of hesitancy on the part of business leaders and managers to deal with emotion, and their official position appears to be to ignore it by diffusing it, reframing it in the guise of rationality, suppressing it, neutralizing it, prescribing it, or buffering it. Neutralizing refers to inventing face-saving rituals such as humor, which is used to diffuse emotion. Prescribing it is seen in organizations that train their employees, particularly those on the front line, to be happy, smiling, and always cheerful when dealing with outsiders. These different methods of minimizing emotion in the workplace are elaborated upon by Ashforth and Lee (1990) and Ashforth and Humphrey (1995) and characterize the exhaustive limits to which business leaders will go to hide, suppress, and ignore emotion in the workplace.

It is no wonder, then, that the function and role of emotion has been overlooked, not only in psychology but also in other fields, such as education and business. As a result, when emotion rears its head, as it does in the classroom and in the office every day, those who are in teaching or in management have no effective way to deal with it. This is quite apparent in a classic article by Oncken (1984), which details the traditional way in which problems—emotional and otherwise—are handled by subordinates: They are dumped on the manager's desk.

RIGHT–LEFT HEMISPHERE COORDINATION

It is quite clear that the right and left hemispheres have different functions, but it takes the coordination of both hemispheres to produce a wholistic response. For example, Skinner (1957) saw language and talking as just one more form of behavior that was learned, through imitation, like any other behavior. But this was a serious error; not only for Skinner but for behaviorism in general.

Vocabulary is learned by imitation and duplication. For example, German children begin speaking in German, Americans in English, and so on. But Chomsky (1971) showed that language was a wholly different process and was not learned or acquired at all. Instead, he showed that the "deep structures" of language, including grammar and syntax, are present from birth but don't develop until two or three years of age. To prove his point, he showed that children of all cultures do not go through a trial-and-error process in putting together words and sentences, and all children, in all cultures, begin to speak at about the same time. If acquisition, learning, and imitation were involved, none of this would occur, and there would be a lot of trial and error before children actually began to speak.

It is quite likely that the structures of the brain that are responsible for vocabulary and learning are quite different from the structures that mediate grammatical rules and syntactic methods, and that the two are coordinated. We typically assign words, vocabulary, and language to the left prefrontal lobe, but another part of the brain—quite likely the counterpart in the right hemisphere—is responsible for the assigning of meaning and also the designation of space and structure. For example, a person who has a left hemispheric lesion from surgery will often report that although they know what they want to say (i.e., the proper word and its context), they cannot generate the actual word. They can "feel" the meaning or perhaps even visualize it, but cannot assign the appropriate word.

Or take, for example, the way that the two hemispheres work together for a man who is lost in the woods. A man in this situation may rely upon his auditory senses, particularly if there is a highway or a commuter railroad nearby. Upon hearing the commuter train come by (whistle blowing, track noise, etc.) the left hemisphere will quickly identify this auditory stimulus: "It is a train." Knowing that the railroad is south of where he is, and knowing that this is the direction that he wants to go, he must then judge the distance from the sound. Since the right hemisphere specializes in spatial relationships, it then becomes apparent that the sound comes from a distance of about a mile to one and a half miles away. Then, as the hiker begins to walk toward the railroad, the sound of the

commuter train gets louder and louder, indicating that he is walking in the right direction and will soon be where he wants to be.

Just as the hiker makes his way out of the woods by attending to
sounds, children attend to the emotional tones of their parents.
From these tones they can draw conclusions. The word "no" does
not always mean no. It can have considerable variation in meaning, depending upon the emotional tones that accompany it. The
right hemisphere specializes in hearing low tones (vowels and other
nonlanguage sounds), whereas the left hemisphere specializes in
hearing tones that are in the higher frequencies (consonants and
finer, more distinctive sounds).

Damasio (1994), quoting Albert Einstein (cited in Hadamard,
1945), has described this relationship between words (left hemisphere) and thoughts (right hemisphere) and how they work together with even more clarity:

The words or language, as they are written or spoken, do not seem to play
any role in my mechanism of thought. The psychical entities which seem
to serve as elements in thought are certain signs and more or less clear
images which can be "voluntarily" reproduced and combined. There is, of
course, a certain connection between those elements and relevant logical
concepts. It is also clear that the desire to arrive finally at logically connected concepts is the emotional basis of this rather vague play with the
above mentioned elements. (p. 107)

The left hemisphere is often characterized as the concrete and
specific side. It deals in specifics, details, particulars, and bits of
information. It is known to string these details together with logic,
which is also characteristic of the analytical left hemisphere. But
its weakness comes when the task also involves the analysis of context, circumstances, or situational variables. Ornstein (1997) has
illustrated this very vividly by including in his book pictures of
Norman Rockwell drawings in which he asks individuals with right
hemispheric damage to describe what they think is going on in the
pictures. What they describe is details. For example, they may see "a
man with a hat on, and one with a bandage on his head, and a lady
with a little boy." What they cannot see, however, is the context, or
fit what they see into the situation, which is supposed to be a doctor's
waiting room with sick people waiting to be seen by the doctor.

Ornstein (1997) gives some other examples that are very helpful
in understanding the different functions of the two hemispheres
but also in understanding how the two hemispheres work together.
He says that one way of understanding the way that the right hemisphere perceives the world is in the same way that a myopic or
nearsighted person sees the world when they remove their glasses.

It is a fuzzy, but also a global representation of reality, where boundaries tend to be shaded and objects blend together, as in surrealistic art. The boundaries are not that clear and distinct. He compares this also to autistic and to schizophrenic individuals, who are unable to formulate a worldview or whose ability to "assemble the world's information into a single sensible framework is absent" (p. 131). A very clear and succinct example is seen in the fact that schizophrenics and individuals with right brain lesions have difficulty with humor. Being able to laugh and appreciate a joke involves not just hearing the words but also in appreciating the often conflicting contexts of the situations in the joke, which is a right brain function.

The right–left brain distinction now appears in the popular literature and is featured regularly on television and in the movies. Left brain people are often seen as "bookish" and right brain dominant people as "creative." I have even seen "professional" presentations where the speaker identified left-handed people as being right brain dominant and vice versa. This is obviously an oversimplification and, if true, would mean that there should never be any left-handed CPAs in the world since right brain people don't do that well with details. Similarly, you would never want to go under the knife with a left-handed surgeon or trust your creative executions to a right hander. But life, and particularly the brain, are not that simplistic.

Recently, Jack Wolfe, Ph.D., an internationally known motivational speaker who commanded big bucks and large audiences spoke in detail about the relationship between the two hemispheres. According to him, there was no relationship. The two hemispheres operated entirely independently. It was to his advantage to separate the two hemispheres in order to simplify his presentation. The example that he gave was that almost everybody talks on the telephone holding the receiver in their left hand, since they are right handed and will want to take notes on the conversation. The lesson to be learned from this was that, since the left ear goes directly to the right side of the brain (crosses over), all the information coming from the telephone call is going into the right hemisphere. Think of the implications. If he was right, there would be no way that colleagues could discuss logical or sequential solutions over the telephone. Business calls would be impossible, and every transaction would have to be in writing. Stock brokers would be unable to take orders over the telephone. But the audience loved it and wanted more. Everyone loves a simple solution. Forget about the fact that the solution creates more problems than it solves. Like Maslow's pyramid, everyone jumped on board and begged the motivational speaker to come back for their next convention. As noted in Chapter 2, the simpler it is, the more likely people will buy it, even if it doesn't work or doesn't explain what is going on. Even psychologists who are deeply immersed in the scientific method and in proving to the world that they are methodologically pure will cite Maslow (Bycio, Hackett, & Allen, 1995; Bass, 1997).

IMPORTANCE OF MAINTAINING RIGHT–LEFT BRAIN BALANCES IN ADVERTISING AND MARKETING

It is important to recognize the roles that both sides of the brain play in advertising. With the advent of computer art and drawing, it is tempting to present absurdities to our audiences, since absurdities appear to get the immediate attention of the right hemisphere. An absurdity is a visual and/or auditory stimulus that departs not completely but partially from reality (described in detail in Chapter 6). For example, with computer art it is very simple to picture a dog sitting at a bar and drinking a beer, wearing a suit and tie, and sitting upright on a bar stool. Computers can even make the dog appear to be talking. Will that capture anyone's attention? You bet that it will. Babies and animals will turn almost anyone's head and are particularly attractive to the right hemisphere, which as we have already stated "thinks" in terms of pictures more than it does in terms of words.

The problem is that the dog sitting at the bar with a glass of suds may be attention getting, but what about the context of the ad? What's the purpose? A boat can be pictured out of context, sitting on an interstate or on the top of a high building. With computers we can put the boat anywhere we want to and thereby create an instant absurdity that will attract the right side of the brain. But the context is not there. For boats, the context is water. And for boat buyers, the issue is water. Taking a boat out of water or a dog out of a dog house may attract the right hemisphere, since it is an absurdity, but for what purpose? The right brain rejects what is not in context or that which is out of character, so that all the work that goes into the formation of the absurdity can be for naught. The seduction of computers which can be used to format absurdities can be useful, or they can be an expensive waste of talent and resources.

Crain (1999) addressed the problem of "advertising's failure to produce results reaching crisis proportions." His complaint is that agencies have gone too far in their creativity and should go back to straightforward ads which tout the features of the product, and not necessarily the benefits. He says that advertising should do what it did years ago, and give consumers a reason to buy the product. He degrades and disparages nonproduct advertising, which may reach the emotions but not the rational reasons why consumers do what they do. Basically, he is advocating that the whole industry take several giant steps backward.

He is right and he is wrong. One of the reasons that advertising's attempts to appeal to the emotions has not worked is because many advertisers do not understand emotions. But they all have computers, and they are thrilled with the capacity that they have to present absurdities ad infinitum, like a child with a new toy or a cook with a new Bass-O-Matic which slices, dices, chops, grinds, bits, clips, parcels, and so on. In *Marketing to the Mind* (Maddock & Fulton, 1996), we warned that the advent of "creative" computer programs would introduce confusion and clutter into advertising, which it now appears to have done in a very short time. There may be so many absurdities and attempts to appeal to the right brain that these "new and enlightened" attempts at advertising are clearly not working. We do not agree that we need to go backward into strictly product advertising. We do feel that emotionally based advertising will work if done right, and we discuss this more fully in Chapter 7 when we deal with personalizations. But if there is a question about how it's done, just look at those who do understand emotion—Hallmark, Michelin, DeBeers, Budweiser, and the like—to remind yourself that emotional advertising does work.

An example of an absurdity that worked was seen in a spot produced for Ford trucks. Two cowboys were riding in a four-wheel-drive F-150 pickup truck across a parched desert landscape with many obstacles, including rocks, logs, streams, and so on. These are the typical obstacles that are met and even sought after by the typical "four-wheeler." But eventually they reach an obstacle that seems insurmountable: a canyon. However the canyon turns out to be not an obstacle at all, as the rider throws a cable across the canyon, lassoing a stump on the other side. The driver then confidently puts the truck's winch in gear and pulls the two walls of the canyon together. The rational, left brain issue? Value. The emotional, right brain issue? Performance. The subliminal cue? There are no limitations with a Ford F-150 four-wheel-drive truck (as long as it has a winch on the front bumper).

IDENTIFYING AND FINDING "RIGHT BRAIN PEOPLE"

It is not unusual to hear people identifying each other as "right brain" or "left brain." Hopefully, this chapter has dissuaded you from attempting to make such a clear-cut choice. The two sides of the brain work together and in harmony with one another. But it is not unusual to encounter individuals who are just naturally endowed with creative skills, not only in advertising but in science, the arts, and medicine. These individuals are often disorganized and illogical in their thinking but at the same time seem to be able to connect and make sense out of disconnected and disengaged events, putting them together almost naturally and forming a *gestalt*. In our work with agencies and other industries we are often asked how they might find a person like that, and what they should be looking for. But it's not easy.

It is clear that schools, from kindergarten to graduate school, heavily favor individuals who are left brain dominant. And professions favor these individuals also because they are initially selected by the professional schools and then matriculated into the professions. Vipond (1996) compares APA style—which is used in almost all of the professions and not just psychology—as typifying and exemplifying this left brain approach. He says that APA style (1) privileges the quantitative method and marginalizes discourse, (2) divorces research methods and ethics, (3) assumes behaviorist principles as basic in human behavior, (4) presents an oversimplified view of science, and (5) devalues literary style, such as the use of the metaphor or resemblance. As Kuhn has described this phenomenon, ordinary scientists labor day after day in their limited paradigms, solving problems like crossword puzzles or mystery plots in a novel, but there is no progress. But for Kuhn (1962), real science is revolutionary and not mundane, and scientific revolutions are the result of a few creative individuals who change the paradigm, eventually dragging the ordinary scientist, kicking and screaming, into the real world. The Copernican, Newtonian, Darwinian, and Freudian revolutions are examples of such rotations and turnarounds in the history of science.

We are often asked how we find people who are more right brain dominant, particularly by agencies and by some schools who appreciate creativity and have a niche for it. Since tests and measurements of human ability are designed by schools for use in schools and in institutions of higher learning, they are, by design, left brain oriented. But there are a few measures that are very adept and proficient at identifying these individuals. The Rorschach ink blot test, which has been in use since the early 1920s, has never been superseded or replaced as the most ingenious and resourceful psychological test ever devised. The Rorschach identifies creative individuals by the way that they are able to integrate various parts of an inkblot into a *gestalt* or a whole image with logical connections between the main body of the blot and all of the subblots. It also assesses the provident and judicious use of color, which is applied to the way an individual handles emotions. There are many other measures in the Rorschach that will single out and pinpoint creative and resourceful individuals, which ordinary tests won't do.

Right-brain-dominant individuals do extremely well in tests of spatial relations, since this is a uniquely right brain function. Because of this well-developed ability, they are often able to bring together, on tests, parts and sections of shapes that appear to be wholly incompatible and inconsistent. In addition, they can see beyond the obvious and prominent features of a product or an object that looks as if it does not belong or fit in, and bring closure to that object. Being able to see beyond the obvious and look into the detached or disconnected is part of the reason they do well on a test of spatial relations, where the task is to select from four choices what a two-dimensional figure would look like when put together into a three-dimensional figure. An example of this type of test item is seen in Figure 4.1.

Conversely, right-brain-dominant people quite often do poorly at logic and in courses that involve logical operations, such as mathematics or statistics. But finding people who are right brain dominant is not difficult; it is simply that tests and measurements have not been devised to identify them. Similarly, and by reputation, it is hard to keep a right-brain-dominant person focused on a task, since they tend to overlook details and incidentals.

And finally, not only do schools and professions seek out, hire, and promote mostly left-brain-dominant individuals, but they are also the most desired quantity in business and industry. This is probably for all the same reasons already given, but also because of the strong tendency of the world's business enterprises to ignore, cover up, and suppress emotional expression in the workplace. We have dealt with that subject in more detail in Chapter 1 and it is a very large and looming subject on the frontier of business, for suppressed and ignored emotion often smolders for a long time before it comes out into the open and bursts into flames.

Figure 4.1
Example of Spatial Relations Test Item

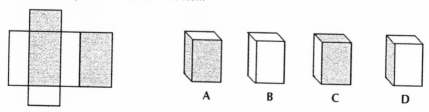

A B C D

Note: The correct answer is C.

REFERENCES

Ashforth, B., & Humphrey, Ronald H. (1995). Emotion in the workplace: A reappraisal. *Human Relations, 48,* 97–126.

Ashforth, B., & Lee, R. T.(1990). Defensive behavior in organizations: A preliminary model. *Human Relations, 43,* 621–48.

Bass, B. (1997). Does the transactional-transformational leadership paradigm transcend organizational and national boundaries? *American Psychologist, 52,* 130–39.

Bycio, P., Hackett, R. D., & Allen, J. S. (1995). Further assessments of Bass's (1985) conceptualization of transactional and transformational leadership. *Journal of Applied Psychology, 80,* 468–78.

Chomsky, N. (1971, December 30). The case against B. F. Skinner. *New York Review of Books,* pp. 18–24.

Crain, D. (1999, January 18). Advertising effectiveness. *Advertising Age.*

Damasio, A. (1994). *Descartes' error: Emotion, reason and the human brain.* New York: Avon Books.

Hadamard, J. (1945). *The psychology of invention in the mathematical field.* Princeton, NJ: Princeton University Press.

Kuhn, T. (1962). *The structure of scientific revolutions.* Chicago: University of Chicago Press.

LeDoux, J. (1996). *The emotional brain: The mysterious underpinnings of emotional life.* New York: Simon & Schuster.

Maddock, R. C., & Fulton, R. L. (1996). *Marketing to the mind: Right brain strategies in advertising and marketing.* Westport, CT: Quorum Books.

Oncken, W. (1984). *Managing management time: Who's got the monkey?* Englewood Cliffs, NJ: Prentice-Hall.

Ornstein, R. (1997). *The right mind: Making sense of the hemispheres.* Orlando, FL: Harcourt-Brace.

Skinner, B. F. (1957). *Verbal behavior.* Englewood Cliffs, NJ: Prentice-Hall.

Vipond, D. (1996). Problems with monolithic APA style. *American Psychologist, 51,* 653.

5

Consumer Resistance

BACKGROUND

It is becoming more and more clear that the traditional ways of getting information from customers are not working. The questionnaire that indicates that a customer is "very satisfied" or "not satisfied" is nothing more than a tracking study, and tells very little about the real intent or motives of customers. When people are surveyed by telephone and indicate that they bank at XYZ Bank because of convenience and friendly tellers, it is often found that they will drive past two or three different banks in order to get to XYZ Bank. Many surveys give out very limited information, and much of what is learned is old hat to management. We typically and commonly hear the complaint that they have already heard it too many times. As a result they stop doing market research altogether. Boldt (1993), who did focus groups for the *Philadelphia Inquirer*, said that "focus groups are like Alice's Restaurant; you can get anything you want" (p. 6).

HOW WE GOT INTO THIS IN THE FIRST PLACE

The reason that traditional formats of market research can no longer provide us with the information that we need is not because of the information revolution or information overload. It is because the methods and techniques that are still in use have outlived their usefulness. At least this may be true of some of them.

SOLUTIONS

Effective marketing research must be the opposite of these meth-odologies that have been introduced into marketing by psychology. It must be directive (vs. nondirective), authoritative (vs. participa-tive), and explanatory (vs. descriptive). All these basic criteria are required in order to break through the very important facade of consumer resistance and to provide the marketer with useful, rel-evant, and worthwhile deliverables.

A problem that occurs when marketers, educators, and others look to psychology for direction and guidance is that psychologists don't study emotion. According to LeDoux (1996), "Our emotions are the blood, sweat and tears, but you wouldn't know this from studying modern cognitive [psychological] research on emotion" (p. 42). He char-acterizes psychologists as very "cold-blooded," since they virtually ignore what people are really passionate about and instead play a giant numbers game with statistics. And yet emotions are the most important consideration for marketers, for it is only through emo-tion that we can understand motivation, and only through motiva-tion that we can understand why consumers do what they do.

Without penetration of the barriers of resistance, we are locked into cycles of rationalizations and justifications that originate on the left side of the brain. This is why it is so important that we recognize consumer resistance, and then develop methodologies that deal with it directly.

RECOGNIZING CONSUMER RESISTANCE

Consumers can't tell you why they do what they do, but this is not intentional or calculated. It is instead the nature of the uncon-scious mind. When a customer is shopping for a $20,000 automo-bile and ends up purchasing a $30,000 one, he or she has to rationalize spending the extra $10,000, or going "over budget." It is consumer resistance that creates this rationalization. Furthermore, the consumer believes these rationalizations, so that he or she has a self-serving benefit. One of the benefits of rationalizations is that they allow people to avoid or ignore many of the real reasons why they made a decision—often an impulsive one—to spend more money than they had to. For this reason—rationalization—people in general and consumers specifically can't give you the real rea-sons why they do what they do.

There is a lot of information in the unconscious mind that is hid-den; not only from others but from ourselves. This information may be too shocking, surprising, disabling, uncomfortable, or queasy, but for one reason or another it is in the mind and it is surrounded by a barrier of resistance. This is especially true of consumer behavior, since most consumer decisions involve spending money, which is always an emotional decision. The more emotional a decision is, the more the consumer has to be defended by their own resistance and, hence, the more rationalizations they generate. Figure 5.1 illustrates this relationship between reason, emotion, and resistance.

In Figure 5.1 it is clear that there is emotion involved in all products. However, there is a continuum from products that involve very little if any reason on the left side to products that involve substantial reason on the right side of the continuum. Examples of left side (emotional) products would be yachts, motorcycles, hot cars, hot boats, casino gaming, sporting and other performance events, floral displays, and flowers. Products that are more central would include kitchen and home products, such as furniture, children's products, clothing, and accessories. Products on the right side would include banks, securities and choice of a securities dealer, nonfiction books, transportation, and so on. It is difficult to classify some products, but all can eventually be classified. The more projects we do that apply Motigraphics, the clearer it becomes which products lie where on the continuum.

Resistance is more formidable and arduous when we are dealing with products that involve less reasoning and deliberation, or less logic. This is where consumers need to accumulate and collect more rationalizations and more reasons for purchasing, thereby fortifying the citadel of resistance. Keep in mind that this fortification or fortress that they erect is primarily for themselves and only sec-

Figure 5.1
Relationship between Reason, Emotion, and Resistance

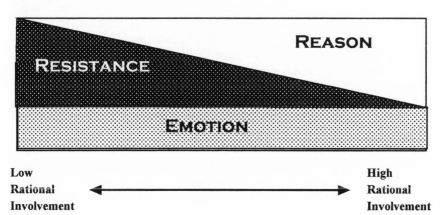

ondarily for others. With that in mind, when a consumer is confronted in a focus group or other market research it stands to reason that they are totally and thoroughly committed to their rationalizations, and therefore their resistance will be hard to break through. For that reason, we offer a new and improved method, the entire purpose of which is to break down the barriers that consumers erect with their rationalizations and justifications and to get around, behind, under, on top of, or beside the resistance. Note that we never say "in front of." The worst way to handle consumer resistance is from the front side. Confrontation only creates more resistance. The methods we offer of getting around resistance involve reducing resistance serendipitously and auspiciously, not directly.

DEFINING CONSUMER RESISTANCE

Two of the major problems with consumer resistance are defining it and recognizing it. When we talk about consumer resistance, we are not referring to sales resistance, which is quite different. Sales resistance deals with the resistance that a customer may have toward a particular person who is trying to make the sale, or toward the product itself. It is product or situation specific. Consumer resistance consists of the barriers and barricades that every consumer has that usually originate on the left side of the brain and which are designed to protect and defend her pocketbook or his wallet. Since very few people have an endless or infinite money supply, there must be resistance at some point. Consumer resistance is made up of rationalizations, justifications, and excuses that are designed to protect and defend the decisions that they make.

A consultant who was selling a program that reduced workers' compensation premiums told me that the first question that he was always asked by the prospective buyer was, "Have you ever sold this program to (this particular industry)?" To use a specific example, he said he was talking to a plant manager in a furniture plant. The plant manager asked, "Have you ever sold this program to a furniture manufacturer before?" The consultant's response was that he had, and when asked who that might be he responded "Flexsteel." The plant manager's immediate response was, "But that's steel furniture, and we produce wood furniture here." Obviously, the product here was workers' compensation, and the same principles would apply in either case with only very minute variations which depended on the safety record of the workforce more than the nature of the product that was being manufactured. Therefore, we can assume that the question, "Have you ever done furniture before?" was related to resistance, not to reality. Most consultants have had this experience. Part of it is explained by the *Adaptation Motive*. If you have done bank consulting, then you have a ticket to do more banks, and so on. But this question is also related to consumer resistance as the gatekeeper for the industry attempts to restrict access to peddlers and vendors.

Consumers in retail situations exhibit the same kind of resistance. They may say, "I'm just looking," or "nothing today, thank you." Both of these are statements which reflect mild to moderate resistance. Whether this consumer can be transformed into a customer depends a great deal on what is referred to in market research as "priming." There are several different ways to prime, and these are discussed in the following section.

One of the reasons that consumer resistance is hard to define is because it is passive. Most of us, when we hear the word "resistance" immediately think of stubbornness or of outright aggressive and oppositional activity. The words that come to mind are words like confrontation, challenge, defiance, and so on. But consumer resistance is not like this. It is a passive kind of resistance that operates almost automatically and instinctively. Therefore, it is difficult to get a handle on. The customer who is "just looking" or who responds, "nothing today, thank you" and who smiles as they say it is offering resistance, but since there is no challenge involved and no conflict it is not easily rebuffed. Furthermore, the smile is misleading.

MANAGING CONSUMER RESISTANCE

There are several ways of dealing with consumer resistance. One way is to use direct confrontation. This is considered by most sales and marketing gurus to be the worst way to deal with sales resistance. However, there are people who sell on the basis of insult and intimidation. This is often seen in businesses that are highly competitive and where the market is overcrowded. In this approach, as soon as the customer begins to demonstrate any resistance at all the saleslady comes across with reasons why they should buy. The more reasons that the saleslady gives, the more intensified the customer's resistance becomes, and the more the saleslady becomes insulting and intimidating. Obviously, this method suits a certain personality style and cannot be used effectively by most people.

A second method of handling resistance is where the seller becomes passively resistant like the customer. This method is used by default in large discount operations like Wal-Mart or K-Mart, and also in large book-selling operations like Barnes and Noble. In the large discount operations there are almost no salespeople, and so the customer is left to fend for themselves. Generally, it is quite difficult to find a salesperson to locate an item, and it becomes frustrating. As some of our research has shown, at times this approach will anger the customer to the point of leaving the store and not purchasing anything. This is more likely to occur in large operations that carry many, many items and which add another variable to the equation: confusion. The array of items and limited number of salespersons causes the customer to become confused and at times, overwhelmed. Wal-Mart, Walgreens, K-Mart, and large-volume stores tend to avoid this by having well-marked and sorted aisles and a situation where most people can find what they want without assistance. Some of the larger hardware stores do not avoid this problem, and so they end up with the problem of angry customers who leave the store.

Generally, the best way to handle consumer and customer resistance is by going with it. Everyone knows that the insult method and any other method of arguing with the customer will, for the most part, only strengthen and heighten the customer's resistance and decrease the chances of a sale. Consider the following example.

During a time when energy producers, like TVA, were increasing their rates and passing them on to their customers—the energy suppliers—the suppliers had no choice but to pass them on to their residential and commercial customers. Residential customers, who often did not read or follow the news, became irate with their bills and would often verbally attack the person who read the meter, since that person was their only contact with the supplier (the local electric company). Many meter readers responded by arguing with the customer but at the same time attempting to maintain a courteous and polite attitude. As rates increased, this became more and more difficult and eventually it was clear that training was needed.

Training was focused on the need to empathize with the customer, indicating that the meter person understood the customer's frustration, but at the same time trying to explain what was happening and why it was happening. This was a situation in which role-playing scenarios were helpful, and through this method the contact persons (meter readers) developed an understanding of how to handle customer resistance.

Contact persons had to learn the fine line between going with the resistance and actually agreeing with the angry customer, who was frequently reduced to calling the company names and shouting obscenities. They also had to learn not to personalize these insults, and to remain calm and cool headed, and this was done through practice. In many of the cases they found that the residential customer had no concept of the relationship between the producer of the power and the supplier, just as many have no concept of the relationship between wholesalers and retailers of goods. This had to be carefully explained. In the process, the company realized that their meter readers were front-line ambassadors for the entire company. As a result, an ongoing training program was established and customer satisfaction markedly increased.

BREAKING THROUGH CONSUMER RESISTANCE

We have found, first in clinical settings and also with consumers, that the method of breaking through resistance can be done either in focus groups or in one-on-one interviews.

Focus Groups in a Talk Show Format

In breaking down resistance in focus groups we have introduced the *focus group in a talk show format*. This is based on the intuitive and visceral appeal of most talk shows. Since we reject the humanistic concept that all group participants have an equal portion to contribute, we take the opinion leaders and those who either (1) know the most about the product or (2) think that they know the most about the product and put them in the position of guest. There may be more than one guest. The guest is an important figure in the focus group and needs to be seated center stage, just as guests are seated on the "Oprah Winfrey" show. The moderator is the paid market researcher, since that person knows the most about how to operate a group and the dynamics of groups.

Rogers (1961) felt that the most effective kind of therapy for clients who had problems was nondirective. His reasoning was that individuals "grow" faster under conditions of what he called unconditional positive regard. These theories led to the belief that all the therapist had to do was reflect what the client was saying back to him or her and the client would eventually see how they really were and that would be the stimulus for change. The therapist, then, was just a "mirror" who reflected the client's feeling back to him or her. Rogers's approach became very popular in the 1970s and 1980s, for it opened the door for almost anyone to become a therapist, since all they had to do was sit and listen. These same principles were adopted to focus groups and focus group leadership, and because all the leader had to do was reflect, almost anyone believed that they were qualified as long as they had the desire. But like other methods of psychotherapy, results were not achieved.

The same guiding principle that defined client-centered therapy defined the focus group, and that was the nondirective aspect. And it still dominates the scene today. But as in anything else, there are positive and negative aspects of this kind of an approach. The positive approach is that it attempts to break down the natural resistance that people have toward talking about why they do what they do, since it sets up a nonthreatening and positive, nonjudgmental environment. The negative aspect is that people who are naturally reluctant to speak can get away with adding little or nothing to the group, whereas the opinion leaders can dominate and hold court for two hours.

The focus group as a talk show format goes with the resistance. It allows the opinion leaders to be the experts and the rest of the focus group participants to be in the audience. They are encouraged by the leader to speak, but only one at a time. They are encouraged to challenge others, and particularly the guests and their opinions. Those who want to talk and dominate get their opportunity. In contrast to the traditional, nondirective focus group, the leader is trained in breaking down and breaking through consumer resistance and getting to the facts and figures.

Since most focus groups meet for only ninety minutes or two hours, a leader who is trained in breaking down resistance is essential. When the focus group is operated in the talk show format this happens, since the leader is an authority, maintains complete and total control over the group members, and concentrates on penetrating the resistance and getting to the facts.

One-On-One Interviews

A second method of breaking down and breaking through consumer resistance is the one-on-one interview, which is usually carried out in a field service facility using a well-trained interviewer. The conduct of these interviews involves some technical expertise. The basis for them is completely outlined and explained in Chapter 15, which describes the interview in depth. These interviews are based upon two major procedures.

First, the interview consists of visualization. Since the right hemisphere of the brain tends to think in pictures rather than words, the respondent is asked to picture and visualize what we have talked about, rather than just think about it. We discourage "thinking" in the traditional sense of the word, and we also discourage the use of the word "remember," although remembering is just what we want the respondent to do. Instead, we ask them simply to visualize the situation that we have placed them in—the supermarket, their kitchen, a restaurant—and then tell us about it. This method of visualization yields information that is much different from what would be seen in a typical market research interview.

Second, the interview consists of repetitive questioning. This is the way that attorneys typically conduct depositions and courtroom testimony. They use a circular procedure that attempts to hone in on the truth. They never accept the first response. If the witness says, "It was good," the obvious follow-up response is, "What about it was good?" If the witness says, "The best part was the trip to Florida," then the attorney says, "What about the trip to Florida was best?" The witness may say, "Seeing old friends that I had not seen for years," and the attorney would say, "What about seeing old friends made this the best part of the trip?" or "What old friends did you see?" The attorney may go on and say, "Which one of the old friends were you the most happy to see?" and "What did you and that old friend talk about?" and then, "What about that subject was important to you?" This circular method of questioning gets to the truth and to the real reasons why people do what they do. It is the only way to get beneath the surface. The combination of visualization and repetition is very effective. But keep in mind that it is not as entertaining as a focus group for your client, and not as exciting. In fact, the repetition can become outright boring and tedious, as the audience in the O. J. Simpson trial and in the Clinton testimony discovered. Depositions and trials are not what they are pictured to be in television dramas, most of which end up in the courtroom. Getting to the bottom line in consumer behavior is work, not fun, but we believe that this is the way it is supposed to be. It would be great if we could just sit down for a few hours and have a friendly chat in a focus group facility and get paid for it, but the client wants more than that for their money. They want results, and they want to hear something that they have never heard before. And they deserve to hear something new, something fresh and something startling. And that's what this type of interviewing delivers. We break through consumer resistance.

SUBLIMINAL CUES REVISITED

In Chapter 3 the whole phenomenon of subliminal cues was introduced. This is a new concept. The whole notion of subliminal cues is based on a discovery of the way that the mind works: People already have cues in their minds about your product (or service) and/or your client's product (or service). Therefore, the task of the focus group leader is to extract these cues and to get them organized, preferably on paper or on a computer. These subliminal cues—good and bad—are clues to what your customer thinks about your product as well as what he or she wants to hear about it in marketing and advertising. Furthermore, these subliminal cues are the basic ingredients for motives.

FOCUS GROUP LEADERSHIP

Ironically, the discovery of subliminal cues makes the job of the focus group leader much easier, even though the process of getting to them is tedious. Because of subliminal cues, the focus group leader is not embarking upon a fishing expedition. Instead, focus group leaders who are familiar with subliminal cues know exactly where they are going and how to get there.

Because of the reality of consumer resistance, focus group leadership cannot be left to chance. Leaders need to be skilled and proficient professionals, operating in much the same way that a surgeon would in extracting damaged or affected organs. Leaders need to know where they are headed and how to get there. And leaders, like lawyers, need never, never, never ask a question that they don't already know the answer to. A leader who asks questions that he or she does not already know the answer to is asking for a very big problem, and that is *surprises*. If there is only one thing that lawyers learn in law school it is the principle of no surprises. Remember, whether conducting large, eight- to ten-member focus groups or one-on-one interviews, most of the time your client is sitting behind the window. Too many surprises, and he or she may no longer be your client.

Too many times we have sat through focus groups, witnessing the beginning and wondering where it was going to end up and what was going to happen. Some focus group leaders are much smoother than others, and have a way of asking questions that does not threaten or cajole. But do they know where they are going, and where they are going to end up? The subliminal cue gives the focus group leader a goal, so that the leader knows where to go, how to get there, and what he or she is looking for.

The obvious question, then, is how do we know when we have found a subliminal cue? Is it experience? Luck? Chance? If this were the case, then we would not be writing this book. A subliminal cue is found when the statement that is made by the respondent fits into one of the motivational categories that we have introduced in Chapter 1 and which we fully expand upon in Part II of this book. A subliminal cue will be recognized when it fits neatly into one of the eleven motives that have been defined. In Chapter 15 we have fully elaborated on this process and we give actual examples of subliminal cues and how they fit into each motivational category and why. Therefore, the process is not guided by luck, the charm of the interviewer, or chance. It is guided by a prescribed procedure, which is what Motigraphics is all about. It is much closer to being scientific and therefore replicable than most procedures that are used in marketing and market research. Results can be obtained by either the most charming or the least charming interviewer, and they can be obtained every time.

REFERENCES

Boldt, D. (1993). Focus group follies. *Bulletin of the American Society of Newspaper Editors,* 4–9.

LeDoux, J. (1996). *The emotional brain: The mysterious underpinnings of emotional life.* New York: Simon & Schuster.

Rogers, C. (1961). *On becoming a person: A therapist's view of psychotherapy.* Boston: Houghton-Mifflin.

6

Absurdities

THE MAKING OF MOMENTOUS, MEMORABLE (BUT NOT NECESSARILY MOTIVATING) ADVERTISING AND MARKETING

Memorable advertising is produced with absurdities and personalizations. An absurdity is something that is rarely seen in everyday reality, but at the same time consists of common, everyday objects. A very simple example of an absurdity is Superman; that is, an individual who flies without wings, power, or any kind of visible support. It is something that we don't encounter in real life, and so it is absurd. However, everyone has wished that they had this power from time to time, and especially during childhood. Some parents can even recall when they had to beckon a child down from a roof at one time or another. The fact that almost everyone has thought of this contingency—flight without wings—makes the absurdity stand out, in the sense that it is not completely and utterly absurd.

In the last few years, computer programs have been introduced that allow us to do anything we want to with images on the screen, and thereby create absurdities. The problem is that with cheap and easy access to these programs, anyone may create just about anything that they want to. The result is that there is an absurdity overload, or clutter. There are so many absurdities on television today that the viewers are beginning to get dazed or indifferent when they see them. Some of them are so abstract or surreal that the viewer doesn't want to take the time to figure it out. This is especially true during prime-time television, where viewers start out the evening or the afternoon by putting their mind into neutral. No one wants to be confronted with a puzzle or dilemma that they have to devote mind power to working out in order to get the point.

In *Marketing to the Mind* (Maddock & Fulton, 1996), we warned about what would occur with an overproduction of absurdities. We said that there would be clutter that would boggle the mind. Right now there are many absurdities, on television and in print. But the great ones are still small in number.

What makes them great? The great ones are the ones that people remember. Like the Coke man who is stocking the shelves in the supermarket and is caught by the security camera picking a Pepsi can from a display cabinet in a convenience store. When he does, the entire display of cans falls over on top of him.

Does an absurdity like this affect people's purchase decisions? Probably not. Absurdities are memorable, but not necessarily motivating. People remember absurdities, but the question that remains is do memorable commercials motivate people toward decisions and action? We don't think so. We believe that what really motivates people is what they can personalize, and not just what they can remember. Personalizations are discussed in Chapter 7 and also in detail in Part II, which reviews the personal motives that make up the target that all advertising tries to aim at. The distance between the bull's-eye and the motive that is being aimed at is the extent to which the marketer has missed the mark. However, absurdities do give the marketer a little extra edge, and that edge is memorability.

It is assumed that everyone and anyone would like to create a great absurdity, because they are so memorable. My mother was always baffled by the fact that as children my brothers and I had difficulty memorizing our multiplication tables and the Gettysburg Address but we could quickly and readily recall a plethora of radio commercials, and particularly those that were set to a jingle. The reason was because of absurdities and access to the right hemisphere of the brain, which often ensures storage in long-term memory. Since almost everyone would like to get their message into long-term storage and memory, we need to take a hard look at how absurdities work.

HISTORY AND BACKGROUND OF ABSURDITIES

In 1972, Federal Express Corporation, now FedEx, embarked upon an advertising campaign that relied heavily upon humor. The thirty-second spots, produced by Alley and Gargano, had the effect of turning the heads of businesspeople and changing the entire timetable by which America (and now the world) does business. These ads ran until the early 1980s and were very effective. In answer to the old question, "Does humor in advertising really sell products?" we would have to give a resounding "yes." But humor was not the only issue here, and may not have been what made this company successful.

A review of a video tape which included all of the FedEx ads that ran indicated that there were two categories of television spots: absurdities and personalizations. Our understanding of how absurdities work and why they work that way is based in part upon descriptions of coordination between the two hemispheres of the brain by Ornstein (1997). His analysis indicates that the left hemisphere is the precise side, whereas the right hemisphere analyzes contexts or large elements of perception and context. It would appear that when an absurdity is delivered it is rejected by the left side of the brain since it is first, a visual, and second, absurd and different. This would imply that the right hemisphere takes over and searches for a familiar context for this absurdity, in order to make some sense out of it. At this point, both the limbic system and long-term memory are consulted; the limbic system in order to assign emotion and feeling to the absurdity, long-term memory to search for similar, recognizable occurrences from the past. Once this contextual analysis is completed, the picture is then sent back to the left hemisphere for a concrete and factual interpretation. Ornstein refers to this as "text and context." He continues

Remember too, that the right brain keeps a number of multiple meanings, for instance of words, and this allows us to get jokes, or to understand the complexity of a poet's words, and on an ordinary level to respond to metaphor and indirection. However when things are understood concretely, and it is time to settle on one meaning and "go into production," so to speak, then the left hemisphere seems to excel. Some learning, like music, most likely involves selecting one of the many alternatives and acting on it. Local and well-defined the left hemisphere's responsibility may be, but with that comes precision. (p. 175)

A personalization is something that people can easily personalize or intimate. It is something that strikes a chord or that goes directly to the heart. Personalizations will be discussed in Chapter 7.

Some of the absurdities seen in the FedEx spots included a voice over which said, "Shipping a package on FedEx is as easy as picking up the telephone." This spot featured a man picking up an entire telephone booth, and another man picking up the entire telephone at home (not just the receiver), half asleep, and attempting to talk into the base of the phone. Another absurdity showed a paper explosion, with gobs of paper careening down a hallway like a tidal wave. There was a fast-talking man who spewed out words like an accelerated tape recording. And, in order to make the point that it's convenient to use FedEx and that they will come right to your office to pick up your package, a FedEx truck drives out of an elevator or right into the office suite.

These absurdities work because they are slight departures from reality, but they are product related. The underlying messages of these absurdities were safety, security, reassurance, availability, simplicity, and practicality. Initially people did not believe that it was possible to get their document or package from Washington, D.C. to San Francisco overnight. Even though airplanes had been around for seventy years, someone or something had to convince them. The absurdities and personalizations worked.

THE WAY ABSURDITIES WORK

The absurdities that got FedEx off to a roaring start worked because of the way that they were processed by the brain. They presented a new, novel, and innovative approach that had not been experienced by the brain before. Since the left hemisphere deals in logic and practicalities, the absurdity is shifted over to the right side of the brain for further interpretation. The right hemisphere uses pictures and gestures in order to communicate. The right hemisphere is also experienced and skilled in dealing with ambiguous, imprecise, and confusing situations. But the right hemisphere does not try to make sense out of these confused situations. What it does is just sort out this confusing information and then send it to the left hemisphere to make sense.

Part of this confusing information is sent to long-term memory, which from what we can determine is also located in the right hemisphere. What occurs then is that the limbic system processes the information that it has received and acts upon it, either favorably or unfavorably. It then sends the message back to the left hemisphere where some action must be taken, based upon the response of the limbic system. If the limbic system sends positive and favorable emotions over to the left side, then the left brain will attempt to make a decision. But this decision is made not with this information only, but with other more rational and logical considerations:

· Can I afford it?
· Is it guaranteed?
· Does it do what I want it to do?
· Does it help me, in some way, to get on with my life?

If the left hemisphere does not get the correct and proper answers to these questions, the overall answer may be "no." But even if it is "no," all is not lost, for the absurdity has been stored in long-term memory where, at a later date, it can be revived and put to use. Unlike advertising and marketing attempts that are not absurdities (or personalizations), the information may not be stored and will not be available for the future.

The first people to be exposed to the FedEx spots in the early 1970s, when interviewed, said that they didn't believe it and in some cases their disbelief and skepticism caused them to postpone using FedEx for several years. But eventually they responded to that original message that had been stored away in long-term memory and became loyal customers. Absurdities are like an investment in the future!

Our deep appreciation for absurdities and personalizations grew out of an early association with FedEx and with an ad agency in St. Louis that specializes in these approaches. Steve Puckett produced a series of spots for a casino with an ancient Roman theme that was destined to move into the midst of midwestern American farmland. The spots showed Roman columns sprouting up out of the ground in the place of soybeans and corn. For a regional brand of chili they produced a spot where father and son were home alone and opened a can of chili, but inadvertently left the uneaten chili on the table when they left the table and the family dog finished it up. At that point, the dog had to be put outside because he was breaking so much wind! These kinds of absurdities and personalizations have lasting and long-term results because they are absurd and because they are product related. Again, this is why we say that an absurdity is an investment in the future.

In *Marketing to the Mind* (Maddock & Fulton, 1996), we included an absurdity from Onan, a division of Cummins Engine Company that appeared in print in 1982. Onan manufactures recreational generators for RVs and boats. In this particular ad, which appeared in *Motor Boating and Sailing* magazine, a fisherman was pictured on a primitive, homemade raft with a makeshift sail. Since there was no wind to power the sail he had aboard a very large, six-foot-high rotating fan which used to be seen in offices. The purpose of the fan was to supply the wind to the sail which would move the raft, but the fan had to have a source of 120-volt ac power. That was the purpose of the Onan, which was also onboard the raft! Here is a picture of a situation that is not only absurd, but also is intimately product related and which appeals to the reader of this particular magazine. It has all of the components of a successful absurdity, not the least of which is memorability.

DO ABSURDITIES HAVE TO BE FUNNY?

There is a lot of controversy about the use of humor in advertising and the argument seems to go on and on, without resolution. Blair and Rosenberg (1994) looked at areas of convergence in advertising to see how humor actually works, but their conclusion was that although it worked better in some areas than in others, "The relatedness of the humor to the ad in magazines does not appear to affect recall performance" (p. 54). However, we know from experience that absurdities do affect recall performance. In order to understand this so that we may become more adept at constructing absurdities, let's take a closer look at the relationship between the two.

The argument against humor has always been that advertising should not be entertaining. If it is, the viewer (or reader) will lose sight of the product that is being advertised and become caught up in the entertainment value of the ad, forgetting the product. Hence comes our warning or dictum that the absurdity should be product related. What an absurdity does is takes two divergent ideas and brings them together, thereby creating a "spark." That spark becomes the embryo of a third and totally new idea, and this new idea is the product of the creative process. Sometimes, when that spark is ignited, a whole revolution occurs, as we have seen in the past 100 years in the various fields of physical science (Kuhn, 1996).

Ericka Fromm (1998) said that in 1932, when she was a student at the University of Frankfurt, she wrote, as part of a psychology project, a letter to 100 scientists and philosophers and asked them each what they experienced during the height of their productive thinking. She received forty-one responses (an amazing response rate), and among them were letters from Freud and Einstein. Freud replied, in a handwritten letter, that he was "unfamiliar with his own thoughts" and could be of no assistance. Einstein, in a slightly longer personal letter, got right to the point and said that he had looked at some principles in basic mechanics and found them to be seriously flawed. He added that the recognition that there was a profound defect here set up a state of psychic tension within him which led to a seven-year search for the answer. He then described the experience of arriving at the answer as a "release," as the psychic tension was dissipated. He concluded

It was always the search for a logically simple meaning of empirically established relationships, propelled by the conviction that there existed a simple logical meaning.

The psychological situation is comparable with the attitude of somebody who wants to solve a puzzle or a chess problem, who is convinced that the solution exists, because the creator of the problem possesses the solution. The only difference lies in that the psychic energy arises from the generality of the problem, and from its root in the relationship to reality. (p. 1198)

This igniting of a spark is the same kind of a situation that is seen in jokes and in humor. Two seemingly unrelated ideas are brought together and create a spark when a new idea is generated. This often happens in the morning, when the mind is not asleep but also not fully awake and the defenses and resistance of the left hemisphere are not fully operational. Creative people will tell you that this is often when they have their most creative and practical ideas.

For Ornstein (1997), a joke is an excellent example of how the right and left hemispheres work together. He states, "We find a joke funny when it brings together two or more unexpected associations. But these associations depend on the overall view and a sense of what is going on" (pp. 106–7). An example might be a sign out in front of a small restaurant that also has gasoline sales which says, "Eat Here and Get Gas." The left hemisphere would interpret this quite literally: It's a gas station that also sells food (or vice-versa). The right hemisphere would discern the incongruity here, the complexity, and the subtlety of the situation and the context. The right hemisphere examines the possibility that there are at least two contexts here: (1) stopping to eat and filling up your car with gasoline, and (2) eating in the restaurant and ending up with gastrointestinal distress. The second interpretation is the one that is funny.

CREATIVITY IN ADVERTISING, SCIENCE, AND OTHER AREAS

Our own interpretation is in agreement with Ornstein (1997) but is more specific. A joke and a creative idea both occur when two divergent ideas are brought together to create a spark. It is quite likely that these two ideas have been "lying around" in long-term memory for some time. For Einstein, these ideas were dormant or semiactive for at least seven years. Then suddenly the spark was ignited!

However, we go even further in examining the content of these divergent ideas. For us, the two ideas must come from two different motivational and emotional systems. We define these motivational systems—eleven of them—in Part II of this book and we elaborate upon them in Part III. These two different motivational systems must be in conflict with each other and be brought together and generate a third idea or concept. In a joke, this is generally referred to as a punch line:

A man stops at a roadside diner for breakfast and the gum-chewing waitress says, "What'll it be?" He responds, "I'll have eggs over light, hash browns, and I could use some kind words." A few minutes later, the waitress brings his breakfast and drops it down in front of him. The man says, "What about the kind words?" She responds, "Don't eat them eggs."

The conflict here is between two motivational systems. The kind words belong to the Spiritual Survival Motive, which deals not only in passion but also in compassion and caring. The response of the waitress, which implies that the eggs are tainted, is related to the Physical Survival Motive.

A man sees an ad in the paper for a late-model Jaguar XJE for $2,000. He can't believe it. He calls the number and verifies that the lady actually wants to sell this car, in mint condition with low mileage, for $2,000. He rushes over to the address that she gives him and looks at the car, then asks if this is really true, or if she is crazy. She assures him that she is not crazy, that she was asking $2,000 for the car, but she has changed her mind and will take $1,000. He finds this even more unbelievable, and questions her again. Slightly annoyed, she confirms the $1,000 price and assures him that she has not lost her mind. She then explains, "The car belongs to my husband, who last week ran off with his secretary to Hawaii. He sent me an e-mail which said 'sell the car, and send me the money.' I am not crazy. As a loyal wife, I'm simply doing what he told me to do."

Note the involvement of both the right and left hemispheres. The left hemisphere notes the ridiculously low price, then sends the information to the right hemisphere which analyzes the context. Again, there are two motivational systems in conflict here. One is the Spiritual Survival Motive, which deals in the elements of family values (marriage and human love). The other is the Territorial Survival Motive, which concerns assets and ownership.

Most jokes involve conflict between the Spiritual Survival Motive and the Sexual Survival Motive, since these two motives are the most incompatible and their juxtaposition in a joke creates the most discord and the most intrapsychic conflict. The problem with most of these kinds of jokes is that they are tasteless and are usually only told by men to other men and not in mixed audiences. Therefore, our third example involves the juxtaposition of the Spiritual Survival Motive and the Territorial Survival Motive. Mixing sexual survival and spiritual survival, which is the framework for most jokes, is left to the reader to discover.

A man in his nineties wins one million dollars in the Illinois sweepstakes, and his daughter and son-in-law are afraid to tell him because of the risk of stroke or heart attack. Good news can often be as shocking to the physical system as bad news. After talking it over, they decide to get the preacher to tell him, since the preacher is used to giving people both bad news and good news. The preacher agrees and on a Sunday after church he comes over to the house, sits on the porch with grandpa, and they talk about trivialities.

Finally, the preacher gets to the point. "Grandpa," he says, "what would you do if someone died and left you a million dollars?" Grandpa didn't even give it a thought. "That's easy!" he said, "I'd give it to the church!" And the preacher dropped dead.

Here we are mixing spiritual survival (church) with territorial survival (assets). These are two motivational categories that usually don't fit together too well and the punch line creates a conflict (psychic tension) out of which comes anxiety and tension which is quickly dissipated by laughter.

Today, most serious thinkers realize that a joke, as well as the creative process, emanates from the collision of two ideas (or subliminal cues) which have been downcast and lying in the unconscious for a number of years. What has not been shown is that creative ideas and punch lines come from the collision of two motive content areas, and we have defined these content areas. They are, basically, the major motives that are found in the unconscious mind. Almost anyone can see the conflict between spiritual survival and sexual survival; for example, in the relationship between a preacher and a prostitute.

In general, what we are saying is that people have a general tendency to pigeonhole information in their minds. We are exposed to mountains of information every day, and somehow we have to sort the information that comes in verbally and visually, just as we have to sort information that comes into the home or office in hard copy. In research that we have done in direct mail, people tell us regularly that the first thing that they do with their mail is sort it. They all have essentially the same categories: junk, bills, ads, coupons, newspapers and magazines, and first-class mail. Similarly, we all do a mental sort. Material coming in includes issues relating to survival, to orientation, to expectation, to adaptation, and to play. These are content categories. They appear to be inclusive of most of the incoming information. Now we can go one step further and say not only that conflict occurs, but it occurs between specific categories within the mind. Furthermore, that conflict causes tension and anxiety, and in some cases the striving to resolve that tension and anxiety either gives rise to a whole new creative idea or to a punch line in a joke. Either way, creativity arises out of tension, and this is consistent with Einstein's definition of the creative process.

Generally, if a joke is funny, people laugh. MacLean (1990) stated that in all of his investigations of the brain, the causes of laughter were the most difficult to find and he eventually said that this would have to be left for later investigations. From our point of view, when two divergent ideas are brought together, psychic conflict occurs. This was verified by Einstein in the letter quoted. When psychic conflict occurs, there are a number of ways to dissipate that conflict, and laughter is one way. Another way, as Einstein has shared with us, is by working out the solution to the conflict—even if it takes seven years!

From what we can determine, then, when two divergent ideas meet and psychic tension is created, laughter is the brain's way of discharging that tension. Therefore, an absurdity, as we have discussed, creates tension. And if this is correct, then those who create absurdities must be particularly careful not to create more problems than they solve. The more intense the conflict between the two ideas, the more laughter will be generated, and there is a good possibility that the basic message will be lost in the translation. This is why we have emphasized the importance of connecting the absurdity with the product, as in the Onan print ad that was mentioned or in all of the FedEx ads that were reviewed earlier in this chapter. Because of the prominence of computer programs and capabilities in creating absurdities, many advertising spots have been created that are not product related and that are not even funny, and where the product itself may become lost in the shuffle and confusion of the advertisement. In this situation, it is usually the client who loses out. This is also why it can be a mistake to use focus groups or other groups of individuals to make the final determination on advertising, since they will be evaluating the spot for its entertainment value and not necessarily for its persuasive value and intent.

The close relationship and kinship between absurdities and humor is often seen in humorous movies and sitcoms. One theme that is used over and over again is the theme of mistaken identity, which is an absurdity which results in humor and laughter. A better and more specific example is seen in many Woody Allen movies, and as an example we pick one of his more popular ones, *Bananas*. In this film, some of the absurdities are

The new president of a Latin American third-world country announces, after successfully overthrowing the old regime, that he is the new president and the official language will be Swedish.

The new president orders the execution, one by one, of the members of a failed coup, and they must take numbers from a rack. Woody Allen hands out the numbers from a "Take-a-Chek" dispenser.

Woody Allen announces to his parents that he is going to South America to become a freedom fighter while they are performing surgery.

In the movie *Take the Money and Run,* Virgil is sentenced to prison for a bank robbery. While in prison he gets into trouble and is sentenced to the "hole," where instead of being in solitary he must spend forty-eight hours with a representative of New York Life. The enormous popularity of movies such as this, and particularly those produced by Woody Allen, is based upon the use of raw absurdities as a basis for humor. Such films allow us to see exactly how humor works and what makes something funny, and also to get a glimpse at the creative process.

CATEGORIES

Our own interpretation of how humor works is consistent with that outlined by Ornstein (1997), but goes further. This is because we have recognized that people have categories in their minds into which they insert information as they receive it. These categories, such as spiritual survival and sexual survival, we have characterized as *motives.* Their importance to the whole process of Motigraphics will soon become apparent. It is when the material that is stored in these motives comes in conflict with other motives that an absurdity is created. When the absurdity is created, the mind has to deal with it, since it has not been seen before. The way that the mind deals with it is through laughter, which is a way of discharging tension and apprehension. This is seen quite often in people who are timid and nervous and who will resort to laughter to cover up their apprehension so that others will not see that they are nervous.

SUMMARY

Absurdities are created because they are memorable. As we have pointed out in this chapter, they are not necessarily motivating, but they are memorable. Absurdities must be related to reality in a tangential way. Otherwise they will just cause confusion and perplexity for the person who encounters them and then, as we have seen, set up a state of apprehension and anxiety. This is what we call the *backfire effect.* That is, what is intended to be persuasive and motivating becomes irritating and annoying. Nothing will cause agitation and outrage in a potential customer more than this.

Absurdities must also be product related. The example of the Onan spot that was run many years ago shows how an absurdity is product related. A more recent example was a television spot by

Totes, a portable umbrella. When people think of umbrellas they think of rain, but in this case the umbrella is used in all kinds of other situations where people are in danger of getting splashed, such as when a 275-pound man cannonballs off of the high board into the pool.

REFERENCES

Blair, M. H., & Rosenberg, K. (1994). Convergent findings increase our understanding of how advertising works. *Journal of Advertising Research, 32*, 35–55.

Fromm, E. (1998). Lost and found a half a century later: Letters by Freud and Einstein. *American Psychologist, 53,* 1195–98.

Kuhn, T. S. (1996). *The structure of scientific revolutions* (3d ed.). Chicago: University of Chicago Press.

MacLean, P. D. (1990). *The triune brain in evolution: Role in paleocerebral functions.* New York: Plenum Press.

Maddock, R. C., & Fulton, R. L. (1996). *Marketing to the mind: Right brain strategies in advertising and marketing.* Westport, CT: Quorum Books.

Ornstein, R. (1997). *The right mind: Making sense of the hemispheres.* Orlando, FL: Harcourt Brace.

7

Paradigms and Personalizations

I was first influenced by absurdities and personalizations when I watched an entire video of ads produced for Federal Express from 1972 to 1981. It was clear after watching it two times that there were two different types of approaches to advertising and marketing to the mind. The first was the absurdity. Almost everyone who saw the "fast-talking man" remembers it to this day. Many remember the "paper explosion" and the truck that made it so convenient for you to use Federal Express that it drove right into your office suite. It was clear that these were absurdities. The other method, which was clearly very different and unique, was the personalization.

No one had ever categorized these ads in this manner. Everyone agreed that they were humorous, and some of them won Clios, Addys, and other awards. But other than describing them as uproariously funny, no one ever looked at what was really behind these spots and why they did what they were supposed to do, and that was to sell people on a new company and a new concept: overnight delivery. It was quite clear that, for whatever reason, they were working.

But advertising, like science, should involve replication. If something works well, others should be able to replicate it. To replicate a method that works we need to know the principles behind the ad that cause it to work, and why it works. Then others can produce an entirely different ad using the same principles and, all other things being equal, it will work just as well as the first one. This puts advertising on the level of science and not just an art, which is where it should be.

Advertising as an art is quite different and puts much more emphasis on creativity and discovery and very little if any on replication. To be realistic, advertising is probably best compared to the profession of medicine. Medicine is a science, but those who practice it have a tremendous appreciation for medicine as an art *and* a science.

SCREENPLAY AND ITS IMPLICATIONS FOR
LIFE AND LIVING

Two small books have had considerable influence and provide the foundation for what is presented here. These books deal with very divergent and incongruous themes. Both are classics in their own right and should be read by everyone, even if the reader has no interest in their respective contents or themes. For although they deal with divergent subject matter, they share a common concern, and that is the concern for the paradigm or framework. These two books are paradigmatic.

The first little book is by Syd Field (1994), and is entitled *Screenplay: The Foundations of Screenwriting*. Some well-known screenwriters have stated that it is the only book that anyone needs to read if they want to write a successful screenplay. Some have even said that there is more information in this little book than there is in a full-fledged master's degree program in screenwriting.

For Field, every screenplay must have a paradigm, or a framework. There are generally three parts to that framework: the setup (Act I); the confrontation (Act II); and the resolution (Act III). According to Field, all drama is conflict, because without conflict there can be no resolution. So Act II is all conflict, and the example that he uses is a well-known film and television screenplay, *The Fugitive*, where the entire drama is driven by the main character's need to bring his wife's killer to justice. This book mirrors lifestyle, since life is filled with conflicts. This is why it is important.

But there is another very important ingredient in Field's scheme: the plot point. The paradigm is punctuated throughout by plot points, which have the effect of changing the entire direction of the drama. Usually, this change is from good to bad or from bad to worse at the beginning of the screenplay, and then back to good again at the end. There are at least two major plot points in any drama: one occurring no more than thirty minutes into the drama and the other occurring from fifteen to thirty minutes before the end. However, the screenwriter may put as many additional plot points into a drama as he or she wants. For example, *Titanic* had a number of plot points, the main one being associated with the sinking of the ship, a historical fact. Other plot points involved romantic involvement and intrigue on the part of the actors and actresses. Since the film was viewed by more people than any other in history, it can be assumed that the multiplicity of plot points had a lot to do with this. Field has noted that if a plot point does not occur within the first thirty minutes of a drama, the audience will quickly lose interest and will either flip channels or give up and go to bed.

I have never watched a movie or read a novel that did not have a paradigm. I believe that there are probably a lot of them that get rejected by producers, and well they should be. A screenplay without a paradigm and without plot points is like a ship without a rudder. If anything like this ever made it to the screen it would be quickly rejected by audiences. Why? Because viewers have to be able to personalize what they see in the movies or on television. If they can't personalize it, the screenplay dies a natural death. The same is true of advertising and marketing.

Television ratings directly reflect the degree to which people can or cannot personalize what they see on the screen. The reason, of course, is that people have plot points in their own lives and they also have a burning desire and need for resolution.

Most of us don't have people shooting live bullets at us, like we see on television, but we do have plot points that at times appear to defy any kind of resolution. Therefore, it is imperative for us to know that others can face insurmountable odds and overcome them or resolve them in the end. This is what survival is all about.

PARADIGMS

People have paradigms in their lives. This is why they watch movies and personalize what they see and hear. They say to themselves, "What would I do in a situation like that?" Men usually define the paradigm in their life in terms of what they do for a living. Upon introduction, a man will generally say, "I'm a plumber," or "I'm a dentist," or "I'm a senior vice president." When men get together in a corner at a party, away from the women, they usually talk about performance. This is their favorite subject, and performance usually defines the paradigm in their life. The job is where they have to perform the most, so in defining themselves in terms of where they work they are defining their life's paradigm. Of the top-selling men's magazines, all are directly related to performance: sexual performance, performance in business, performance in automobiles, sports, recreation, and so on.

Women also have a paradigm in their lives which they define in terms of home, family, children, and grandchildren. Top-selling women's magazines—*Better Homes and Gardens* and *Family Circle*—attest to this. Lifetime Television—which is dedicated to women and women's concerns—almost always features screenplays that are dedicated to this paradigm. Although some may object and make reference to exceptions to this paradigm, there are exceptions to everything, but in this case the magazine circulation figures don't support the exceptions.

An example of the importance of a paradigm is seen in the novels of Danielle Steel, an extremely prolific writer. She has a paradigm which is extremely appealing, and it is repeated in every one of her books. Basically, her paradigm consists of a woman who is living with/married to/engaged to/working for a man who is insensitive. She may actually have no romantic attachment to this insensitive man, but somehow he is in her life. A plot point occurs in which a sensitive man comes into her life, and resolution occurs when the insensitive man is replaced by the sensitive one. In our research, we asked over 200 women to describe their husband in one word, and the word that over half of them used was insensitive.

In the movie that was made from a book by Garganus (1996), the oldest living Confederate widow gives a speech at the very end of her life. She is very convincing when she says that "of all the things that I've done in my life, and of all that has happened to me, the greatest pleasure of all was being a mother and a grandmother." She was talking about the framework or paradigm of her life, from a retrospective point of view.

The point that is often missed by many people is the importance of having a paradigm or a framework in their lives. Both Syd Field and Danielle Steel, as well as John Grisham and others, illustrate the importance of a paradigm to all of us. Day after day, people search obituaries (among the most popular features in most newspapers) in order to read about people who died that they did not even know, to see if they had a paradigm in their life and, if so, what kind of a paradigm it was. In talking to many of these people in newspaper research that I have done, I firmly believe that they were looking for one for themselves. For what other reason would they turn first to the obituary section and read about the deaths of people that they did not even know? When asked about this they responded, "You never know. There may be someone in there that I knew." This is the phenomenon that Fleischman (1990) calls *meaningful death*.

Successful and Not-So-Successful Paradigms

The second classic book that should be read and digested by many is by Thomas Kuhn (1996), and is entitled *The Structure of Scien-*

tific Revolutions. In this book, the author shows how important a paradigm is for achieving success in science, and traces successes and failures during a time that science and invention were attempting to build credibility and generate results. One example that he gives is in the evolution of electricity during the eighteenth century:

The history of electrical research in the first half of the eighteenth century provides a more concrete and better known example of the way that a science develops before it acquires the first universally received paradigm. During that period there were almost as many views about the nature of electricity as there were important electrical experimenters: men like Hauksbee, Gray, Desaguliers, Du Fay, Nollett, Watson, Franklin and others. All of their numerous concepts of electricity had something in common—they were partially derived from one or another version of the mechanico-corpuscular philosophy that guided all scientific research of the day. In addition, all were components of real scientific theories; of theories that had been drawn in part from experiment and observation that partially determined the choice and interpretation of additional problems undertaken in research. Yet, though all of the experiments were electrical and though all of the experimenters read each other's works, their theories had no more than a family resemblance. (pp. 13–14)

Kuhn stresses the importance of paradigms in the development and history of science back to the study of motion before Aristotle and the study of statics before Archimedes, and in many other fields. His conclusion is, "History suggests that the road to a firm research consensus is extraordinarily arduous" (p. 15). Interestingly, Kuhn has doubts and expresses these doubts when it comes to paradigms in the social sciences. He states, "It remains an open question what parts of social science have yet acquired such paradigms at all" (p. 15).

If you accept the notion that a paradigm is essential, the reason many of the social sciences, and particularly sociology and psychology, have failed to deliver results to marketers, educators, and practicing psychologists is because of the lack of a viable paradigm. Without a paradigm, results are not forthcoming. Psychologists felt that they had a paradigm in behaviorism, and although that hope vanished in 1959, there were many who still cling to it in spite of its overall inadequacy to explain or predict human behavior and also in spite of its oversimplification of human behavior. More recently, psychology invented "cognitive psychology," which is actually just behaviorism in disguise, so that, although the name had changed, the paradigm (or lack of) remains the same (LeDoux, 1996). This whole subject is very controversial and is discussed in more detail in Chapter 2.

In the field of criminology, which is a subfield of sociology, the absence of a paradigm led to large losses in terms of human life.

However, the mayor of New York, Rudolph Giuliani, and his police commissioner, William J. Bratton, saw crime fall to its lowest level in twenty-five years as a result of their efforts and leadership. Their crime czar, Jack Maples, made a "wager" with all of the sociologists and criminologists in the metropolitan colleges and universities. Maples said that he would love to get all of the criminologists together in one room and have them put their grant money in the middle of the floor in a big pile, and then declare a winner, where "winner takes all." What he was referring to was their paradigm versus his. The paradigm that has been in effect since the Johnson administration crime report of 1967 is that inner-city crime is the inevitable product of racism and poverty. This "enlightened" view held that little could be done until the social conditions were dealt with. In contrast, Maples, Bratton, and Giuliani were working within a paradigm that said the way to reduce crime is with more police and more arrests. The reason they were so gleeful is that it looked like, after twenty-five years of an enlightened paradigm, the added police and policing approach was the only one that really worked. Horowitz (1995) summarizes the results that were achieved in New York subways alone: "Today, riding the subways is a wholly different experience from what it was five years ago. Serious felonies are down sixty-four percent, and robberies are down an extraordinary seventy-three percent. Each day, some 3.5 million people take the subways. There are fewer than twenty reported crimes" (p. 23).

Although neither side "won" (in the sense that the criminals will always be with us), the mayor and his staff declared a victory. And the results are very visible. The statistics speak for themselves. The criminologists, without a paradigm, were able to muster very little statistical support for their approach to the treatment of crime and criminals. The fact that they still receive financial support, in terms of big dollars, is more closely related to the emotional appeal of their pitch than it is to the bottom line, which refers to the considerable reduction in crime statistics and the feeling of safety and security that one feels when walking the streets of New York City.

WHERE WE GO FROM HERE

In this book we put forward a paradigm. It is a paradigm or a framework for motivation that works. The reason that we know that it works is that we have drawn much of our material from advertising which, when done right, works. Our belief is that the people who dump millions of dollars into advertising each year do it because they know that it works, and when they spend that kind of money, they better know that it does. If a thirty-second spot on the Superbowl costs $1.6 million, then the sponsor better know what motivates the people who are going to be exposed to it.

We have, for our paradigm, also relied heavily upon the research that has been conducted on the brain during the late 1980s and early 1990s. And, of course, we also present empirical evidence to support our assertions that the paradigm does indeed work.

LOST AND FOUND

Shorter (1998) gives an interesting account of how medicine in general and psychiatry in particular had a paradigm, lost it, and then got it back again. He traces the beginning of the history not to Freud, as most historians do, but to William Battie in 1758. Battie was an Englishman who worked out a complicated explanation of mental illness based upon muscular "spasms" that led to "laxity" of the blood vessels of the brain, which in turn caused "obstructions" of those vessels and a consequent "compression" of the nerves. This, in turn, resulted in delusions. According to Shorter, Benjamin Rush (1812) said that "the cause of madness is seated primarily in the blood vessels of the brain, and it depends upon the same kind of morbid and irregular actions that constitute other arterial diseases."

During the nineteenth century, German scientists dominated the work in this area, but with their primitive microscopes and other equipment they were unable to make much of an impact. The general failure of their paradigm opened the door for all of the social theories, particularly those of Freud, who came along at the right time. Freud's psychoanalysis had great appeal for both doctors and patients. Doctors in particular, who were tired of working in "asylums," could apply psychoanalysis in their offices and work for themselves. Psychoanalysis came to the United States when Freud visited Clark University in 1909, and a fashionable therapeutic bonanza followed. But with the work that took place during the "decade of the brain" in the 1980s and 1990s, we learned much about the role of neurotransmitters and some brain structures that we knew nothing about before. The paradigm then shifted back again to physical and chemical explanations for mental illness, and medications like Prozac and Xanax began to produce obvious and lasting results. Patients no longer had to spend hours and fortunes looking for repressed childhood memories. They did not even need a psychiatrist. Most depressed and anxious patients today just visit their family physician for treatment of mental and emotional problems. The treatment has come full circle, and early pioneers like Battie and Benjamin Rush proved to be on the right track. The paradigm was physical, not metaphysical or mental. The treatment was chemical.

MOTIVATION

The paradigm introduced here has to do with motivation. It is interesting that the "science" of psychology has been around for 100 years and has yet to produce a functional paradigm, especially with regard to what motivates people; that is, what makes them do the things that they do. Although we are in the process of building a space station, we have gone through the process of impeaching a president, and we have made enormous strides in conquering space during the last half of the twentieth century, we still don't understand what makes people do some of the things that they do. But the answer is straightforward: We just don't understand ourselves. Human behavior is only a little less mysterious than it was in the days of Rush and Battie, and our understanding of motivation has moved forward at a snail's pace.

WHAT PEOPLE PERSONALIZE

The master of personalization was Leo Burnett. He realized that what people personalize was other people. When television became a household fixture in 1954, it was apparent that what people wanted to see on television was other people. They were particularly interested in seeing their faces. At some level, Leo Burnett knew this when he created (1) the Jolly Green Giant, (2) the Marlboro man, and (3) the Pillsbury Doughboy. These characters and personalities represented a breakthrough in advertising and marketing, for now people had a way to associate with a product that had no real strong brand identity.

For example, in 1954, Marlboro was basically a cigarette for women and was one of the few brands that was filter tipped at the time. It was lackluster, at best. Goodrum and Dalrymple (1990) write

The Marlboro campaign, believed by many advertising professionals to be number one among the all time greats, started in 1954 when Phillip Morris moved an uninspired account to Leo Burnett in Chicago. By 1954 there were already six filter tip cigarettes on the market. Marlboro then had a red paper "beauty tip" to camouflage lipstick, came in a white pack bearing the slogan, "Mild as May," and, not surprisingly, sold mostly to women. It held less than one quarter of one percent share of the cigarette market.

Burnett decided to go for the macho. The agency redesigned the pack to a flip-top box, changed the color to strong red and white, and chose the cowboy as the most effective shorthand symbol for the masculine image. (For the first ten years the cowboy always had a tattoo on the back of one hand.)

The original photographer of the series, Constantin Joffe, recalls that "the most successful Marlboro men were pilots, and do you know why? Because pilots seem to have a little wrinkle around the eyes."

At the time of this writing, the Marlboro series is the longest running modern campaign and has better brand identification and recall than any other advertising theme in the marketplace. (p. 198)

Burnett took Marlboro and changed the gender so that it became a man's cigarette. Prior to that time, very few men if any smoked cigarettes that were filtered. He then put the Marlboro man in a setting where every man would like to be: in the wild yet untamed (almost) West, where people took the law and other things into their own hands. The Marlboro man, as seen in Chapter 3 on subliminal cues, was anything but an absurdity. He was very real, and he embodied many of the qualities that most men want: independence, free thinking, liberty, autonomy, and freedom. This is paradigms and personalization at its best.

The Marlboro man, introduced in 1954, is still running strong today. In an era in which cigarette manufacturers and the tobacco industry are under attack from all sides, the Marlboro man has come forward to save them. His presence and visibility in all media (in which cigarette advertising is legal) has increased considerably. Not only is the Marlboro man the strongest and most visible personalization in advertising and marketing, but he is the most visible symbol in advertising and marketing in America (Goodrum & Dalrymple, 1990). It is quite clear that the Marlboro man represents all the qualities that have been listed and particularly autonomy.

But these are not the only qualities that people personalize. The Jolly Green Giant was part absurdity and part personalization. There was also a rational part to the Jolly Green Giant and that is that he was big. He was a giant. And what people want when they purchase food is quantity. They want to make certain that they are getting their money's worth. The Jolly Green Giant is still around.

Finally, it is quite obvious why the Pillsbury Doughboy is personalized. He is cute. He is personalized for the same reason that people personalize the Michelin baby in the tire or babies (and puppies) in any advertisement. They are cute and lovable. And, like the Marlboro man, the Pillsbury Doughboy is still around. He vanished for a short time, but prudence and foresight brought him back again. Some things are timeless, and it just doesn't make sense to attack or ignore a national icon or idol.

The Pillsbury Doughboy, the Marlboro man, and the Jolly Green Giant are more than idols, however. They are subliminal cues. Do people actively think about the Pillsbury Doughboy when they go to the dairy case to pick up that tube of biscuits? Not necessarily. But they do carry that subliminal cue around in their unconscious mind, which has a whole lot to do with their choice and decision to use one brand over another, particularly if everything else is equal— which it usually is.

Ascribing subliminal cue status to the Marlboro man, the Pillsbury Doughboy, and others makes a lot more sense than referring to them as idols or icons. The latter implies that we worship these fictional characters, whereas ascribing subliminal cue status merely states that we are influenced by them, quite heavily, each time we go to the supermarket or the gas station. Other subliminal cues that people can personalize include the Michelin baby, Ronald McDonald, various cartoon characters who from time to time lend themselves out for an endorsement, Michael Jordan, the Budweiser talking lizards, Smokey the bear, and various tigers, including the ones that go into your gas tank and into your cereal bowl.

THE CONSTRUCTION AND FABRICATION
OF PERSONALIZATIONS

Every marketer would like to transform his client's image or product into a subliminal cue, and one of the first ways to do that is with absurdities and/or personalizations. But keep in mind that absurdities, although making advertising memorable, don't necessarily motivate people to make their moves toward the product. On the other hand, personalizations do motivate and they are memorable. So even though absurdities have a rightful place in advertising and marketing, they have a more limited role than personalizations.

In the original ads sanctioned by Federal Express Corporation, some of the personalizations have remained unforgettable, even though it has been over ten years since they were shown on national television.

At a corporate board meeting with everyone present from the company, the CEO congratulates everyone for a job well done; everyone except Smith, who sent the package on the wrong carrier. Smith is spotlighted within the large crowd.

After being guaranteed several times by Dingbat Air Express that his slides will be in Chicago when he arrives, the next scene shows the presenter making pictures of animals with his fingers on the screen. FedEx still uses this paradigm today.

The aging CEO, who cannot find his way out of the building, can still dial Federal Express on the phone. ("It's so easy, even a CEO can do it.")

Smith is hiding under the desk as his boss walks up and down the hall, looking for him, and shouting that the package never got there.

A rubber duckie manufacturer, after stressing the importance of the package getting there tomorrow, is assured that it will by Dingbat Air Express. The next day the rubber duckie plant is boarded up with a sign "out of business."

These television spots are probably just as relevant today as they were many years ago when they were first shown, because of personalization. Who has ever arrived at an important business meeting and found that items that were crucial to the presentation had never been shipped, or were shipped to the wrong address? Who has ever feared being singled out at a meeting in front of peers and strangers? Who has never been dressed down by the boss; or, if not dressed down, who has never feared that they might be? Who has never looked at the CEO as a bungling old fool, and thought about how much better they could do the job if they were in that seat? These are the things that people personalize.

In a way, absurdities and personalizations have similar mechanisms. Both create tension. The absurdity introduces something that has not been seen before and which represents a slight departure from reality. This creates tension in the brain which struggles to define what it is looking at. The personalization creates tension by introducing us to a concept that is frightening or intimidating but real in the sense that we have all personally experienced it or known someone close to us who has. In both cases this psychic tension, as Einstein described it, needs to be discharged. The purpose of laughter is the discharge of psychic tension, which is almost always created in humor but is also seen in many other ways, as in the structure of scientific revolutions (Kuhn, 1996).

It should be quite clear that advertising executives, and particularly people like David Ogilvy and Leo Burnett, understand human motivation, emotion, and passion. And they have the proof that advertising works, and what kinds of advertising works, and why. This is why we have relied on advertising as our paradigm and framework for human motivation, and not upon psychology. Advertisers have been busily trying to serve their clients, because if they don't, and if customers quit buying, they won't have a client and, like the man who manufactured rubber duckies, they will find themselves out of business. Therefore, we look to advertising to tell us what motivates people and what people really want.

However, we will also be adding another chapter to the book that was first written by Leo Burnett and other pioneers. We not only describe and define human motivation (Part II) but we show how it is measured (Part III). Measurement is important, for as Lord Baron Kelvin stated, "Until you've measured something, you don't know what you are talking about." The measurement of motivation tells us what is important and what is not. Furthermore, the measurement of human motivation, desire, and passion gives us a handle on such elusive concepts as brand equity, brand identity, brand loyalty, and brand preference, for in most of these cases these concepts represent the amount of consumer emotion that is involved in the product (Feig, 1997). Once we are capable of measuring the motives, then we become capable of talking realistically and practically about brand equity and other concepts that are meaningful and important but have never been operationally defined.

STORYTELLING AS AN IMPORTANT PARADIGM IN ADVERTISING

David Wolfe (personal communication, November 27, 1998) describes the importance of storytelling in marketing. Storytelling is certainly a form or format of personalization. For Wolfe and for other storytellers, the story is a way to help people process their lives. From the fairy tales that were mentioned in Chapter 3 to the parables of Jesus to the Mahabharata and the Bhagavad Gita to the early tales of the bard of Lake Woebegone, these stories and poems are ways that people process their lives. And, as Wolfe has stated, "Every good storyteller knows that the way to reach people's interest is to capture their hearts before getting into their minds." This is personalization at its best. He goes on to state that marketing that works best is less about features and more about appealing to people's dreams, fantasies, and feelings that relate to who they are and where they want to be in their lives. He mentions some well-known examples, to which we have added a few, that are directly aimed at helping people to process their lives:

- The U.S. Army beckons recruits with the incantation, "Be all that you can be"; the Corps with the mantra, "The change is forever." Can you think of any better directive or offering for helping people to process their lives?
- New Balance shoes says, "Achieve the new balance" (to your life).
- Macintosh computers started fourteen years ago to beckon people to "think different." The campaign is still running strong today.
- People still remember the 1983 commercial for Coke when the attitude of "Mean" Joe Greene was throttled and reversed in a thirty-second spot by an eight-year-old kid and a can of Coke.
- The Marlboro man, who helps people process their lives by adding the qualities of autonomy, independence, and freedom.

- Federal Express, which in 1972 showed people in business how to be heroes by getting the shipment, the document, or the letter there the very next day at a time when fax machines were unheard of.

The would-be successful marketing executive needs to ask, "How does my brand help people to process their lives?" How do marketers, with their product(s), help people to process their lives? Is it done with strategic planning? With relationship marketing? With absurdities? With psychographics? We don't think so. It is done with personalizations.

RELATIONSHIP MARKETING

Wolfe (personal communication, December 3, 1998) has also dealt with the issue of relationship marketing, which received a lot of attention during the mid- to late 1990s. For him, relationship marketing is the ability of marketers to empathize with their customers; that is, to understand where they are coming from. In order to empathize with our customers we need to understand or strike an accord with them as to what they want. This is another form of personalization. Customers often develop strong emotional attachments to products. I once took one of my pet ducks who had an injured web to the veterinarian, and the duck was unusually patient with the vet and with the way she was being handled. When I asked the vet about it, he said, "The duck knows that you are trying to help her." It impressed me that a professional who seemed to have a caring way with animals would say this, and so I wrote to a veterinarian at a large southern university who said that she answered questions about animal health on the World Wide Web. I asked her if the duck could actually "know" that we cared about her. Her response was that this was nothing but anthropomorphism and that people tend to do that with animals. My point is that I received a left brain opinion from the vet at the university and a right brain opinion from the vet who actually cares for animals on a day-to-day basis. Who was right? Does it really matter? The point is that people develop emotional attachments to their products just as they do to their pets and animals. In effect, they build empathetic relationships.

One example of empathy is the "sad story." Most men will topple or disintegrate when a woman starts to cry. They have no idea how to respond. Similarly, most woman will give in to a man when he has a sad story. They want to mother him back to his normal state, and will often stay with him as long as is necessary. This is empathy. In the same way, Wolfe says that customers develop empathy with products.

Consumer response to Tylenol when the brand was threatened by a sociopath who put poison in the containers demonstrates how empathetic connections can develop between customers and a brand. Johnson & Johnson, the parent company of the brand, invited Mike Wallace of "Sixty Minutes" into company meetings where the problem was being discussed and solutions sought. Press conferences were held to discuss the problem in public. Consumers eventually came to view Tylenol as a victim and responded empathetically, just as the woman who hears a man's sad story. Tylenol ended up with a larger market share after the new tamper-proof containers arrived on store shelves. In sharp contrast, when their cars were reported as suddenly lurching forward, causing injuries and death, Audi blamed the drivers and, when they did, they subsequently saw their U.S. market disappear. When the consumers saw that Audi was defensive and making excuses and accusations, their response was anger, not empathy. There are no products that are devoid of emotion.

WHY ARE MOTIVES SO IMPORTANT?

One of the questions that we are regularly asked is, "Why are motives so important?" I am always stunned when I get this question and at first had to grope for an answer. What stunned me was that I just always assumed that what motivated people was the bottom line in sales, in psychology, and in marketing. What else is there?

It occurred to me that perhaps the reason for this question has been that, over the years, motives and motivations have been basically ignored and overlooked, with the exception of Maslow's hierarchy. But what is even more questionable and puzzling is that long after people accept the fact that Maslow's hierarchy does not explain anything that marketers can use, they still cling to it tenaciously and the loyalty to this structure is unwavering. Perhaps this is because, as Watson (1996) has pointed out, the graphic is so appealing in its simplicity that the material is accepted uncritically and its shortcomings are never even contemplated. Even psychologists who are steeped in the scientific tradition and for whom the issue of psychology as a science is never even considered still feel compelled to show that their theoretical approach is consistent with and supportive of Maslow's theory (Bass, 1997; Shapiro, Schwartz, & Astin, 1996). This contradiction or paradox should be seen at the very least as a contradiction in terms or, in our own terminology, as an absurdity.

Motives are important, not only because they move people to action, but, in Wolfe's terminology, they help them to process their lives. And these motives are highly personal, which is one reason that they are not readily shared. You can't ask people what it is that motivates them because they cannot tell you. But marketers and psychologists alike should not allow this to minimize the importance of motives. Also, motivations are a first cousin to emotions, and consumers will never admit that they buy anything on the basis of their emotions. According to Feig (1997), this doesn't mean that the marketer should be prevented from measuring consumer motivation. He adds, "You just have to pry the information out of them by showing them various kinds of real-world stimuli" (p. 44).

Unfortunately, and until now, there has been no way to "pry the information out of them." We will elaborate upon the motives that we have introduced in Chapter 1, but we also intend to show how they are measured with Motigraphics and then to give a step-by-step analysis of how these emotions and motives are "pryed out" of the consumer in a unique intervening process. The result of the process is that we come face to face with raw consumer motivation and emotion.

Why is this important? Because emotions drive motives, and motives drive customers toward decisions, judgments, selections, alternatives, choices, and preferences. It is these motives, that your customers cannot talk about directly or verbalize, that constitute the engine that drives the train or the wing that gives the lift to the choices that they make. And it is the emotions that allow consumers to personalize the brand and to incorporate the brand into their lifestyle. If anyone ever asks you, "What's in a (brand) name?" the appropriate response is "emotion."

SUMMARY

There is a tendency on the part of advertisers today to want to use absurdities because of the technological breakthroughs that are available in animation and other areas. Many have seen the ad showing the young boy on the beach who sucks his Pepsi with a straw until it is absolutely dry and then gets himself sucked into the bottle. His sister summons her parents and says, "He's done it again." This is obviously an absurdity, and it has tremendous appeal. There is no question that it promotes memorability and name recognition. But just because a person remembers the ad, the product, and the stunt is no prediction that he or she will buy the product. It takes more than memorability and recognition.

On the other hand, personalizations go "straight to the heart." Hallmark commercials, Coke commercials, and others pull at the heartstrings in order to get a commitment. These are personalizations, and they do motivate. The customer is looking for some way to process his or her life, and advertising that goes directly to the emotions comes closer than anything else to dealing directly with motivation.

The mainstay of this book is personalizations, which consist of the motives that will be defined and described in Part II. People hold very tightly and securely to that which is personal, private, and intimate. They firmly believe in that which is private, introspective, and subjective. Not only do personalizations motivate, they commit. It is at this level that the casual user is separated from the committed user. It is at the level of personalization that loyalty, fidelity, allegiance, and devotion are established, and this is what intrinsic motivation is all about.

REFERENCES

Bass, B. M. (1997). Does the transactional–transformational leadership paradigm transcend organizational and national boundaries? *American Psychologist, 52,* 133.

Feig, B. (1997). *Marketing straight to the heart: From product to positioning to advertising—how smart companies use the power of emotion to win loyal customers.* New York: American Management Association.

Field, S. (1994). *Screenplay: The foundations of screenwriting.* New York: Dell.

Fleischman, P. (1990). *The healing spirit.* New York: Paragon House.

Garganus, A. (1996). *Oldest Confederate widow tells all.* New York: Ballantine Books.

Goodrum, C., & Dalrymple, H. (1990). *Advertising in America: The first two-hundred years.* New York: Abram.

Horowitz, J. (1995, August 14). The suddenly safer city: How Giuliani and Bratton cut the murder rate 37% and overturned 30 years of thinking about law and order. *New York Magazine,* pp. 20–25, 82.

Kuhn, T. S. (1996). *The structure of scientific revolutions* (3d ed.). Chicago: University of Chicago Press.

LeDoux, J. (1996). *The emotional brain: The mysterious underpinnings of emotional life.* New York: Simon & Schuster.

Shapiro, D. H., Schwartz, C. E., & Astin, J. A. (1996). Controlling ourselves, controlling our world: Psychology's role in understanding positive and negative consequences of seeking and gaining control. *American Psychologist, 51,* 1234.

Shorter, E. (1998, September). How Prozac slew Freud. *American Heritage,* pp. 43–53.

Watson, T. J. (1996). Motivation: That's Maslow, isn't it? *Management Learning, 27,* 447.

PART II

HUMAN MOTIVATION

8

The Structure of
Human Motivation

BACKGROUND

The work that we have done with the unconscious or Silent Side
was started in treatment situations with posttraumatic stress disorder that was encountered in troops who were engaged in active
combat in Vietnam and also those who had been returned stateside for psychiatric treatment. It was noted that a large number of
individuals who had severe anxiety attacks, fatigue, depression,
and other symptoms were reacting not only to the trauma of the
situation but also to other traumas that had been encountered earlier in their lifetimes. It was as if the trauma of battle was automatically linked to an earlier trauma involving an accident, severe
illness, medical emergency, or near death experience. This was an
important finding, for it helped to explain why some GIs were im-
pervious to the trauma of battle and others had to be quickly removed from all action. Although there was not a lot of time for
treatment in Vietnam, a lot of extensive testing was done and decisions had to be made quickly as to whether they could be returned
to battle or sent stateside for rehabilitation.

We continued to apply this methodology in the private practice
of psychiatry and had very satisfying results. Our best results were
with patients who had somatic or psychophysiological problems,
which is a disorder where the mind converts anxiety, depression,
fear, and other negative emotions to physical symptoms. This was

the same kind of problem that we had seen on a more intense basis in Vietnam and in those who were being returned to hospitals stateside for evaluation and treatment.

We found early on that in order to interpret and add meaning to what was happening to a patient who, for example, had chronic, unretractable headaches for which there was no physical or medical cause, it was necessary to go into the unconscious mind in order to solve that problem. As we entered the unconscious mind it became more and more apparent that there was a structure there that helped us to make sense out of what had previously been called irrational, crazy, or bizarre. But the structure that we found went beyond that. It also helped us to explain why people make the decisions that they make—good and bad—and how those decisions lead to choices, preferences, and options. We were able to find out and describe how people adapt lifestyles and choose certain kinds of vocations and careers or mates. After all, it has been known for a long time that the choice of a marital partner, vocation, and other major decisions in life are not all made at the conscious level. Anyone who has been a parent and watched their children make choices that were clearly wrong can understand this and appreciate this observation.

Out of the observations that were made, not only with Vietnam vets but also with people who were having psychological problems, it was only natural that we began to chart what we saw. And out of these charts a blueprint began to arise that showed us that certain categories within the mind were often in conflict with each other when major and minor decisions had to be made.

Whenever we present information on the Silent Side of the mind the question always comes up, "Well, where did you get this stuff? We've never heard it before." This is why we have added this brief background section, to show where "this stuff" comes from. In a way, this puts us in the same category with Maslow, for he also developed a theory of motivation from observations that he made on his patients. Maslow's theory, as we have shown, has gone a long way in making its way into the annals of psychiatry and psychology, since it consists of a very memorable graphic: the pyramid. We too have constructed a pyramid, which we have identified as the building blocks of human motivation. So what is the difference between our approach and Maslow's approach? Why is one any better—or worse—than the other?

Figures Don't Lie

There are three major differences between Maslow's approach and the one presented here, and we will briefly review each one of them in this chapter, showing how we have gained support for the building blocks of human motivation. We have gone beyond Maslow (1) in generating statistical (empirical) support for the building blocks, (2) in appealing to recent research on the brain and brain structures, and (3) in a reliance upon advertising and marketing, where we believe that there is already an appreciation and understanding of motivation and emotion.

PROCEDURE

The procedure that we relied upon was research that was conducted entirely outside of our ordinary, day-to-day research with consumers and with products. We wanted to validate our observations on people who were not psychiatric patients and not consumers who happened to be shopping for a particular product at that time. As a result, we relied upon evening students in an adult program, most of whom were working toward either an undergraduate or graduate degree. There were 100 evening students, ranging in age from twenty-one to sixty-five, in this group. A second group consisted of production workers in a hospital, a large web printing plant, and an auto parts production firm. There were 100 individuals in this group, whose age ranges were approximately the same as the students.

Although there were more than 200 people who were originally involved in this research, cuts were made so that the research sample adequately represented race (white and African American) and sex in proportion to the distribution in the population. Research was carried out in three locations in Tennessee, Arkansas, and Oklahoma.

The procedure involved filling out a 200-item questionnaire that was in a semantic differential format, as shown in Figure 8.1. In this format, respondents are simply asked to circle or check the "O" that most closely agrees with, in this case, the way that they feel about the movement of time. The procedure took about forty-five

Figure 8.1
Semantic Differential Format Example

	Disagree Stronly	Disagree Somewhat	Disagree Slightly	Agree Slightly	Agree Somewhat	Agree Strongly	
Time goes fast when you are having fun	O	O	O	O	O	O	Time goes slow when you are having fun

minutes to complete. The items that were included were statements regarding what we considered to be motives, such as the Orientation to Time Motive. Some of the questions within corresponding categories were as follows:

The Orientation Motives

    Orientation to Person

        I'm not the kind of person that criticizes others

        I am a person that likes a lot of privacy

        My whole life revolves around my family

    Orientation to Time

        I make the most of the time that I have

        I like to sleep late on weekends

        I feel a sense of urgency most of the time

    Orientation to Place

        I would like to quit my job and move away

        I am ready for a vacation

        I enjoy eating out at different restaurants

The Survival Motives

    Spiritual Survival

        When they play the National Anthem I get goose bumps all over

        I believe in a higher power that hears me

        My job is more than a vocation; it's like a "calling"

    Physical Survival

        I only eat healthy foods that are low in fat and cholesterol

        I always "buckle up"

        I would not live in a home without a burglar alarm

    Territorial Survival

        I check the market three times a day

        In my job I am more competitive than most

        The Cardinals are "my team"

    Sexual Survival

        I would give up watching the Superbowl for good sex

        I would rather be sexy than intelligent

        I choose clothes that are sexy and seductive

The Adaptation Motive

        I do what other people do

Testimonials influence me more than they should

I smoke because most of my friends do

The Expectation/Resolution Motive

I feel like I will eventually be "discovered"

I think that I have a chance to win the lottery

I trust my doctor and will do whatever he recommends

The Play Motive, which was added later to the building blocks, was not included in this analysis of the motives. However, and as we will see in Chapter 13, this motive was derived from observations made by brain researchers, particularly MacLean (1990), and has substantial neurological and commonsense support.

The purpose of gaining empirical (statistical) support as we have is to allow replication of the procedure. Replication of a procedure is one of the paramount tenants of science, and without replication the researcher is working in a vacuum. Although this particular chapter, which is concerned with statistical support, may not be of interest to everyone, it is the key that allows us to transition into these motives that we have observed and to apply them in a much broader and wider context, such as with consumers, in management paradigms, and in other contexts which are seen in the Appendix.

RESULTS

Based upon the confirmatory factor analysis that was carried out, the following twenty factors were yielded which closely approximated the motives and their elements that we have used to support our research:

The Survival Motives (% of Total 35)

Spiritual Survival (passion)   % of Total = 9.2

0.83   Prayer is more important than sports

0.80   Reading the Bible in schools should be allowed

0.70   Families that pray together stay together

0.57   We will be punished or rewarded for what we do in this life

0.57   My family is more important to me than my work

Physical Survival   % of Total = 4.0

0.78 I eat anything that tastes good

0.70 The air I breathe is OK

Territorial Survival (female)   % of Total = 2.7

0.81   I really feel appreciated for what I do

0.58   A career is more important than anything else

Sexual Survival   % of Total = 6.0

      Gender (female)

0.80   I love getting flowers

0.74   I like feeling feminine

0.59   I like to wear a lot of jewelry

0.57   I have lots of perfumes at home

0.46   I like to be treated special

      Impulse   % of Total = 8.2

0.86   I want a car with lots of power (vs. a safe car)

0.82   I want a car that is fast and hot

0.82   I would rather be sexy than intelligent

0.41   I choose clothes that are sexy and seductive

0.47   I would rather be with friends than with family

0.68   I like making quick decisions

0.60   I never plan to slow down

0.41   My family consumes me

      Gender (male)   % of Total = 2.7

0.78   My actions don't influence how I feel about myself

0.43   I never read anything about glamour

0.41   I don't like antiques

0.37   I don't like to read romance novels

      Inhibition   % of Total = 2.0

0.76   I am cold most of the time

0.41   Love is worth more than money

0.40   I enjoy going to museums (vs. night clubs)

The Orientation Motives (% of Total 26.5)

Orientation to Person (self)   % of Total = 14.7

0.74   I consider myself up to date

0.73   I remain aware of all current fads

0.72   A person's career is what makes that person

0.40   What you eat is what you are

0.70   I love to shop

0.61   I like living in the big city (vs. living in a cabin in the woods)

0.58   I like to wear whatever is in style

0.53   I like a fast pace

Orientation to Place   % of Total = 6.0

0.77   Getting away from it all relieves me

0.67   I need to escape more than most people

0.74   I like a change of scenery

0.51   I like to get in the car and just drive

0.38   There is much more in life than what we see before us

Orientation to Time   % of Total = 2.5

0.78   Marijuana should be legalized

Orientation to Circumstances   % of Total = 3.3

0.76   Drugs help me to gain perspective

0.67   I like being part of the "good old boy" network

0.45   A drink at the end of the day helps me to forget

The Expectation/Resolution Motive (% of Total = 8.4)

0.88   You can't always trust a doctor

0.81   I think that the future looks good for me

0.72   People should be able to choose their own doctor

0.70   I don't trust just anyone to operate on me

0.63   I question my doctor

0.45   You can't trust just anyone in this world

Pessimism

0.81   I have to look out for myself

0.58   I always wear seat belts

The Adaptation Motive (% of Total = 5.1)

0.80   I want what everyone else has

0.75   If the majority does it, it must be right

0.56   I like reading articles about what others think

Factor 17 was omitted because it dealt with a single item, gun control, and although this may be related to the Spiritual Survival Motive (passion), it cannot be assumed that everyone who is interested in the issue of gun control is passionate or fanatic about it, although many gun-control proponents are fanatic.

The results of this factor analysis clearly supported the overall importance of the first two Motives, Orientation to Person and Spiritual Survival, which was consistent with what was predicted. For one thing, it was consistent with the fact that Motigraphics, in projects that we have carried out in various products and services, almost always has found the Orientation to Person Motive to contribute the most variance. The Spiritual Survival Motive is often the next. Of course, the way that the motives "stack up" in terms of building blocks will vary from project to project. For example, the

Sexual Survival Motive is generally not involved in studies done on banks and banking.

The fact that the Orientation to Person Motive usually comes out at the top in almost all products and services is consistent with the way that consumers weigh benefits. In other words, one of the first questions that they ask themselves when they anticipate a purchase is, "What's in it for me?" Similarly, the second question might be, "What's in it for my family?" This second question relates to family values, which is an element of the Spiritual Survival Motive. The answers to these two questions clearly relate to benefits that the consumer sees in the product that he or she is purchasing. Hence, Silent Side research is clearly a process which investigates benefits and not features. Note that benefits can only be understood by understanding the mind of the consumer or customer. This means getting inside their heads and working through the same processes that they work through as they anticipate a purchase. The methodology for doing this is found in Chapter 15, on interviewing.

LOOSE ENDS

The factor analysis described gave us direction in the establishment of the building blocks of human motivation, which were presented in Figure 1.1.

Most of the motives that appear in the building blocks are clear and straightforward, but this is not the case with the Spiritual Survival Motive. This motive is discussed in detail in Chapter 10. It is clear that the word "spiritual" could have many different implications and therefore the motive itself could become a "dumping ground" or a wastebasket category for anything that did not fit into any of the other ten categories. To prevent this, we employed elements established by Fleischman (1990). These elements provide us with operational definitions of the Spiritual Survival Motive, and they are as follows:

Element	Meaning
1. Witness significance	Belief that a higher power listens, understands
2. Lawful order	Belief in the basic order of the universe and world that we live in
3. Wholeness	Involves affirmation and acceptance of the person
4. A sense of calling	A universal need for importance, to feel like work and life is relevant, connected
5. Membership	Part of a network that affirms, accepts, and legitimizes the person and his or her beliefs

6. Release	Renewal and release of new power
7. Human love	A vital element—love, bonding, and marriage overcome fear, pain, and loss; also includes patriotism, love of country
8. Sacrifice	The ability to go beyond one's self; often used to "bargain" with a higher power
9. Meaningful death	The goal of any spiritual program, organized or unorganized
10. Inner peace	Translating self-centeredness, worry, and responsibility into peace

We have not employed these elements arbitrarily. Fleischman (1990) spent twenty years looking at various religions around the world. In his words, these elements are found on almost every page of every religious document ever produced: the Koran, the Old Testament, and so on. In addition, we have factor analyzed these elements and found an almost one-to-one relationship between the elements that Fleischman discovered and the structure of the factors in the factor analysis.

An operational definition allows us to define something in terms of how we go about measuring it. These elements are not discretely ordered or measured, but they do come much closer to this goal than the overall motive of spiritual survival. They also allow us to restrict the content that would go into the spiritual survival category by establishing a criterion for each entry into the category. In addition to these ten elements, we have added one additional and very useful element, and that is the element of family values. In many cases the motivation to buy something grows out of a need to do something for one's family, particularly in women. Although this element is actually a subset of number 7, human love, we have found that it is referred to so often in our work with consumers that it is most efficiently and effectively handled separately and in its own category.

In order to partially remove the spiritual survival category from a strict and literal interpretation of religion, we have been inclined to define it in terms of what people are passionate about. In this way we get access into their emotions and motivations and not just into their thoughts. In a separate factor analysis, we had 103 items on lifestyle, of which 20 were concerned with what people are passionate about. We had a category marked "X" on the answer sheet, and whenever test subjects saw X they were to think in terms of what it was they were most passionate about in their lives. Since this category could have been embarrassing to them, they were not asked to spell it out and were given no further direction than to mark their preference on a five-point scale. For example, to the statement, "I would not want to go on living without X," they could choose "Strongly Disagree," "Moderately Disagree," "Neither Agree nor Disagree," "Moderately Agree," or "Strongly Agree."

Respondents in this study were asked to indicate their preference with regard to X on a questionnaire that measured their response to issues in spiritual survival. The X questions all grouped themselves into one motive, which accounted for almost 18 percent of the variance on the factor analysis. This indicates an extremely robust factor, and also indicates that passion and emotion are indeed very important elements. In the system that we are presenting here, the elements that have been defined by Fleischman (1990) can be used to define passion, since each one of them specifically describes what people are generally passionate about. For example, many of the activities involving recreation are aimed toward achieving peace of mind, which is Fleischman's element number 10. In another example, it is not unusual for people to elevate their job or vocation to the level of a vocation to which they feel called, which is Fleischman's element number 4. When this occurs, their job becomes an obsession and fixation, and, as a result, passion and emotion become issues. We then define the job in terms of spiritual survival rather than territorial survival, since this is the only way that we can understand or explain the person's fixation with the job.

Several exploratory factor analyses were conducted in order to more clearly define categories before we conducted the final confirmatory analysis that has been reported on. All were supportive of the factors that have been described. On one, however, an additional factor was seen which could only be labeled as religion. This factor was clearly associated with the Spiritual Survival Motive, but had not been seen before. In keeping with the traditional definition, religion is definitely a part of spiritual survival. In our initial research, we measured the Spiritual Survival Motive in terms of the importance of religion in people's overall lifestyles. However, as we worked with various products and services, we found that people became emotional and passionate over many issues and not just religion, and hence it made common sense to expand this category and include issues involving more than just traditional religion and religious beliefs.

BEYOND FACTOR ANALYSIS AND
EMPIRICAL (STATISTICAL) METHODS

We have included empirical methods as support for our observations and findings, but do not rely on them solely for this support. For example, we have already shown that the Play Motive, which was not included in the factor study, has been included in the building blocks because of neurological findings and because of plain common sense. According to MacLean (1990), there is a motivation toward spontaneous play in all humans and in lower animals with a paleomammalian (mid) brain. This suggests that play originated in the limbic system of the brain, but MacLean at the time of his writing was uncertain about the origin of play. Nevertheless, we feel that it surely belongs as one of the essential building blocks of human motivation, simply because of what we see all around us.

Knowledge of evolutionary processes and the results of many studies of the brain in the late 1980s and into the 1990s has played an important role in the construction of the building blocks of human motivation. This is one of the major sources of our findings. For example, one of the fundamental groups of motives that we have found to be essentially responsible for the variance in human behavior is the Orientation Motives. Essentially, orientation is an important function of the brain which is believed to be relegated to the frontal and temporal lobes of the brain. We have found that orientation, as a motive, has not only the function of keeping us in tune with the world around us but also is vitally concerned with self-concept, self-control, happiness, recreational choices, leadership, and a myriad of other activities that are all aspects of consumer behavior. Many of these activities will be explained in Chapter 9, where the Orientation Motives are discussed in detail.

A third source of support that we have derived for these motives, in addition to empirical methods and neurological research, is advertising. Advertising executives, creative people, and others involved in advertising have had an intuitive sense of motivation from the very beginning of the art. Because of this intuitive sense they have won the loyalty of clients and over the years have built a huge industry in the United States. We typically rely on advertising agencies and people when we want to know how to do something. Sometimes they are wrong, but more often than not they are correct in what they tell us to do. As a result, we trust them. All that we have done in Silent Side research is to take this one step further in moving toward a more scientific and replicable method; one which can be repeated over and over again. It is our desire to see this method as complementary to the substantial contributions already made by the advertising industry, and not competitive with it.

MOTIVES AND THEIR ELEMENTS

The motivational elements of the Physical Survival Motive are food, air, and water. This is easy to understand. The motivational elements of the Spiritual Survival Motive are, among others, passion, love, peace of mind, and witness significance, somewhat harder to understand but still more specific and more concrete than the motive itself. The elements of the Sexual Survival Motive are impulse, inhibition, and gender. The single most important element of the Orientation to Person Motive is self-control. Table 8.1 references the motives and their respective elements, as well as the emotions and the benefits associated with each. Each one of these motives will be handled in separate chapters.

At this point it is important to say that the notion of expectation has been more thoroughly researched than any of the other motives in psychology. Much of this research deals with animal expectation (Hull, 1943; Tolman, 1932). The work of Rosenthal and Jacobsen (1968) dealt with human expectation and is well known. Rosenthal and Jacobsen showed that when teachers are informed that students are "dull" or "slow" they will have predetermined expectancies. The results are that the students who are "dull" will not do as well as students who are supposed to be "bright," even when the two groups are matched evenly in terms of IQ and achievement. Both Vroom (1964) and Kelly (1955) were also early pioneers in the area of human expectancies, as well as Festinger (1957) and Lewin (1951). Other motives and elements receive support not only from empirical methods (factor analysis) but also from the literature.

The Orientation Motives: Person, Place, Time, and Circumstances

For over 100 years the psychiatric mental status test has been applied in clinical settings whenever neurological impairment was suspected. It generally seeks to establish stability and/or orientation in three areas: person, place, and time. We have added a fourth area: circumstances, or the person's knowledge of the present situation. Orientation to circumstances assesses not only who, where, and when but also addresses what. The psychiatric mental status test consists of a clinician (psychiatrist, physician, nurse, etc.) asking the patient if he or she knows who they are; where they are; the time, date, and day; and why they think they are here (in this situation).

The mental status test assesses a person's mental *state*. Hence, it is a noun. What we have done is turn this mental state into a motive or action verb. This is often done in the English language as in the transition from party (noun) to partying (verb). Whereas a noun signifies a state or a status and will name something, such as the quality of a person's life (mental status), a verb denotes action. Therefore, when we talk about motives we are talking about action, since motives compel to action.

It is reasonable to assume that humans are concerned with orientation, even though they do not actively think about it or contemplate

Table 8.1
Motives, Elements, Emotions, and Benefits

ORIENTATION MOTIVES	ELEMENTS	EMOTIONS	BENEFITS
Person Orientation	Self-Control	Self-Esteem Self-Confidence Self-Image	Acceptance Well-Being, Image
Place Orientation	Where	Escape Involvement, Renewal	Gain Perspective, Refresh Renewal and Relief
Time Orientation	When	Escape, Urgency Beat & Timing, Seasons	Relief, Nostalgia Escape (from time)

SURVIVAL MOTIVES	ELEMENTS	EMOTIONS	BENEFITS
Spiritual Survival **(Passion)**	Family Values, Inner Peace, Lawful Order, Wholeness, Belonging, Witness Significance, Affirming Acceptance, Calling, Membership, Release, Human Love, Sacrifice, World View, Meaningful Death	Love Passion Dedication Perfection	Dedication Perfection Achievement Long Life Freedom from Pain Helping Others
Physical Survival	Food, Air Water, Shelter	Health and Wellness Security Safety	Security Protection, Safety Strength
Territorial Survival	Performance Assets, Income Career, Competition	Security	Achievement Power Control, Status
Sexual Survival	Gender (M/F) Impulse (bad) Inhibition (female) Impotence (male)	Masculinity/Femininity Sex & Aggression Fear Security	Reproduction Enjoyment Self-Expression Performance, Pleasure

ADAPTATION MOTIVE	ELEMENTS	EMOTIONS	BENEFITS
	Imitation Learning Testimonials	Security Confidence Self-Assurance, Low Risk	Status & Belonging Achievement Acceptance

EXPECTATION/ RESOLUTION MOTIVE	ELEMENTS	EMOTIONS	BENEFITS
	Resolution Closure Future	Anticipation, Anxiety Trust, Hope	Commitment, Confidence Belief, Closure Organization

PLAY MOTIVE	ELEMENTS	EMOTIONS	BENEFITS
	Urge "Good" Impulse Notion	Fun, Laughter Winning Competition	Creativity Relief Victory

it. After all, we are dealing with the unconscious, not the conscious mind. About the only time orientation actually becomes an issue is when people see someone who is disoriented, as in neurological impairment, dementia, or in senility as seen in Alzheimer's syndrome. Encountering an older person who is in such a state is a reminder to anyone about how fragile life is and how quickly we can lose our mental capacities through no fault or failing on our own.

There are many references in psychiatry to the mental status examination, its purpose, and how it should be conducted (Goodman, 1967; Friedman, 1972; Seltzer, 1994). It is well established as an assessment tool in psychiatry. However, there are no references in the literature to states of orientation as motives. This is where our approach to human behavior differs from any other.

To introduce the notion of orientation to person, place, time, and circumstances, we use the illustration of Phineas Gage (Damasio, 1994), who in 1846 was working on the railroad in Vermont and, while tamping dynamite with a tamping rod, encountered an explosion which blew the tamping rod through the base of his skull and out the top of his head, lodging itself in his brain and causing frontal and temporal lobe damage. What is of interest here is that following this very traumatic and shocking accident he was still able to walk to the closest town, three miles away, and consult a physician. Obviously, the physician, a local general practitioner, had never seen this phenomenon before, or even read about it in medical school, and was amazed by the fact that Gage was walking and talking.

There was apparently damage to the ventromedial region of the left frontal lobe, eventually disrupting Gage's ability to attend to a task and perform calculations. Loss of function in these areas usually denotes impaired mental control. But of even more interest was the fact that behaviorally he became a different person. As a railroad foreman he supervised others and was in a leadership role. As such, he could always be depended upon to be prompt, efficient, and reliable and also to make good judgments. Following the accident, he became unreliable and had to be prompted by someone else in order to do almost anything. He had little regard for time. His ability to plan for the future was compromised. He often made a fool of himself in social situations because of his inability to assess contexts. As his coworkers said, he was a "different person."

Damasio (1994) photographed and measured Gage's skull, measuring not only the angle of the tamping rod but the trajectory and orbit of its impact. Damasio then found several of his own patients who had damage to a similar area of the brain due to tumor compression. He found that these patients had become disoriented in several spheres. One patient in particular had to be prompted to go to work (orientation to time) and when he got there he failed to make productive use of his time (orientation to time). The patient could no longer be counted upon by management to perform the appropriate action when he was expected to (orientation to circumstances). He also lost most of his good judgment and, according to his friends, "became a different person." The point is that disorientation set in, and when it did Damasio's patient was not motivated to do his job. In fact, he was demotivated at times, and at other times he was fully motivated. He was inconsistent and unreliable. After Gage's accident, he wasted time, which was totally out of character for him. Just as Gage had wandered off and appeared to have no real interest in working, Damasio's patient exhibited the same traits. In our way of looking at things, both patients had become disoriented and when they did, their pattern of motivation changed drastically.

When many people encounter an elderly patient who has Alzheimer's or senile dementia, they will retract and say, "I hope I never get that way." What we are reacting to is that person's state of disorientation to what is going on around him or her. Surely if a simple migratory bird can orient itself to fly south in the winter and north in the summer, if a fish can find its way around the ocean, it is reasonable to expect that people also have an orienting device, albeit much more sophisticated. We believe that it is this orientation device within the bird brain that not only orients but also motivates the creature to make this migratory journey, season after season and year after year. Is it not reasonable, therefore, to conclude that people also have a much more sophisticated orientation and disorientation device that motivates them to move from place to place, to make good or bad use of their time, to be attentive (or inattentive) to the circumstances around them, and, above all, to maintain self-control? Further, is it not reasonable to conclude that staying oriented is exhausting? We quickly tire of the same place all the time, whether it is home, work, or even a vacation place. And even though we are not conscious of this need to remain oriented and fixated, it still becomes a chore. This is why people coin phrases like, "Stop the world, I want to get off." It is what they are referring to when they talk about stress, or pressure or fatigue. Even if you don't know it or feel it directly, remaining oriented to the world around us day after day is fatiguing and it takes its toll.

How then do we remove the fatigue? The logical conclusion is that we disorient or disconnect, which is a very powerful motive that is intimately connected to survival. Even God, the Bible tells us, created the world in six days but disconnected on the seventh day. Most of us do the same thing. Vacations, days off, trips, time off, time out—all of these are ways of getting disconnected or disoriented.

There are four Orientation Motives: Orientation to Person, Orientation to Place, Orientation to Time, and Orientation to Circumstances. They are listed in order of importance. When a person loses orientation because of brain damage or senility, it is lost in reverse order. They lose their orientation to circumstances first, not knowing what they had for breakfast that day. Loss of orientation to time is next, not knowing the day, date, or season. Loss of orientation to place is third, not knowing where they are. Loss of orientation to person is the last orientation to disappear. We feel that this sequence is important because it gives us an idea as to the order of importance of each orientation, thereby helping us to establish the relative position of each motive in the building blocks of human motivation (see Figure 1.1). These four orientations are introduced and discussed as motives in Chapter 9.

The Survival Motives: Physical, Territorial, Spiritual, and Sexual

Factor analysis strongly confirmed all four of the Survival Motives but, as discussed, the Physical Survival Motive did not get the support that was expected. The Physical Survival Motive included the basic elements of food, air, and water.

Sexual survival guarantees the survival of the human race, and there are no real questions about its rightful place in the building blocks of human motivation. Sexual survival and the other Survival Motives will be discussed in Chapter 10. The Sexual Survival Motive includes the elements of sexual gender, sexual inhibition, and sexual impulse. These elements all received support in the factor analysis. However, since the element of sexual inhibition by custom almost always refers to women, we have added a fourth element, impotence, which by custom always refers to men. Interestingly, in Chapter 10 we will provide support for the fact that there are many more impotent men than there are inhibited women, which is contrary to popular belief.

Epstein (1994, 1998) is concerned with a theory of motivation that includes the truths and the essentials of psychoanalysis but at the same time is consistent with Darwin's principles of evolutionary science. He presents this as Cognitive–Experiential Self Theory. The problem is that CEST is inadequate in explaining human behavior and motivation since it overlooks two very essential elements of survival: sexuality and spirituality, the two things that people are most passionate about. The fact that sex is a critical element of survival is not even arguable, since it guarantees the existence of the race. The fact that he has overlooked this in his theory leaves a critical flaw. Conversely, when we talk about spirituality and its most visible element, passion, we encounter more controversy and resistance. However, when spiritual survival is left out of the equation there are many elements of human behavior and motivation that cannot be explained. Epstein's approach typifies the psychological approaches that LeDoux (1996) brands as "cold-blooded," since ordinary, day-to-day emotions are left out in the cold and ignored, and people are treated, in theories like CEST, as robots. Cognitive psychology is simply an attempt to convert feelings and emotions to thought, with the eventual goal of converting these thoughts into a framework that can be explained in terms of learning theory. This is why we say that cognitive psychology is just another way of promoting learning theory and behaviorism.

The Territorial Survival Motive, like the Orientation Motives, is seen in most animals. It therefore follows from evolutionary theory that if lower animals demonstrate this motive, as when a bird sings or flaps its wings or when a dog urinates around the perimeter of his territory, that humans would also have a territorial motivation, albeit much more sophisticated. The elements of the Territorial Survival Motive in humans include assets, income, career, competition, and greed. This motive is discussed more fully in Chapter 10 along with the other Survival Motives.

Other Motives

The Expectation/Resolution Motive, which was supported in factor analysis, has extensive support throughout the literature and will be presented in Chapter 12. The Adaptation Motive, which is the motive to do what others do through imitation and learning, has also had extensive support in the psychological literature, but not by the same name. In psychology, learning and imitation are two concepts that have been used to account for most behavior. In this approach, imitation and learning are fundamental ingredients of the Adaptation Motive. In advertising, the Adaptation Motive has been used and overused in the form of testimonials, status seeking, spokespersons, and endorsements. The Adaptation Motive represents the major emotional appeal that has been used by advertisers in the past, although not defined as such. It is reviewed in Chapter 11. The Play Motive, which was not included in any of the factor analyses that were carried out but which was added because of common sense and because of the findings in neurological research, is reviewed in Chapter 13.

REFERENCES

Damasio, A. (1994). *Descartes' error: Emotion, reason and the human brain.* New York: Avon Books.

Epstein, S. (1994). Integration of the cognitive and psychoanalytic unconscious. *American Psychologist 49,* 709–24.

Epstein, S. (1998). Cognitive-experiential self-theory: A dual process personality theory with implications for diagnosis and psychotherapy. In R. F. Bornstein & J. M. Masling (Eds.), *Empirical perspectives on the psychoanalytic unconscious*. Washington, DC: American Psychological Association.

Festinger, L. (1957). *A theory of cognitive dissonance*. Evanston, IL: Row, Peterson.

Fleischman, P. (1990). *The healing spirit*. New York: Paragon House.

Friedman, A. M. (1972). *Diagnosing mental illness: Evaluation in psychology and psychiatry*. New York: Atheneum.

Goodman, J. (1967). *The child's mental status examination*. New York: Basic Books.

Hull, C. L. (1943). *Principles of behavior*. New York: Appleton-Century-Crofts.

Kelly, G. A. (1955). *The psychology of personal constructs*. New York: Norton.

LeDoux, J. (1996). *The emotional brain: The mysterious underpinnings of emotional life*. New York: Simon & Schuster.

Lewin, K. (1951). *Field theory and social science*. New York: Harper & Brothers.

MacLean, P. D. (1990). *The triune brain in evolution: Role in paleocerebral functions*. New York: Plenum Press.

Rosenthal, R., & Jacobsen, L. (1968). *Pygmalion in the classroom*. New York: Holt, Rinehart & Winston.

Seltzer, B. (1994). Psychiatric symptoms in Alzheimer's disease: Mental status examination vs. caregiver's report. *Gerontologist*.

Tolman, E. C. (1932). *Purposive behavior in animals and men*. New York: Appleton-Century-Crofts.

Vroom, V. H. (1964). *Work and motivation*. New York: Wiley.

9

The Orientation Motives

It's all right letting yourself go as long as you can let yourself back.
                                                                —Mick Jagger

ATTENTION, PERCEPTION, AND ORIENTATION

Another word that is often used for orientation is *attention*. We
need to pay attention to something before we can actually orient to
it. Attention involves many different areas of the brain, but particularly a small group of neurons in the brain stem known as the
reticular activating system. The job of the reticular activating system of the brain is to receive information and then project it out to
different parts of the brain, activating those other parts of the brain.
The reticular activating system can provoke or ignite large parts of
both hemispheres or small parts, depending upon what is needed.
   Ramachandran and Blakeslee (1998) have quoted Marcel
Mesulam of Harvard University with regard to an interesting theory
that he has regarding attention and perception. We have already
seen that the right and left hemispheres have different functions.
We recognize the left hemisphere for dealing with language and
rational thinking (logic) and the right hemisphere for dealing with
the emotions and with contexts. One distinguishing difference is
that the left hemisphere deals with specifics and details, whereas
the right hemisphere is more wholistic and expansive. Mesulam
says that the right hemisphere, which has an important role in the

wholistic aspects of vision, has a broad "searchlight" of attention that encompasses the entire left and right visual fields. On the other hand, the left hemisphere has a much smaller searchlight which is confined only to the details of the world. This is another example of how the two sides work together in attention and orientation.

An example of how this works would be in driving home from work. The right hemisphere will generally be focused upon the familiar sights that we see every day on that drive: other cars, terrain, interstate exits, and bridges. On the other hand, the searchlight in the left hemisphere may be acutely attending to a news item on the radio, or there may be a police officer on the side of the road operating a radar gun and immediately the smaller searchlight on the left side attends to that and takes appropriate action. In another illustration of how this works, I have asked over 300 people who came to my office how they got there from their home, and only about half could give me accurate directions that I could follow if I wanted to take the same route. This indicates that the smaller searchlight is engaged in some other activity and the facts that I would need to make that trip are not available to those who made the trip.

Orientation, attention, and motivation come together in a conjoint package and the relationship is seen very clearly in the child who exhibits attention deficit hyperactivity disorder (ADHD). A teacher will typically describe the child as uncaring and unmotivated, unwilling to do his work, or completely distracted from what he should be doing.[1] A parent describes the ADHD child not as unwilling but unable. We do know that Ritalin is effective in controlling this condition until the child reaches about eleven or twelve years of age, but we don't know why it works. In adults, Ritalin has the opposite or paradoxical effect. In terms of the searchlight metaphor, the ADHD child appears to have an impairment in terms of the way that the reticular activating system is projecting the world to the various parts of the brain. Both searchlights are working, but it is as if the whole brain is responding rather than specific parts of it.

In one of the offices where I work there are lights which are inset into the ceiling. When these lights build up heat they go into a "time out," but it never happens all at once; they go off and on individually. I asked the maintenance staff to repair it but after several attempts they gave up. It is at best a very minor annoyance, and I am never working in darkness so it's very easy to ignore. However, I noted that when a child is in the room who has been diagnosed or is suspected ADHD, he will lose attention to whatever task he is working on every time a light goes off or comes back on. A "normal" child may lose attention to task the first or second time that this happens, but then it becomes a nonissue for him. But for the ADHD child it is never a nonissue, and each time the lights blink on or off he will turn his head in the direction of the light that blinked.

Do we say the child is inattentive or unmotivated? He appears to be both, and at this point it is really not important that we separate these two terms, only that we recognize that perception, attention, and motivation are all very closely interrelated to each other and don't work independently. In order to be motivated to do something, we first have to see it and perceive the possibility of doing it.

THE ORIENTATION MOTIVES

As stated in Chapter 8, orientation as a motivation or motivational system represents a whole new way of looking at things. The medical profession has long recognized orientation as a mental state, or status. What we have discovered is that orientation in humans is also a motive that is closely related to survival.

Since we have known for a long time that there are four orientation states, it follows that there are four Orientation Motives:

Orientation to Person

Orientation to Place

Orientation to Time

Orientation to Circumstances

These motives have been confirmed in factor analysis, and with the exception of circumstances, which was added by us, have been an essential part of the medical mental status examination for over 100 years. The medical mental status examination asks a person if they know their name, where they are, why they are here, and the day of the week. The exam can be that simple, or it can become more complex. It is typically used to examine elderly people to see if they qualify for nursing home admission.

We also know that these motives have an order of importance, and we described this order of importance in Chapter 8. The orientation that is lost first, circumstances, in either an accident or the onset of senile dementia, is considered the weakest. The orientation that is lost last, person, is considered the strongest and most potent. We know this from examining people who are in the process of losing their orientation because of the aging process.

Orientation to circumstances is the weakest or least important motive, since it is the first area in which demented patients lose their bearings. They may insist that they be taken home when they already are at home. Or they may be in a nursing facility and believe that they are at home. My grandmother, when she was in her mid-eighties, was weak and frail and would have to have the assistance of several men to get up the stairs or come to the dinner table. But if the door was left open she would bolt out and be on her way. The police would pick her up two or three miles from the house. When asked where she was going, she would always reply, "home." When asked where home was, she would always reply "Portsmouth, Ohio," which was about 600 miles from where we lived.

Orientation to time is the next most fragile mental state, and hence the next most fragile motive. Nursing homes will typically put a large clock in the room of each patient, but this has very little effect. As demented patients get older they regress in time, since long-term memory remains intact much longer and is more robust than short-term memory. An elderly person often can recite incidents from very early childhood by chapter and verse but are unable to tell you what they had for breakfast that morning.

Orientation to place is the next to the last mental state to disappear, and this is often the criteria for nursing home admission. Orientation to place refers to a physical place as opposed to circumstances, which refers to what is going on around a person. If a person does not know where they are, then they are unable to act on behalf of their own safety, find a fire exit, or know what to do when an alarm is sounded. Knowing where you are is an essential ingredient of orientation.

Orientation to person is the last mental state to disappear and therefore is the strongest. The major element here is self-control. When viewed as a motive, orientation to person shows up as the strongest motive, both in everyday experience and in terms of the factor structure that we uncovered in our research and which is presented in Chapter 8. Similarly, in many of the projects that we do with consumers which emphasize benefits rather than features, the Personal Orientation Motive will come out as the one that is the most salient and accounts for the most variance. The elements of this motive may change from project to project, but the motive itself usually comes out on top in most of the studies that include Motigraphics. Another way of looking at the Personal Orientation Motive from the customer's perspective is by saying, "What will this (product, service) do for me?" or, more precisely, "How will it help me to process my life?"

By looking at the sequence that older people go through when they begin to lose their perspective we can learn a lot about motivation. One thing that we learn is how important these mental states are. Another thing we learn is how fragile they are. A third thing that we learn is that it takes a lot of mental energy, substance, and vigor to stay oriented each day and, conversely, if we lose this energy and vigor we stand the chance of becoming more and more disoriented to life, living, and our surroundings.

GETTING MOTIVATED

Remaining oriented (and therefore motivated) takes energy. Interestingly, very few people are consciously aware of this but they do make reference to it from time to time. They might say, "I've had it," or "It's too much for me," or "Stop the train, I want to get off." Most people when they say this don't really mean it, but it is a veiled reference to how exhausting the process of remaining oriented and remaining motivated can become. The overall and overwhelming popularity of idiot-level prime-time sitcoms is a testimonial to this need to disorient or disconnect. An attorney once told me, "I read briefs and depositions all day long, and listen to testimony in court. When I get home I want to find the most low-level, imbecilic, and dim-witted program I can find so that I no longer have to think." What he was talking about is how he disconnects (disorients) from the real world at the end of the day. He does not want to come home and engage in any kind of an activity that will take more mental effort. Staying oriented is like being on "alert" all day long, and that's why it's tiring and monotonous.

Although these four orientations serve us as motives, motives and motivations can also be disorienting. The attorney who watches idiot-level sitcoms wants to disorient from the day's events. The adolescent who goes to a theme park and jumps off the Free Fall fifty or sixty times in one day wants to disorient himself or herself from the scary events that surround adolescence. Watching a sporting event, such as NFL football, can be extremely disorienting, especially if the viewer has an emotional investment in the team or teams that are playing. More often than not, the motive is to disorient, not to orient oneself. This is what vacations are all about.

THE ORIENTATION TO PERSON MOTIVE IN CONSUMER ACTIVITIES

When a woman says, "I have nothing to wear," the typical male response is, "You have a whole closet full of clothes!" I always make a point of introducing the Orientation Motives with this metaphor when attempting to illustrate the Personal Orientation Motive, since everyone understands it. What married man has not heard a woman say this before?

When a woman says "I have nothing to wear," she is talking about the particular occasion and the dress style that she feels would be appropriate. A woman has many, many choices in terms of what she wears and this is the part that men don't understand. Using the searchlight metaphor, a woman goes into the clothing section of a large department store and will do a right-hemisphere "broad sweep" of hundreds of items, each of them suggesting to her a different personality style or flair. On the other hand, a man will use the smaller left-hemisphere searchlight and will focus on a particular item or items. For this reason it takes a woman a lot longer to shop for clothing and this is why men become so impatient with women who are shopping. Conversely, when men's items such as ties are available in large selections, our research has shown women will often make the choice because they are better equipped for making these selections than men. One reason is that they have more experience in picking out clothing since they work with a much larger selection. Another reason is that a tie is one of the few items that a man wears that is colorful, and women have more experience with color than men. And since color is usually associated with emotion, this may also suggest that women are in closer touch with their emotions than men, which is the reason why they would be more qualified to pick out a man's tie. These differences between men and women are not experiential or environmental; they are neurological. In other words, the differences are hardwired into the brain.

In any and all articles of clothing for women—even in those articles that are unseen—there are considerable and extensive selections available since there are considerable variations in the types of person that a woman may want to be: sexy, brilliant, beautiful, racy, glamorous, alluring, attractive, breathtaking, cute, foxy, comely, gorgeous, stunning, voluptuous, and so on. Since the Personal Orientation Motive is intimately related to a woman's character (and also to a man's), women dress primarily for the benefit of other women and secondarily for men, although they may say that it's the other way around. Women have more choices today than they have ever had before in terms of how they want to appear, and therefore more kinds of characterlogical displays and exhibitions are possible.

Cosmetics and hairstyles do the same thing for a woman that clothing does. They allow other women and men to make inferences about the character of the person who wears the makeup or who commands a particular type of hairstyle. An adolescent girl often will appear entirely inappropriate in terms of the amount of makeup that she has applied to her face, and this is because the whole area of cosmetics is new to adolescents, but also, and more important, the adolescent is defining her character and substance, and cosmetics help her toward this definition. The period of adolescence is a time of confused and uncertain identity, and cosmetics aid and assist the adolescent girl in finding and establishing that identity and moving more smoothly through the transition from childhood to adolescence. If some of the cosmetic manufacturers recognized the importance of the role of cosmetics in adolescence they might target this market as a specialty, in much the same way that some marketers targeted allergenic reactions or dry skin.

Brief Case History

A large supermarket chain had considerable difficulty when an equally large mass marketer of clothing, tools, auto accessories, and just about everything else also took on a line of grocery items. Our research found that women preferred the mass marketer because grocery shopping, which is normally a chore, gave them an excuse to look at the new styles and fashions which changed almost weekly (orientation to person). Even though they might not purchase anything (and usually didn't), they wanted to have the opportunity to look and dream. The grocery chain did not have the opportunity and furthermore did not want to get into the fashion business, but at the same time wanted to remain competitive.

Recognizing that the trip to the mass marketer and perusal of fashions was motivated by the Personal Orientation Motive, we recommended that the cosmetics department in the grocery store be upgraded and separated from the rest of the store by a tent structure that had an aura of privacy and distinctive lighting. In addition, a cosmetologist was placed in this area who dispensed advice and reassurance in areas involving cosmetics. Keep in mind that both clothing and cosmetics, for women, are related to the Personal Orientation Motive, and this motive is the strongest in the building blocks (see Figure 1.1). Although this small innovation did not reverse the trend, it did bring some previous customers back from the mass marketer, since the Personal Orientation Motive was the issue in both clothing and in cosmetics. Furthermore, it showed the grocery chain where they would need to make future innovations and changes: in areas that involved the Personal Orientation Motive but not necessarily in fashions or clothing.

THE PLACE ORIENTATION MOTIVE

When a woman encounters depression she will often go out and purchase new wardrobe items. This should make sense, for in terms of the previous discussion a woman defines her identity or her personal orientation by what she wears and how she appears.

When a man encounters depression his first impulse is to change circumstances as in quitting his job and finding another one. His next impulse is to change location (orientation to place). This is because in America and in many other countries in the world, a man's identity or his personal orientation is tied up in what he does for a living. But since he does not realize this, he often feels—erroneously—that if he moves, changes jobs, or goes someplace else, things will change and he will feel miraculously better. Like the woman who buys a new wardrobe when she is depressed in order to change her worldview, the change is only temporary.

An example of a temporary change of place—or pace—is when people go out to eat rather than eating at home. The way that kitchens are equipped today there is little if any reason to eat out. If food were the main reason that people chose to eat out (change in food preference), many supermarkets cater to this motive and desire. Supermarkets now have precooked recipes on hand that need only to be microwaved, and a person can have the same delectables that they might find in a restaurant. But food and taste is only a small part of the reason why people eat at restaurants. A more compelling reason is disconnecting to place, or disorientation.

Henry Ford, in a 1919 interview with the *Detroit Free Press,* said that his primary reason for going into the automobile business was because "everybody wants to get where they ain't, and when they get there they want to get back home again." Henry Ford was talking about disorientation to place; a motive that compels and coerces a lot of people.

Ever feel like an entirely different person when you are on vacation? Did you do things that perhaps you wished you had not done when you got home? Spent more than you should have? Ate more than you should have? Bought t-shirts, jackets, or caps with the name of the place you visited in order to extend the experience and make it last longer? This is what souvenirs are all about. We take a three- or four-day vacation and go to one of our favorite places. We come home and would like that special feeling to last a little while longer. So we buy some souvenirs that identify the experience, often with a brand name and logo. Hopefully, when we get back home again, days or perhaps weeks later we can wear that t-shirt or cap and bring back the same feelings and emotions that were encountered on the three- or four-day vacation. We may not be able to go back again, but at least we may be able to recreate the time that we were there or, more important, relive the feelings and the emotions of that special time.

THE TIME ORIENTATION MOTIVE

As we begin the twenty-first century it is more apparent than ever that time is a critical motivator and many of us have difficulty in keeping up. Ever since the advent of the Information Revolution, when computers "took over," time has been a problem. Part of the reason is that computers do everything so quickly and we can't keep up with the speed. Everything moves so fast. Nothing ever stands still for very long. And in keeping with the old saying "haste makes waste," there is nothing we can do about the haste, but it's up to us to clean up the waste. Much of our time is spent every day in correcting errors and mistakes that are made in the haste of the computer-driven generation. Time is of the essence.

One of the absurdities presented in the Federal Express spots referenced in Chapters 6 and 7 was the fast-talking man. The fast-talking man, who appeared circa 1983, was a harbinger of the times that were coming. The message was that it's getting harder and harder to keep up. The fast-talking man was an absurdity, but also a personalization. Who, in 1983 and even more so today, could not personalize a world that was moving so fast that everything was spinning out of control? The antidote to this is time disorientation. There are many activities that allow us to block out time or escape from time. Perhaps the most vivid of these activities is entertainment and casinos, which are two of the fastest growing industries in America. Entertainment, in all of its forms and formats—organized sports, concerts, television, computer games, computers, DVD, CDs, and so on—exists in order to help us to lose track of, disorient or disconnect from time. We continue to invent more and more ways to disorient ourselves and escape from the constraints that time imposes upon us.

Federal Express is successful because that's what they sell: time. They allow us to buy time right down to the last few hours before a proposal, a document, or a product deadline is imposed. People will pay big money for time, and if that's true, then time is, like person and place, a powerful motivator.

Malmo (1999) has put his finger on the Time Orientation Motive in a way that makes sense and adds some perspective to this very important motive:

Marketers talk about the constantly changing motivations of consumers, yet there is one over-riding consumer motivation that has not changed since the first caveman had a full belly.

People will pay for products and services that save time. Saving consumers time has, does and will continue to drive more categories of the world's economy than any other single motivation.

People pay more for cars than horses because cars save time. They pay more for airplane travel than train travel because airplanes are faster.

Innovations in products and services that save time are the ones that create the biggest opportunities and outdate the status quo performers the quickest.

You've read plenty about those companies, those industries that suffered competitors to stunt their growth, even make them obsolete. The airlines did it to the railroads. The personal computer industry did it to IBM.

Yet there are more examples on the other side of the fence about which you have read a lot less. These are companies in the mature categories that understand the consumer motivation to save time, that see competition coming and are smart enough to create that competition themselves.

These are the companies that reinvent themselves and redefine their categories.

One example is Kellogg, once known only as a breakfast cereal giant but now known simply as the breakfast giant.

USA Today featured a research study by the NPD Group on the breakfast habits of a panel of 5,000 Americans. To the surprise of no one, breakfast in America has become all about convenience. Once convenient, quick, cold breakfast cereal is no longer convenient enough for everyone.

Breakfast finger foods such as Pop-Tarts and Nutri-Grain Bars and other such bowl-less and utensil-less breakfast options are growing fast. You probably already know that Pop-Tarts and Nutri-Grain Bars are products of Kellogg.

What you may not know is that these and other such finger foods now account for twenty-five percent (1.4 billion) of Kellogg's worldwide revenues. While Kellogg's cereal sales were declining seven percent in the first nine months of last year, Pop-Tart sales were up ten percent and Nutri-Grain grew by seventeen percent.

As all people, tribes and nations progress along the journey of becoming civilized, they increase their inventory of wealth and possessions and decrease their inventory of time.

Time, Timing, Emotion, and Motivation

Almost all disciplines include in their theories an analysis or partial analysis of how people perceive time, but psychology has been completely silent about the concept of time as an emotion and as a motivation. Carstensen, Isaacowitz, and Charles (1999) have devoted considerable space and effort to a discussion of time and its relationship to motivation. These authors have recognized that scholars of physics, anthropology, astronomy, and philosophy have all written extensively about people's perception of time and how psychology has been "conspicuously silent about the topic." For these authors, time changes with age. As people get older they become increasingly aware of the fact that time is running out, and the whole concept of time changes from open-ended to closed-ended. As a result of this, interests, activities, and behaviors all change. When there is a realization that time is limited, there is an avoidance of unpleasant activities and people focus on the present rather than the future or on the past. This shift in turn leads to a focus on the intuitive and the subjective rather than the planful and the analytical. And although these authors do not go very far beyond behavior, they do conclude that people's perception of time is an important ingredient to human motivation, which is the approach that we have always taken in Motigraphics. "Because we believe that time is fundamental to human motivation, we then consider the broader implications that boundaries on time may have for theory building in psychology" (p. 166).

A few years ago I read an article in the *Philadelphia Inquirer* in which the author said that as a child he always spent his summers on the New Jersey shore. My experiences were similar. He went on to say that in those days, when he was eight, nine, and ten years old, his memories were clothed in brilliant sunshine and the summer days seemed to go on and on as if they had no end. He then explained this by saying that as we get older, each day that we live actually becomes shorter and shorter in terms of our perspective, since it is perceived within the structure of our entire lifetime. A woman who is eighty years old perceives a day as much briefer and shorter than a woman who is twenty-five years old. This difference in perception has an effect upon urgency, exigency, and pressure.

CASINO GAMING

Casinos and the entertainment industry as a whole are growing very fast in America. Casinos gross more money than all video rentals, concert receipts, and receipts from all organized athletic activities combined. Casinos sell disorientation. Disorientation to time, place, person, and circumstances. This is not by design, because most casino operators and owners have no idea what they are selling, or why they are so successful at what they are doing. Consider an example.

In June 1990, the voters in Tunica County, Mississippi approved casino gaming along the banks of the Mississippi River. Casinos were erected very quickly and during the first few years, when the dust was still settling, there were losers and winners in the race to see who stayed and who didn't. Within the first three years four casinos bit the dust. Interestingly, and not by coincidence, all four of the casinos that folded had windows in them. Similarly, there are no clocks in casinos. If you ask anyone about this they will quickly tell you that the reason casino management doesn't put clocks in casinos is because they want people to play longer. But that's not the reason. We can safely assume that anyone who goes to a casino today has some personal method of telling time.

So what's important about windows and clocks? The importance of eliminating these features is that over the years casino management has figured out that the more that the casino disorients people, the more they are likely to stay and the more they are likely to return the next time. Some casinos build a virtual fantasy land around the customer. They have figured this out via a process of elimination and by intuition. Casino gaming disorients people in all four spheres: person, place, time, and circumstances. Casinos sell disorientation. We have seen this phenomenon come out, over and over again, in Silent Side research.

Disorientation to time occurs because there are no clocks, no windows, and no references to time. The most successful casinos are dimly lit, dark, and isolated so that the only reference to time is the player's own stomach. However, most players are so transfixed by the game and their involvement in it that hunger is not even a remote consideration.

Disorientation to place occurs in several ways. The restaurants are lavish and food is delectable. There is also an unusual auditory stimulus in the background that could be called "music" but is only remotely associated with any kind of music that has ever been popular or on the charts. There is lighting that in and of itself is disorienting and not similar to any kind of place that you have been before. The lighting and the music are fast-paced and are designed to build excitement and expectation.

And finally there is disorientation to person, which we have discussed as the most powerful motive of all. Disorientation to person was usually reserved for the big-time high rollers who were "regulars" at the casino. These were the people for whom "perks" were invented. Perks included upgraded room and dining facilities, trips to and from the airport, private flights to and from the casino from wherever they happened to live, and entertainment, both public and private.

However, much of this changed when Bill Bennett and Bill Pennington took over Circus Circus in Las Vegas in 1974. Jay Sarno had been the manager and his whole pitch had been to high rollers. Bennett and Pennington were both businessmen, and they brought a new concept to Las Vegas and eventually to casino gaming nationwide. They introduced a new demographic to the market: low rollers. These new owners believed they could draw people to the casino with cheap rooms and cheap food and with slot machines. To the amazement of many, their marketing plan worked like a jewel. In a way, they had discovered the disorientation motives, and particularly the Personal Orientation Motive. Treating ordinary people like big shots goes a long way, not only when they are winning big but especially when they are losing.

Although Circus Circus is no longer a key player, the concept that Pennington and Bennett brought to the party—that is, bringing middle Americans to the casino instead of limiting the games only to higher rollers—is still very much alive. And it is alive in middle America, where casinos have sprung up like weeds in what used to be bean fields, cotton fields, and corn fields. The success of these casinos is based upon the entertainment that they provide, primarily to low rollers and middle- and low-income players. But their success is also based upon the recognition that all customers, regardless of where they live, have similar motives to (1) disorient and (2) expect to win. Remember, motives are a blueprint for successful marketing. The only major difference is that instead of bringing high rollers to the casino, the casinos are now going to the low rollers.

Not long after the casinos opened in Tunica, Mississippi, a story appeared in the Memphis *Commercial Appeal* which told of a young African American man. At twenty-four he was promoted to vice president of a large local bank and it looked as if he had a very promising career in banking ahead of him. However, he had started gambling at one of the Tunica casinos. He happened to start his gaming career with a long winning streak, and amassed around $75,000. At the point when he was at the very top, casino management started Plan I of the personal disorientation, which was to treat him like the big shot he felt that he was, since he was richer by $75,000. He received special dining privileges, room privileges, and other perks that ordinary people did not receive. At this point his luck turned against him, and he began to lose about as fast as he had won. This is when Plan II went into effect, which was a much more elaborate upgrade of Plan I. Plan II included private jet charters to the sister casino in Las Vegas or Atlantic City, chauffeured limousine service from his own home to the Tunica casino, and other first-class treatment while he was in the casino. As a result, he continued to play and, as luck would have it, continued to lose. Eventually he got in so far over his head that he staged a one-man holdup in a bank across the Mississippi River in West Memphis, Arkansas. Upon getting the money he jumped into his car and headed back across the bridge to Memphis, with the West Memphis police behind him and the Memphis police waiting for his arrival on the Tennessee side of the river. He stopped in the middle of the bridge, left the money in the car, and jumped down into the swift and swirling river below.

In states where it is legal, casinos are allowed to give away free alcoholic beverages, and this is probably the best of all methods for intensifying disorientation to a person. Once an individual loses track of who he or she is, there is no telling what he or she will do to remain in the game. Tunica casinos have representatives of local banks and car dealers who have cash in hand and will readily and willingly give it to any gambler who asks, in return for the car title. Unlike Las Vegas, the majority of gamblers in Tunica are "low rollers"; the kind that were introduced to the industry by Bennett and Pennington. In most cases, the only backup they have when they get into the hole is their home or their car. By this time, they are totally and completely disoriented to who they are, where they are, and even the day of the month, and they are willing to do anything in order to stay in the game.

O'Brien (1998) quotes Steve Wynn, the "impresario of Mirage Resorts and the most influential figure in the casino business" and probably the first casino professional who recognized the "real" motivation behind casino gambling and gamblers:

I tell you that there are no suckers in a casino. It implies ignorance, and more importantly it implies that there's a predator involved, which has to be me. All you've got to do is find one customer at the Mirage who can't tell you that the house percentage is against him; find one person there who's there to make a living, who thinks that they can win in the casino as a matter of fact as opposed to being pure luck. . . . These people are here for diversion. (p. 45)

It would follow from this brief lesson on casino gaming that the more an owner or manager disorients a customer, the more successful the business will be. Our research has shown that this approach is successful in restaurants, in the fashion industry, in auto sales, in theme parks, and in many other industries and businesses. The more powerful the disorientation motive (personal orientation being the most powerful), the more successful the business. To echo Steve Wynn, "These people are here for diversion." We might add and clarify somewhat by saying, "These people are here for diversion, disorientation, and disconnection."

THE ORIENTATION TO CIRCUMSTANCES MOTIVE

We have found in almost all of our research, including research with consumers and with volunteers, that the Orientation to Circumstances Motive is the weakest of all of the motives because it is situational and transient. The circumstances of the day can often be obliterated with one drink at the end of the day and completely obliterated with two drinks. This is often the case; that is, that people come home from work and the daily ritual is first to have a drink before doing anything else.

In the mid-1960s, the New Haven Railroad ran commuter trains from New York's Grand Central Station to Bridgeport, Connecticut. The train served the bedroom communities outside of New York City. One day, railroad management made the announcement that they were going to terminate services on their bar car because it was not living up to their expectations in revenue. No amount of screaming, yelling, weeping, or wailing on the part of the commuters impacted the decision. As a result, a group of commuters got together and approached railroad management, asking if they would allow them to provide their own car. When management agreed, the commuters purchased their own railroad box car and turned it into a club car by putting some wooden benches and old chairs that were donated by some of the "founders." They hired their own bartender. With no heat or air conditioning in the car, they were very uncomfortable, but the opportunity to disorient was more essential than personal comforts. Nothing fancy, but it did the job; it helped commuters to wipe out the circumstances of the day. So we say that the Orientation to Circumstances Motive is the weakest in the chain and it is, but this illustration shows that there are no really "weak" motives; all of them are strong in the sense that they account for large portions of human behavior.

We have defined two elements of the Orientation to Circumstances Motive: pace (of life) and convenience. It is a sign of the times that most people, in conversation, will talk about how their life is almost out of control and how they can't keep up with the frenetic pace. In addition, the entire motive in almost all shopping, and certainly as important as price (which is a rational motive), is convenience.

The motivational phenomenon behind Lynn Hickey Dodge explains why Lynn Hickey (1995) became the world's largest Dodge dealer. He simply slowed the pace and simplified the circumstances when it came to making the decision to buy a car. Recognizing that car buying was one of the two most important decisions that a consumer makes, he disabled the PA system on the car lot and gave all the salespeople pagers. He recognized that the constant interference from loud speakers and nonessential announcements interrupted the concentration of the customer at a time when concentration and focusing was upon a critical task. He also was one of the first automobile dealers to discontinue classified advertising in the newspaper, since in the automobile business this is another cause of clutter and confusion for the car buyer. By simplifying the circumstances surrounding car buying (a complicated transaction), Lynn Hickey became the largest Dodge dealer in America.

In our own experience, a supermarket bank was doing quite well in its association with a national chain of supermarkets. However there was a concern on the part of management that no real "serious" banking was being done. There was plenty of traffic, but most of it consisted of check cashing and miscellaneous transfers; no loans or mortgages were being made. Our research found that the real problem here was that the banks were located in the "fast lane" of the supermarket, and that people were reluctant to do any serious banking in the midst of the confusion that often swirls around the checking lanes and exits from the supermarket. Traffic was great, but most people will resist balancing their checkbook or dealing with serious money matters in the middle of a mass of noise and confusion. In addition, in this project we had customers draw a picture of a "real" bank and a supermarket bank, and found substantial differences. The real bank had pillars, a vault, and tellers who were often middle-aged men and women, or at least they were remembered in this manner. Recommendations consisted of leaving the bank in the fast lane but enclosing it so that people could actually walk into the bank and remove themselves from the clutter and pace of the fast lane. This change increased the volume of serious banking. Another recommendation consisted of placing pillars in the bank, giving it the appearance of a real bank. As one manager said, "That was a really expensive recommendation, but well worth it."

SUMMARY

The Orientation Motives (Person, Place, Time, and Circumstances) are easily taken for granted, but need to be at the foundation of every marketing plan. When walking up or down a flight of stairs, we never stop and think about what we are doing; if we did, we might trip ourselves and fall down the stairs. We don't think about orientation, but because we don't think about it there are many consumer and other human behaviors that go unexplained and unaccounted for. This is precisely why, when you ask people why they do what they do, they cannot tell you.

The more disorientation is a part of the big picture, the more motivating the product or service is to the customer. This is true in most markets and in most business sectors, except when the business requires orientation as opposed to disorientation. Just consider all of the businesses that have become successful by selling the most precious commodity of all—time.

Motives are blueprints for success in marketing. When a product or service is designed to appeal to the realization that people have a need to orient or disorient, that product or service is headed for success. What motivates people is what moves people. Motives are the hot buttons.

NOTE

1. The gender-specific pronoun is used in this case since over 80 percent of the patients that I have seen with this diagnosis are boys.

REFERENCES

Carstensen, L. L., Isaacowitz, D. M., & Charles, S. T. (1999). Taking time seriously: A theory of socioemotional selectivity. *American Psychologist, 54,* 165–81.

Lynn Hickey Dodge. (1995, September–October). In *Automobile Dealer Magazine.*

Malmo, J. (1999, February 1). Many will pay extra to save more time. (Memphis) *Commercial Appeal.*

O'Brien, T. L. (1998). *Bad bet: The inside story of the glamour, glitz and danger of America's gambling industry.* New York: Time Books.

Ramachandran, V. S., & Blakeslee, S (1998). *Phantoms in the brain: Probing the mysteries of the human brain.* New York: William Morrow.

10

The Survival Motives

The trouble with the rat race is that if you win, you're still a rat.
—Lilly Tomlin

SCIENCE, SOCIETY, AND SURVIVAL

The major sources of support for the observations that are made in this book include empirical support, support from the neurosciences, and observations of advertising as a motivational "art form." It is also reassuring to know that everything that we have said so far is consistent with scientific findings of the past and the present, and particularly with evolutionary theory. The fact that the Silent Side research methods include survival, orientation, and other basic issues lends considerable scientific credibility and consistency to this method, not only with science but also with common sense. In other words, this is what motivation *should* be all about. We do what we need to do, every day, in order to survive and stay oriented. The faster the world moves, the more obvious this becomes and the more prominent the need to spend some time that is disoriented and disconnected from the day-to-day rat race.

When we look at primitive societies, it is clear that survival was an everyday event, but it is not so clear when we look at our own lives. This is because we tend to equate survival with physical survival, and in doing this we miss the point of what survival is all about. In this chapter, we will see that physical survival plays a small but very important role in our lives, and there are other categories of survival that are in some cases less important and in other cases more important than physical survival. In any case, we cannot look at motivations, as Maslow or the behaviorists have, without considering the essential elements of survival and orientation or, for that matter, adaptation (which follows in Chapter 11) and expectation (which follows in Chapter 12).

OVERVIEW OF THE SURVIVAL MOTIVES: THE FOUR Fs

There are four Survival Motives which shadow or are roughly equivalent to what Ramachandran and Blakeslee (1998) refer to as the four Fs: fighting, feeding, fleeing, and sexual behavior. Feeding is associated with the Physical Survival Motive. Along with drinking, clean air, and good health, these are the elements of the Physical Survival Motive. Fighting is associated with the Spiritual Survival Motive, for, as we have defined spiritual survival, it is closely associated with whatever a person happens to be passionate about. And we fight for what we believe in and what we are passionate about. In fact, we are willing to die fighting for what we believe in. Fleeing or running is associated with the Territorial Survival Motive, as in trespassing, territorial imperatives, or in running away or perhaps running to a new and exciting career opportunity. Finally, sexual behavior is associated with the Sexual Survival Motive and the four elements of sexual survival: gender, impulse, inhibition in women, and impotence in men.

The four Fs may be validated with dreams. My research of dream analysis with psychiatric patients has shown that the content of any and all dreams will fall into one of these four categories exclusively: feeding, fighting, fleeing, and sexual behavior. All dreams can eventually be interpreted on the basis of one of these four content areas. To be more expansive and specific at the same time, all dreams in any language and in any culture will consist of these four categories, no more and no less. This is a form of crosscultural validation. Often a dream will consist of only one of the four Fs or motives, but at times dreams will run together and include more than one, or at least it will seem as if more than one is included. Another way to look at this is to say that dreams are about survival.

Our discussion of survival as a motive will include the four Fs and the four motives that have been listed in the survival category, since they are parallel, overlapping, and equivalent.

THE SPIRITUAL SURVIVAL MOTIVE

Passion

The elements of the Spiritual Survival Motive may at first seem to be complex and complicated, but in fact they only serve to simplify things. Just as the elements of physical survival are food, air, and water and the elements of sexual survival are gender, impulse, and inhibition, the elements of the Spiritual Survival Motive are

1. Whatever people are passionate about.
2. Paul Fleischman's ten elements, introduced in Chapter 8 and discussed in more detail here.
3. Religion.

The first element, passion, is highly idiosyncratic. When people are asked what they are passionate about they will give many different responses, but in research where we have asked people to do this, each respondent usually hones in on a single response. This is because they know exactly what their passion is in their life, what they are willing to fight for, and how far they are willing to go to protect it.

In our research, we had a 103-item questionnaire, and ten of those items consisted of "X." Respondents were told that X is "whatever you are passionate about in your life right now." What resulted from this analysis on passion was a very robust, clear-cut, and unambiguous factor that we called passion and grouped under the area of spiritual survival.

Passion, of course, could be negative or positive. Love is associated with passion most of the time, but certain hate crimes can also be classified as "crimes of passion." A person can take a position on the building blocks of human motivation either at the center or at the extreme left or the extreme right. The center indicates moderation. Figure 10.1 illustrates these various positions. An example of an extreme position in spiritual survival may be seen in a romantic relationship. On the right side of this block in the building blocks is possessive love, punctuated by stalking, frequent calling, frequent gifts (with hidden obligations), and extreme, pathological jealousy. What one might refer to as love or passion on the extreme (severe) left side is "love" which is characterized by neglect and indifference, which is seen in some marriages. The extreme position on the left side is characterized by disregard, forgetfulness, ignoring, neglect, and insensitivity. The extreme right side,

Figure 10.1
Severity Scale: Human Motives (Lateral)

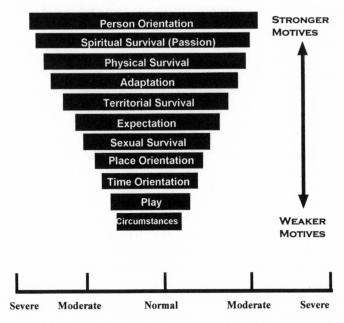

where there is pathological jealousy, could even lead to crimes of passion, including physical abuse and possibly even homicide. The extreme left side will typically lead to divorce, as love is proclaimed but never demonstrated.

The middle position represents the most desirable position on the building blocks of human motivation within the motive of spiritual survival. The implications of these various extreme positions on the building blocks with regard to criminal behavior, law enforcement, and leadership are discussed in more detail in the Appendix, where we consider implications of this general approach to motivation that are not related to advertising and marketing.

Passion does not lend itself easily to measurement in terms of traditional psychometric methods. Perhaps this is why psychology has overlooked passion: It cannot be fitted into discrete categories and measured on a seven-point scale. However, the method of interviewing and data collection that we will review in Chapter 15 is tailored to uncovering what people are passionate about. The method is effective because consumers tell stories or generate scripts in their own words, and these are then subjected to an objective scoring procedure, as opposed to a subjective one that is given by the respondent when he or she circles a category on a five-, seven-, or nine-point scale. Adaval and Wyer (1998) have discussed the relative superiority of data that are generated in a narrative form by the respondent rather than in the form of an unorganized list, and although they applied this to an external brochure that was being reviewed, it is assumed that the same principle would apply in this context (i.e., when the consumer generates his or her own narrative in relation to the product).

Fleischman's Elements of Spiritual Survival

Table 10.1 shows the results of a factor analysis carried out on Paul Fleischman's ten elements of spiritual survival (Fleischman, 1990). The results shown in Table 10.1 represent a very robust factor analysis and this is as it should be. Fleischman spent many years researching the various religious beliefs of people in various countries and corners of the world. The research was in the form of naturalistic observations. He found similarities between all religions, similar to the way that Chomsky (1968) found support for similar grammatical structures which underlie all of the world's languages. The elements listed in Table 10.1 are essential to the Spiritual Survival Motive. The purpose of these elements is to assist us in defining passion on an individual basis and what people are passionate about. When Fleischman was sent a copy of the output of this factor analysis, he said that he was not at all surprised at how perfectly it turned out, since these "elements stand up and scream at you from every page of the Old Testament, the New Testament, the Koran, the Bhagavad Gita, and every other religious document that has ever been written" (personal communication). In other words, they are timeless. Neither technology, postmodernism, nor any other "insight" from the modern world appears to have any effect on the importance of these essential elements.

Although all of the elements will not be discussed here, two were found to be of vital importance in our discussion of leadership (Maddock & Fulton, 1998). The first was witness significance, or the universal belief that there is a higher power that looks out over us, understands and empathizes with us, and knows what we are going through. A glance at Table 10.1 indicates that this is by far the most important of the elements, since it accounts for the most variance. When the element of witness significance is applied to plant management, we showed that there was a discernible and significant difference when the plant manager was seen on the plant floor every day by workers. It made a discernible difference to Wendy's (hamburgers) when Dave Thomas himself appeared in the advertising, inviting anyone who was watching to stop in for a ham-

Table 10.1
Results of Factor Analysis on Fleischman's Elements of Spiritual Survival

Factor #	Factor Name	Variance Accounted for (%)
1.	Witness Significance	11.3
2.	Membership	7.8
3.	Renewal and Release	4.5
5.	Sacrifice*	3.3
6.	Lawful Order	3.1
8.	Affirming Acceptance	2.6
9.	Affirming Acceptance II	2.5
10.	Renewal and Release II	2.4
11.	Human Love	2.2
12.	Calling	2.1
13.	Inner Peace**	2.0
	Total Variance Accounted for	43.8

*Factor 4, pace (of life), was the only factor that was not part of the ten elements of spiritual survival, but accounted for 3.7 percent of the variance. This issue is addressed by Fleischman (1990) in his book and lectures.

**The one factor that was not accounted for in the first ten was meaningful death. Some of the variables that appeared to describe this variable were grouped with lawful order in factor 6.

burger. When Chrysler was in big trouble and needed to pull off a miracle to survive, it made a big difference for Lee Iacocca himself to appear in all of the ads, assuring and reassuring viewers or readers that he was overseeing the whole process and that he personally was building quality into products. Similarly, Romero (1994) who belittles, degrades, and denounces almost all casino advertising (since it is all alike), states in his book that the only effective casino advertising that he has ever encountered was an outdoor (billboard) for Caesar's that simply stated, "He's here!" These are all examples of how the element of witness significance can be applied in situations that we encounter every day. The fact that some advertising is totally simplistic and yet at the same time totally effective is based upon the element of witness significance.

In the area of leadership, which is a thoroughly researched field, the element of witness significance was also seen as essential. Not only did it come out as the first factor in other factor analyses that were conducted by other researchers (Bass, 1997), but was also shown to be one of the two most important factors involved in leadership and management, albeit by another name, such as "charisma."

A second element of spiritual survival, membership, accounted for 7.8 percent of the variance and was also a very important contributing factor, not only in our research on leadership but in the research that has been carried out by others. A number of studies (Maddock & Fulton, 1998) in leadership show that when management instills a sense of belonging, constituency, and membership to large groups of employees, most of them will jump on board and become committed to the organization. In the same vein, when union organizers appeal to that same sense of belongingness and constituency, employees will jump on board. People want to be members of an organization and a group of people that thinks, acts, and believes the same way that they do. This is one of the major reasons behind church attendance, and the same concept can be applied to organizations and to consumer appeals. The results in both cases (witness significance and membership) are generally overwhelming and performance on the part of people exceeds all expectations when these two elements are part of the organization.

Fleischman (1990) discusses other elements, such as sacrifice, that are all essential elements of the Spiritual Survival Motive. The Marine Corps, which depends heavily upon all of the elements of the Spiritual Survival Motive in its training, has found that the element of sacrifice—the willingness to die for one's country—is one of the most cohesive factors in Marine Corps training, in boot camp and beyond. When the Spiritual Survival Motive is incorporated into advertising it has a lasting and permanent impression, as in DeBeers's "Diamonds are forever"; Michelin's "You care about what's riding on your tires"; or Hallmark's "You care enough to send the very best." Similarly, the Marine Corps, using focus groups, has found that their appeal to spiritual survival has had a lasting and permanent effect, as seen in "The change is forever." We have also asked people in research if they would enter a burning house to save someone that they love (sacrifice) if they knew there was only a fifty-fifty chance of survival, and the affirmative response is over 92 percent. This is an affirmation of their willingness to choose spiritual survival over physical survival.

One of the most pervasive motives in Fleischman's (1990) structure is inner peace. We have asked people why they would purchase a yacht or a beach condominium for $200,000 to $300,000 and then only use it once or twice a year. When we ask this, they are perplexed, since they cannot respond directly to the question. We do this in order to demonstrate that all human behavior is not that easily explained. However, when the boat or condo owners are interviewed using Silent Side methods described in Chapter 15, the response that we always end up getting is "inner peace." It would be interesting to know how many boat, RV, and beachfront condo salespeople really know what they are selling, and whether they know the real value of their product. For some reason, we find inner peace on the water. We break our necks and open our wallets to get to the beach. Waterfront property, when you can find it, is more expensive than ordinary property. Malmo (1999) said that people will pay anything for time. We believe that they will pay even more for inner peace.

Beckwith (1997) asks the question, "What are you really selling?" He did not do an empirical study, but we have appealed to advertising and marketing just as strongly as we have appealed to empirical studies. Beckwith said that McDonald's figured out that people weren't buying hamburgers, they were buying an experience. When Burger King tried to compete with them by positioning themselves as flame broiled and not fried, it didn't work. That supports our previous observations that McDonald's was never in the hamburger business. Our own research has gone one step further than Beckwith, and has shown that what McDonald's is selling is a specific kind of experience, and that is family values, which is another one of the elements of the Spiritual Survival Motive. Without it, most of the marketing phenomena that are encountered would be unexplainable.

The complete structure of motives and their corresponding elements is found in Table 8.3. Since motives are abstract in nature it is difficult to talk about them, let alone define them in a research project. Therefore the elements that are associated with motives are listed in table form, since this makes them much easier to identify and recognize.

Neurological Support for Spiritual Survival

We have received some statistical support for the Spiritual Survival Motive, which is usually the most controversial of the motives that are presented. But support is also available from other areas, and particularly from those who have made extensive and invasive studies of the relationship between the brain and behavior.

Ramachandran and Blakeslee (1998) report on a Canadian psychologist, Dr. Michael Persinger, who used a device to administer intercranial self-stimulation (ICSS) to parts of his own temporal lobe and, for the first time in his life, experienced God in a very intense religious experience. These researchers also note that this is not unusual, and that "every medical student is taught that patients with epileptic seizures originating in this part of the brain can have intense, spiritual experiences during the seizures and sometimes become preoccupied with religion and moral issues, even during the seizure-free or interdictal periods."

It is not unusual in many fundamentalist and Pentecostal churches to see the opposite phenomenon; that is, where the religious experience occurs first, usually in terms of charismatic preaching, and seizures follow on the part of some of the members of the congregation. Quite often these pseudo seizures will carry over and persist, outside of the church or religious environment, whenever emotional experiences or stress is encountered. Under these conditions medical care is often sought out and the findings are usually equivocal.

Ramachandran and Blakeslee (1998) suggest that it is possible that the human brain has a specialized neural circuitry which mediates religious and spiritual experiences, and they base this on the observation that "the human belief in the supernatural is so widespread in all societies all over the world that it's tempting to ask whether the propensity for such beliefs might have a biological basis" (p. 183). Either way, they feel that certain areas of the temporal lobes as well as the limbic system are involved in this seizure phenomenon.

Ornstein (1997) also argues convincingly for a neural substrate of religious and spiritual experience. He says that since the right brain is involved primarily in a more sweeping, universal, and large-scale view of the universe as a whole (broad searchlight; see Chapter 9), it perhaps has a role in developing the overall meaning of life's situation, even above and beyond the physical world that we now see. Ornstein goes on to talk about the training that many religions give in meditation and contemplation that goes well beyond the verbal; many experiences being movement or music oriented and therefore considered nonrational by many psychologists and other pseudoscientists. For Ornstein, these kinds of nonverbal exercises are engaged in by members of all religious persuasions, some more than others, and they are peculiarly right brain kinds of activities. A simple example is closing the eyes during prayer. I see a dichotomy between religious groups that employ these more nonverbal methods of involvement and those religious groups that are strongly and vigorously committed only to verbal and rational methods. One group is worshiping from a left brain perspective and the other from the perspective of the right brain. In terms of any of the measures of success that are usually recorded in religious institutions—income, membership, level of activity, evangelism, and so on—when the verbal versus the nonverbal groups are matched, those that stress experience, involvement, and personal magnetism win hands down over those who stress and emphasize only left brain involvement.

MacLean (1990) also talks about the experience of a religious or spiritual phenomenon under the conditions of limbic seizures and manifestations of psychomotor epilepsy, which he says may account for a dissociation between intellectual and emotional mentality. He then presents an epistemological impasse: "Hence, it would appear that the manufacture of belief in the reality, importance and truth or falsity of what is conceived depends on a mentality incapable of verbal comprehension and communication. It is one thing to have a primitive, illiterate mind for judging the authenticity of food or a mate, but where do we stand if we must depend on that same mind for belief in our ideas, concepts and theories?" (p. 579).

THE PHYSICAL SURVIVAL MOTIVE

The elements of the Physical Survival Motive are food, air, and water. We might also add the element of personal safety and good health, which brings into focus the place of health care in our motivational structure. When we started our research in 1978, most people were not concerned about what they ate, what they put in their bodies, and why. Cigarette smoking was allowed everywhere and there was no undue concern with the dangers of second-hand smoke. Food was packaged attractively, but the requirements about truth in ingredients, as seen in package labeling today, were not that stringent. Crime was not an issue, at least to the extent that it is today. Most homes did not have burglar and theft alarms, although people were starting to buy them and take them seriously. In summary, we were not that concerned with physical survival, just as today we are not that concerned with the Orientation Motives, even though we do act upon them every day.

Just as the lower animals are concerned with physical survival, so are we. But until recently we spent very little of our waking time thinking about it. That has changed dramatically. The individual who walks or runs three or four miles every day is engaged in this exercise strictly because of the need to maintain his or her physical survival. The individual who gives up smoking and is still aware of the need for a cigarette every passing minute is consciously aware of his or her own need for equilibrium at the level of the Physical Survival Motive. The same is true of those who go on rigorous diets, who select only very limited and discriminating foods, and who regularly and religiously are checked by a physician for any possible signs or symptoms of disease.

As we have stated several times in this book, for Maslow (1970), physical survival was the bottom line. But there are also those who ignore their physical survival, and so Maslow's description of motivation cannot be taken seriously. When I was discharged from the Navy, I was smoking nonfiltered Lucky Strike cigarettes and paying fifteen cents per pack. The thought of becoming a civilian and paying thirty-five cents a pack was to me very foreboding. I therefore quit smoking, which I now feel was a wise decision for reasons other than money. In 1999, people pay $3.50 to $4.00 for a pack of cigarettes and think nothing of it. Soon the price will rise to $4.50 and $5 in order for the cigarette companies to pay off the lawsuits that they have encountered. But of those that I have asked about their future plans, none feel that the price will deter them from smoking. When it comes to cigarette smoking, price (cost) is truly not an issue.

Smoking originates with the Adaptation Motive (Chapter 11). The Adaptation Motive tells us to do what our peers are doing. Our research has shown in most cases, people start to smoke because other adolescents who are friends of theirs are smoking. But smoking is continued for an entirely different reason: because of addiction and because of the Physical Survival Motive (taste). This is why the Adaptation Motive is almost tied for third place with the Physical Survival Motive on the building blocks of human motivation. At times, as in the decision to start smoking, it is even more important, and this needs to be discussed.

Earlier in this chapter we discussed the fact that people make lateral moves upon each motive in the building blocks of human motivation. If they move out too far to the left or right they may become ineffective or radical and irrational, respectively. But they also can move up and down the building blocks by shifting the blocks into a different order or configuration. This happens quite frequently, and is called a *vertical displacement*. The cure for the problems that arise out of vertical displacement is called the *vertical fix*.

The ideal place for the various motives to line up is as shown in Figure 1.1. A vertical displacement takes place when a person makes the decision to start smoking because their friends are smoking and they say that "it's cool." The Adaptation Motive is placed above the Physical Survival Motive. The same transition takes place when someone decides to drink and drive—because all of his friends are doing it—or to use recreational drugs. Whenever the blocks get out of order vertically, a problematic and difficult situation arises, and either minor or, in most cases, major problems arise within an organization. This is because priorities are shifted around and have to be put back in order again. Whenever a motive is displaced vertically, it needs to be put back in position again. This is the vertical fix, and it is the job of management and leadership to keep the blocks in the correct and proper order.

THE TERRITORIAL SURVIVAL MOTIVE

Animals are territorial. It only stands to reason that we have inherited this tendency from the lower animals who preceded us on this planet. Territoriality—along with other motives that have been discussed—are the legacies that the animals have left us.

Territorial Survival and Personal Orientation: Women

We have a tendency to confuse territorial survival with the Personal Orientation Motive. It has already been noted that men often define themselves (personal orientation) in terms of what they do for a living. "Hi there. I'm Fred. I'm a plumber. What do you do for a living?" Quite often, this is the way that conversations begin. In the past, women were sent to college strictly for the purpose of finding a "good man," who was defined in terms of his education and his ability to sustain her and his would-be family comfortably. A secondary benefit of a college education for women was status, which is discussed more fully under the Adaptation Motive.

For women, the territory has always been the home, and in ages past when men dominated societies because of their ability to hunt and feed the family, women remained at home and awaited the hunter's return. Although this scenario has changed markedly over the centuries, the magazines that women read still support the idea that women's major interests still lie with home and family.

Farrell (1986) describes home and family as a woman's "primary fantasy." He backs up his claim by looking at magazine circulation figures. When he did his research in 1985, *Better Homes and Gardens* and *Family Circle* were the leading women's magazines. *Better Homes and Gardens* had a paid circulation of 8 million and, in 1995, 7.6 million. Similarly, *Family Circle* in 1985 had a paid circulation of 7.1 million and in 1995 it was 5 million. Most magazines have lost circulation in the ten-year period from 1985 to 1995 and are continuing to lose circulation today. To us this suggests that a woman's primary orientation and the way that she defines herself is not only by what she wears but also by the condition of her home and what is in it. This is certainly not true of all women, but there do seem to be three primary areas by which women define themselves: dress, home and food (cooking). In studies we have done with consumers in various areas, women have typically responded that other people will judge them by (1) what they wear,

(2) what they serve when guests are in the home, and (3) the condition of their home when guests are invited in and/or the overall outside appearance of both the home and the grounds around it.

It is concluded that there is considerable confusion between the Territorial Survival Motive and the Personal Orientation Motive, at least in terms of the importance of the home and the grounds around it. In a study that we did on garage doors, the manufacturer felt that builders were his primary market. But as it turned out, the woman who was having the home built (new construction) had more to say about the garage door than anyone else. Furthermore, it was impossible not to talk about front doors and their overall importance to the entire house, because even though the respondents were told that the study was on garage doors they continued to want to insert the subject of the front door and its importance to the home.

In the 1960s, Ernst Dichter (1964, 1971), who was the first psychologist to deal with unconscious motivations in consumers, recommended that home builders install a large, 12- to 16-inch dish-type doorknob in the middle of the door of every home so that homeowners could "hug" their home. His rationale was that the largest purchase that most people ever make is their home, and they should have some way to hold on to it, which is the way that we demonstrate our affections for most of our possessions. There are not that many of those dish-style doorknobs being installed anymore, but they can still be seen on homes that were constructed in the early 1960s. Nevertheless, Dichter introduced a lasting concept for today. Just as it was years ago, the front door displays the "personality" of the home, and thence the personality of the homemaker. It is decorated appropriately in the colors and decor of the season and announces to anyone and everyone who passes by that "we are in the holiday spirit." As a result, our garage door client started a business in front doors and was very successful. Not only did he find a new market—women—but he also found a new product—front doors. Motivational research often "opens new doors," as it did with this project.

Territorial Survival and Personal Orientation: Men

According to Farrell (1986), the motivations that underlie men's behavior are quite different than the motives that underlie women's behavior. This should come as no surprise. The leading men's magazines when Farrell did his research in 1985 were *Playboy* (4.2 million) and *Penthouse* (3.5 million), which strongly supports Farrell's observation that the primary fantasy of men is to have sex with a beautiful woman. In 1995, the paid circulation figures for *Playboy* still remained strong in spite of the fact that all magazine sales in every area, men's and women's, were depressed. However, the figures for *Penthouse* showed a marked decrease in circulation. We believe that this is because of the explosive growth of pornographic literature now available for men on the Internet and on videotapes, which are more effective and more realistic than still pictures or any kind of print media.

What we are attempting to show is a confusion between the Personal Orientation Motive and the Territorial Survival Motive for men, just as we did for women. What we have ended up showing is a confusion between the Territorial Survival Motive and the Sexual Survival Motive, which creates another problem. It is not unusual for men, and especially for those over forty or forty-five, to want to redefine themselves in terms of having a beautiful woman on their arm when they appear in public. Sex may be secondary to the public appearance with a beautiful woman. This is a personal orientation issue but is expressed in terms of a territorial imperative. In men, as in women, there is also considerable confusion between the Personal Orientation Motive and the Territorial Survival Motive.

For Farrell (1986), both men and women have primary and secondary fantasies. The primary fantasy for women is home and family; for men, to have sex with a beautiful woman and to display that beautiful woman on their arm. The secondary fantasy for women is beauty, which accomplishes the purpose of the primary fantasy to attract a man who will provide for that home and family. Women are taught as little girls that the more beautiful they are, the better chances they have of attracting a man. Hence, the best-selling women's magazines in the secondary-fantasy category for women are *Cosmopolitan, Glamour, Seventeen,* and *Teen*, in that order. These magazines, like the ones that emphasize home and family, also pay very close attention to all of the areas that we have related to personal orientation for women: cosmetics, clothing, fashion, and, to some extent, food and family.

The secondary fantasy for men is also designed to support the primary fantasy. If the primary fantasy in men is to have sex with and display a beautiful woman, then the secondary fantasy, according to Farrell (1986), is performance. All of the next-best-selling magazines for men, as well as all of the remaining magazines for men down to the lowest-selling magazines on the list, are concerned with performance. This is because the men who are the best performers are able to attract the most beautiful women. The top-selling men's magazines in the secondary-fantasy category in 1985 were *American Legion, Sports Illustrated, Boy's Life,* and *Forbes*. These magazines deal with military performance, sports performance, preparation to perform, and business performance, respectively. In 1995, these figures changed considerably, but the basic theme remained the same. Two of the top-selling men's magazines appealing to the secondary fantasy in 1995 were *Motortrend* and *Field and Stream*, replacing *Forbes* and *Boy's Life*. Again, the major themes represented are automobile performance and hunting performance.

In summary, according to Farrell (1986), the primary fantasy of a woman is home and family and the method of achieving this fantasy is through beauty. For men, the primary fantasy is to have sex with and display a beautiful woman and the way to get a beautiful woman is with performance.

By the year 2005, we predict that magazine sales will continue to drop at an even steeper decline, primarily because of the Internet as well as other methods of communication. But the themes that have been discussed will remain the same. The important and enduring lesson is that although there are surface changes in technology and in sophistication, the underlying issues, which are rooted in the unconscious, never change. These underlying issues are those that are associated with the eleven motives described in this book and their order of importance for men and for women. They are permanent, durable, and eternal. Ten thousand years ago a woman's place was in the home and a man's place was in the field (or the woods). Today it is considered incorrect to make such a statement, and yet many women (who often make better managers than men) find that, especially after they have a child, their preference is to be at home rather than at work. Could this be just another example of confusion between personal orientation and territorial survival? We believe that it is.

Sports and Athletic Contests

Nowhere is the confusion and perplexity that exists between motives more clearly seen than in sports and athletic contests. It has created a whole new culture or society, called *soccer moms*. The best way to look at this confused and confounding picture is to start at the very beginning, when children are around four or five and begin to play in an organized rather than disorganized manner. This is when they move from self-play to team play. Often this begins with T-ball. The next step beyond this is pee-wee and eventually little league ball, and this is the level at which parents usually get involved.

We are referring to the Play Motive, which is more fully discussed in Chapter 13. Since children take very naturally to play, T-ball is intriguing and exciting to them. But as they move up within the hierarchy of organized children's sports, a tighter and more rigid structure is imposed upon them. With structure comes the automatic involvement of parents, who then quite naturally want to add more closure to the games. In order to do this, the parents and coaches (most of whom are parents) look toward the only model that they know of, and that is big league, organized college and professional sports. In imitating this model, the children's games are moved up a few notches in the building blocks of human motivation, in this case to the level of the Territorial Survival Motive.

At the territorial survival level, organized sports for children become what big league college and professional sports are supposed to be: territorial. Teams represent real places; they have a home turf and fans who show up for the games are usually associated with that turf. Sporting events at this level become battles between turfs, all of which are vying for a championship. But by the time the children's sports arrive at the territorial level they find that big league professional and college sports have already moved beyond this. Most professional sports have moved onward and upward to the level of spiritual survival, representing passion, and even beyond that to the level of the Personal Orientation Motive. At the level of the Personal Orientation Motive people define themselves and their existence in terms of the team that represents them.

We have already shown some support in this chapter for how the Spiritual Survival Motive is often weighted more heavily than the Physical Survival Motive. Teams like the Dallas Cowboys, the Chicago Bulls, the Notre Dame Fighting Irish, and the New York Yankees have a way of pulling at people's passions and, as a result, compete in a different realm or sphere which can only be described as spiritual and extremely passionate. Notre Dame is unique in that it has the ability to appeal to fans who have absolutely no connection with the university and never have had, the so-called "subway alumni."

In the spring of 1997, more than 600 people left their homes under six feet of water along the banks of the Ohio River in order to attend the SEC playoffs in Memphis and to see the Kentucky Wildcats play and capture the NCAA championship. What's more important, physical survival (basic shelter) or Kentucky basketball (spiritual survival; passion)? Further support for the fact that organized athletics often function at the spiritual level is provided by Chidester (1996), who shows that organized professional baseball meets the criteria of an officially established religion at all levels. This was reviewed in Chapter 2.

When an activity reaches the level of spiritual survival and passion, established boundaries often disappear, and this happens quite frequently in organized athletics, from T-ball all the way to the Olympics. In 1998, it was discovered that there were substantial payoffs between Olympic officials and the city of Salt Lake, with reference to hosting the Winter Games in that city. At the University of Mississippi in the mid-1990s, certain alumni chose to ignore established boundaries. When promising young quarterbacks and other players came to town to tour the campus they were often treated to alcohol and adult entertainment, even though they were minors. In another incident, seventeen high schools in one large southern city were all found to be involved in recruiting and offering money to promising young basketball players, and some schools even paid moving expenses for their entire family and paid rent and bought groceries for them. It was also found, in this same city and in several surrounding states, that promising young players were not made to follow attendance rules, and most were placed in special education classes so that their grades would not be an issue when it came to meeting eligibility standards for school athletes. Several parents even agreed to divorce, so that one of the divorced mates could move to another state with the child who was an athlete and meet the new state's eligibility standards; all for the opportunity to play for a team that was more competitive. That way the child would not have to remain on the bench for one year in the new state before becoming eligible. All of these activities, which were documented within a one-year period, represented successful attempts to remove the boundaries that exist within high school and college athletics, because when organized sports ascend to the level of spiritual survival, the end justifies the means. This is true in any spiritual activity. In other words, when sporting activities and athletics are elevated to the level of the Spiritual Survival Motive, all bets are off and the rules that govern the game—and the ones that govern what goes on outside of the game—don't apply.

The Transposition of the Territorial and Spiritual Survival Motives

A common and typically encountered example of the shifting and confusion between the Territorial and Spiritual Survival Motives, outside of organized athletics, is seen in the workaholic. The workaholic works eighteen hours per day, seven days a week, in spite of the fact that he or she does not need the money and is at the stage in life where he or she could comfortably retire if he or she wanted to. But he or she won't even consider retirement. He or she has spiritualized his or her career or vocation, and this is the only way that dedication and devotion can be explained. Note that it usually takes the insight that is derived from Silent Side research to explain and understand this behavior. Most people pass it off as "irrational," but Silent Side research specializes in irrational behavior and what it means.

Spiritualization of a career, job, or vocation that rightfully belongs in the category of the territorial survival area creates many problems. One of the most difficult and problematic situations is when a boss or owner has spiritualized his or her own position (which is often the case) and then expects everyone else—at least those in senior management positions—to do the same thing. This is a hard problem to solve, because it may involve going against the owner or the boss, who probably got where he or she is because he or she spiritualized the work. But not everyone else cares to be or wants to be where the boss is. Somehow and in some way, the boss needs to be able to come to understand this and see people for where they are (on the building blocks of human motivation) and not where he or she is. It takes a special kind of a person to explain this to the boss, and also a thorough understanding of the building blocks of human motivation.

The Elements and Ingredients of the Territorial Survival Motive

The elements of the Territorial Survival Motive are career and vocation, as well as money, assets, greed, competition, and ownership. Although greed is usually seen in a negative context, in this circumstance it should not be. It is natural human emotions and motives that cause people to want to hold on to what they have and, if possible and feasible, to extend their boundaries beyond what they already have in order to have more.

The forces underlying the movement of the Dow Jones Industrial Average can appear mysterious and nefarious. When the numbers move in either direction for the day, ten different "experts" will offer ten different opinions as to what is happening. We have never done research on the markets, but we suspect from what we have done in the past that the movement of the markets is only symbolic of what is happening at the unconscious level on the part of those who move the markets. It is altogether possible that these forces could be uncovered and quantified, through Motigraphics. Obviously, these forces are unconscious and defy rational interpretation, but greed is one of these forces. There are elements and ingredients of greed that Motigraphics should be able to define and quantify. When and if research is done on the unconscious side of the market it will add a third dimension to "head and shoulder" and other patterns and templates that are seen on the charts. It would also add a substantial dimension to prediction of what the markets would do in the future, replacing the guessing game and chaos that is now in place.

THE SEXUAL SURVIVAL MOTIVE

The Sexual Survival Motive consists of four elements: sexual impulse, sexual inhibition, sexual impotence, and sexual gender. Whenever the conversation turns to sex and sexuality, the cardinal rule that we always impose is to define what is being talked about. Is it gender, impulse, impotence, or inhibition? Failure to define what you are talking about will result in confusion and usually in misunderstanding.

Sexual Impulse

The element of sexual impulse is often referred to as the "bad" impulse. This is because people publicly display displeasure, distaste, and aversion to the sexual impulse when it is expressed in public. Privately we are not certain what their real feelings are, but we believe there are some clues. The "good" impulse is an element that is associated with the Play Motive that will be discussed in Chapter 13. To say that it is "good" implies a judgment which is misleading. It is merely an impulse, such as the impulse that a woman has to cook or that a man may have to eat at a restaurant rather than eating at home. Play is impulsive, as we will see in Chapter 13, just as sex is impulsive.

The "bad" impulse that is generally associated with sex and sexuality, in contrast to the good impulse, is very, very bad. All kinds of problems arise from it. Homicides arise out of the sexual impulse. There are many rules and regulations, many of them recent, that absolutely forbid it. For example, the expression or the display of the sexual impulse is forbidden in most workplaces. The display of a sexual impulse can consist of something as simple as a woman wearing a short skirt or a partially transparent blouse in the workplace. It does not have to be as complicated and complex as the actual display of sexual organs or the open discussion of sexual fantasies at the water cooler or in the break room. The open display of sexual impulse may consist of using the Internet at work to view pornographic materials. In seminars, we have had objections from individuals about the use of the word "bad" in association with the sexual impulse, but we believe that it is warranted and justified. This is because of the way that it is treated by the public and by those who make the rules and regulations.

In 1985, Calvin Klein found out about the "bad" impulse in print ads for jeans that used actress Brooke Shields. Because of her age and the suggestive nature of the ads, nationwide outrage was ignited and more rules were laid down (Kuriansky, 1995). But as Kuriansky noted, sex still sells. And as we might add, it always will, because it is a part of the Silent Side and one of the eleven essential motives.

In 1998, a similar controversy erupted with Abercrombie and Fitch, who allegedly published catalogs with pictures of nearly nude adolescents in compromising positions. As in the case of Calvin Klein, whenever the element of sexual impulse is exploited it causes all kinds of dilemmas, predicaments, and other indictments and prosecution.

Is the Open Expression of the Sexual Impulse Always Bad?

We are beginning to see some substantial evidence that suggests when people react to the expression of the sexual impulse with disgust and disdain, they actually feel quite differently in the unconscious or Silent Side. Let's look at three examples.

Graceland, Elvis Presley's Home

In 1979, I carried out research on Graceland mansion, the home of Elvis Presley. Prior to Presley's death, visitation was limited to just a few people each day; one hundred at the most and perhaps a few more on weekends. There were no formal plans to open the mansion to the public. This was just after Presley's death. However, it was noticed that after his death large crowds began to gather at the gates, a phenomenon that had not been previously observed. Since the executors of the estate did not feel that this would be a lasting phenomenon, they were unwilling to pay for us to do the research. However, they did give us permission to proceed on our own. Our interest in doing this, at the time, was to show that Silent Side research could "predict the unpredictable."

Visitors on both sides of the Atlantic and the Pacific, who had spent their life savings to come to Graceland, were interviewed. These people were the really committed, passionate followers and from them we hoped to identify the motives that attracted them to Graceland. Their motives were very powerful and were quickly identified. Basically, they had lived through an age of sexual inhibition, and Elvis, by his public television appearances, had done in public what they feared to do and were afraid to do in private. Elvis not only dispelled this nonsense and condemnation about sexual impulse but he blessed it when he added hymns and sacred music to his repertoire. Typically, he would present songs like "Jailhouse

Rock," which was pure impulse, and then close a concert with sacred hymns and spirituals, such as "Just As I Am."

What a combination! The evidence of the research was overwhelming. I called a meeting of the executors and presented a time line of projected visitation to Graceland from 1981 to 1991, without the advantage of any previous visitor statistics. The executors of the estate, when they saw it, could not even wait for the meeting to end. Within a month, work began to make Graceland a destination for visitors from around the world. Today, Graceland is the second most visited home in the United States. Also, since Elvis Presley died before he accomplished his mission here on earth, he became a martyr, taking his place alongside the only other martyrs of the twentieth century, Martin Luther King and John F. Kennedy.[1]

The Impeachment of the President, 1998

There have been only two presidential impeachments. The first, in 1868, was ostensibly because President Andrew Johnson had terminated his Secretary of War when Congress had voted against his termination. The real reason given by historians was because President Johnson, in exercising his chief executive's powers, had attempted to bring the Southern states back into the union and establish solidarity and unity, and there was overwhelming opposition to doing this.

The second impeachment, concerning Bill Clinton, was said to be because he lied under oath. Many believe that the real reason was because he openly displayed his sexual preferences in the Oval Office of the White House, which is a sacred, sacrosanct, and consecrated part of America. Therefore, he was confusing and transposing the Spiritual Survival Motive with the Sexual Survival Motive. This is not a good transposition to make, as Calvin Klein discovered. It's fine to place children inside of rubber tires and talk about love (Michelin), but it's not fine to put them in a pair of tight jeans and imply sex!

In spite of nationwide expressions of disgust and revulsion regarding Bill Clinton's behavior, ratings of his presidency just kept climbing (*Time*, 1998). At the height of his impeachment hearings his ratings of public approval surpassed those of President Ronald Reagan when Reagan's ratings were at an all-time high for his presidency. In the White House Rose Garden, immediately following Congress's decision to impeach, there was what appeared to be a large pep rally. Instead of sadness following the decision to impeach there was an air of happiness, mirth, and merriment. Congressmen and others attended, expressing public support and determination for the ongoing and future victories of the Clinton presidency. Just the opposite of what one would expect—or is it?

Anwar Ibrahim of Malaysia

There is a lesser-known character, Anwar Ibrahim, who was the Deputy Prime Minister of Malaysia, a very conservative and predominantly Muslim country, who faced ten counts of adultery, sodomy, and homosexuality, which included sodomizing his own brother. In a country that is predominantly Muslim, sexual charges are an anathema and an absolute curse. In spite of this, Ibrahim, who was believed to be the victim of a plot orchestrated by his political rival, became a folk hero in this conservative country of twenty-two million people. Thousands demonstrated for his release and for the resignation of his rival, so that Anwar would be reinstated (Butler, 1998).

How much of an issue is the sexual impulse, and what is the explanation for what appears to be a schizophrenic response in all three of the cases mentioned? It is our belief that although the element of sexual impulse is an issue at the conscious level, it appears to be a nonissue at the unconscious or Silent Side level. At least it is somewhat less of an issue. Obviously, if it involves someone else's spouse, boyfriend, or girlfriend it is an issue and there is little doubt here. But in this case it seems to be more of a territorial, spiritual, and personal orientation issue than it is a sexual issue.

Any discussion of the Sexual Survival Motive and sexual impulse needs to consider the higher-level Spiritual Survival Motive. The two are often in conflict with each other. This was demonstrated in Chapter 6 when absurdities were discussed. Conflicts between two motivational levels are usually experienced by the mind as absurdities and, as such, create anxiety and agitation. Anxiety and agitation is then dissuaded by laughter. The purpose of laughter is to serve as a personal defense mechanism. This explains the proliferation of Clinton jokes before, during, and after the impeachment proceedings and inquiries. But as Freud (1963) has shown us, jokes can be very close not only to reality but also to disaster.

The "bad" segment of the "bad" impulse is imposed by the Spiritual Survival Motive, and this interaction produces guilt, regret, and even remorse at times. From the three illustrations cited, it would appear that anyone who can assist in removing or extracting this guilt is going to make us feel better. One way to make everyone feel better is with a public acknowledgment (preferably by a well-known personage) that he or she experiences the same kind of sexual feelings that we all do. In spite of this, they have made it as a leader, an authority, or a master of some type. In a way this all represents a paradox, but if it results in making people feel better than they felt before, no one seems to care what it is or how conflictual it may appear to be. The point is that the leader who gets into these dilemmas is experienced as human and is seen as having shortcomings, like we all do. Therefore, he or she becomes more popular instead of less popular.

The situations that we have described are not comparable to the bad impulse of homicide. One reason is because most of us do not experience a homicidal impulse as often as we do a sexual impulse, if it is experienced at all. Therefore, the circumstances surrounding the O. J. Simpson case were not at all similar to those surrounding the events that we have described where the sexual impulse was the issue.

Sexual Inhibition and Sexual Impotence

We have many words in our vocabulary, such as "promiscuous," which applies primarily to women, or "virile," which applies primarily to men. The words describing the elements of sexual inhibition and sexual impotence are two sides of the same coin. Both describe the fear of sex.

Interestingly, whereas women are almost always positioned in the popular literature as the ones who are inhibited and disinterested in sex, there are many more men who fit this category than women. This is verified by the large number of sexual paraphilias and other disorders that apply only to men and not to women, and which are designed to create sexual arousal without involving sexual intercourse. This is an interesting phenomenon and includes exhibitionism, fetishism, frotteurism, voyeurism, tranvestic fetishism, and pedophilia (American Psychiatric Association, 1994). Two other paraphilias—sexual masochism and sexual sadism—are shared by men and women but are believed to be much more prominent among men. Where sadistic and masochistic impulses are acted out, the female is more likely to be a passive observer than a participant. In many cases she may be paid to administer either the masochistic or sadistic treatment, and in these situations her involvement is strictly financial. The predominance of sexual paraphilias among men as opposed to women strongly supports the observation that there are more impotent men than there are inhibited women. The reason for this is that men are much more likely to get involved in sexual and quasisexual situations when they are children, and it is when they are in those situations that they receive and process, unconsciously, subliminal cues that are related to sexual behavior and sexual organs. These cues eventually become completely subliminal, but remain active in the unconscious, often sending warning signs about possible dangers to the sexual organs. This is because the original subliminal cue is usually associated with some kind of injury or wound involving the sex organ. These warning signs may persist for a lifetime, forcing a man who is victimized by them to seek sexual outlets in nontraditional places and formats, such as those listed. All of them, as noted, are either substitutions or alternatives for sexual intercourse. At times they serve the male as precursors to sex; that is, something that he must do in order to either commence or complete sexual intercourse. Our own unpublished research, using instruments designed to assess the strength of the sex drive, showed that the sexual appetite of women is almost double the sexual appetite of men, and the primary reasons for this difference are the sexual element(s) just discussed, inhibition and impotence.

There were articles from Reuters news service (Miller, 1999) that were released on the same day regarding sexual inhibition; one that supports our assertion about inhibition and the other that seems to refute it. In the first article it was stated that sexual dysfunction (due to sexual inhibition) is widespread in the United States and is found in 43 percent of the women who responded to a survey and 30 percent of the men. It is our contention that more men are sexually inhibited (and therefore sexually dysfunctional) than women. However, we believe that these results are easily explained by the fact that men who are engaged in some kind of a paraphilia or perversion, such as exhibitionism or chronic exposure to pornography, do not consider themselves to be dysfunctional, even though they may not be having sexual intercourse in the traditional sense. The fact that there are so many paraphilias and alternative methods of sexual fulfillment for men strongly supports the fact that men are more inhibited and fearful of sex than women.

The second article states that U.S. television is "overloaded" with sex and reports on a study by the Kaiser Family Foundation of 1,351 subjects, indicating that 56 percent of all shows on television have sexual content, with an average of three sex scenes per hour. This finding strongly suggests our observation regarding inhibition, and may be responsible for many Americans becoming spectators to the sport (sex) rather than participants.

Just as there are products to appeal to sexual impulse, such as Calvin Klein jeans, there are products that sell to the element of sexual inhibition and sexual impotence. Viagra is probably the best known of all products that sell directly to men's sexual impotence. Many years ago it was the Charles Atlas bodybuilding kit, which appeared on the inside back cover of many magazines and comic books. But probably the best known and most widely used products that sell directly to sexual impotence are pornographic literature, videotapes, websites, and other media that serve as unnatural and artificial substitutions and alternatives for sexual intercourse. This is not meant to imply that all of these products are sold strictly for this reason. They are not. A couple may watch a video in order to potentiate sexual intercourse and make it more intimate and more exciting, and in this case the product would be selling to sexual impulse rather than inhibition. But it is believed that many of these publications and other media are basically sold to the element of sexual impotence as a substitution for sexual fulfillment and completion, because of fear, which is the basic cause of both impotence and inhibition.

There are also products for inhibited women. However, these products are fewer in number since there are fewer inhibited women than there are men. Most of the products for inhibited women involve clothing which lacks color and which covers, rather than exposes, most of the body.

Sexual Gender

The third element of the Sexual Survival Motive is sexual gender. Sexual gender focuses on the differences between men and women and how these differences play out in our society. There is a decided effort on the part of the media, fashion designers, and opinion leaders to minimize gender differences between men and women. This effort is welcomed by some and disliked by others, although the fashions and clothing in the stores today reflects gender similarities a lot more than it does gender differences.

In spite of the efforts to minimize the gender gap, gender differences remain and any change will be very slow and laborious. The element of gender is a legitimate part of the Silent Side of human motivation. Just as we see strong support for spiritual issues in the unconscious and over generations, we see similar support for gender differences. We may see significant changes occurring all around us in technology and other areas, but the unconscious generally remains the same, year after year and century after century. The Silent Side, which is the emotional, motivational, and unconscious side, is responsible for maintaining the various differences that distinguish and differentiate between the sexes.

SUMMARY: THE SURVIVAL MOTIVES

How much influence do the Survival Motives really play in our lives? Are they archaic vestiges from the past, or are they vibrant, dynamic, and vigorous motives that affect our daily lives? Anyone

who has ever been hungry, sexually deprived, seriously ill, or passionate about human love and then lost it knows the response to
this question. The Survival Motives are very much alive and active. Anyone who has ever lost a job and did not know where to
turn knows that the Physical Survival Motive is alive and vibrant
in the unconscious mind.

Try this experiment. Go to the grocery store right after eating a
big dinner, shop, and when you get home add up the bill. Then do it
again, only this time after you have not eaten all day. See what
occurs. The Survival Motives—Spiritual, Physical, Territorial, and
Sexual—shape our purchasing behavior every day. The only reason people deny this is because they don't see it or feel it. It's on the
Silent Side. We are very hesitant to admit that things that we can't
see, feel, and touch can direct, guide, and govern our lives, lifestyles,
and purchasing habits.

How do we know that the Spiritual Survival Motive is more potent and more powerful than the Physical Survival Motive? Isn't
this asking us to take a leap of faith? In my clinical office, I have
seen several patients who, after losing their husband or boyfriend
in a break up, would sit at home, smoke three packs of cigarettes a
day, and burn their underarms with each one of the lit cigarettes.
This behavior was puzzling to me. Why would the loss of a boyfriend or spouse generate this kind of behavior? I asked several
colleagues who had seen the same thing, but none of them had an
answer or even a clue. And then one day it occurred to me that it
could be explained right out of the approach that we are talking
about in this book: Spiritual pain is more intolerable and unbearable
than physical pain. When a person is faced with a deep-rooted spiritual loss (love) and the pain is seemingly unbearable, what could be
more distracting from this spiritual pain than a shift away from spiritual pain and toward physical pain? Physical pain masks spiritual
pain. After all, the mind cannot focus on two things at same time,
and this is particularly true of pain (Bryan, 1985). It's a physical
and mental impossibility. We are not suggesting the burn treatment as a cure for lost love or for anything else. No matter how you
look at it, pain is pain. However, most of us will shift our attention
when we are in a painful situation. The depressed woman purchases
a new outfit and sometimes a whole new wardrobe (spiritual sur-
vival/personal orientation). The man who is passed over for promotion seeks a new job (territorial survival/place orientation).

By integrating survival into our approach and more specifically
by integrating spiritual survival into our approach, we become more
and more capable of handling our own emotions and motivations
as well as the emotions and motivations of others. This is true not
only on a personal basis but also on a scientific and logical basis.

NOTE

1. The Silent Side operational definition of a martyr is someone who dies before he or she completes his or her mission. John F. Kennedy, Martin Luther King, and Elvis were the only Americans in the twentieth century who fulfill this criterion. Whether Princess Diana meets this criterion is still undetermined. By this criterion, the only martyr in the nineteenth century was Abraham Lincoln.

REFERENCES

Adaval, R., & Wyer, R. S. (1998). The role of narratives in consumer information processing. *Journal of Consumer Psychology, 7,* 207–45.

American Psychiatric Association. (1994). *Diagnostic and statistical manual of mental disorders* (4th ed.). Washington, DC: Author.

Bass, B. M. (1997). Does the transactional–transformational leadership paradigm transcend organizational and national boundaries? *American Psychologist, 52,* 130–39.

Beckwith, H. (1997). *Selling the invisible.* New York: Warner Books.

Bryan, W. J. (1985). *The chosen ones: The art of jury selection* (special ed.). Glendale, CA: Westwood.

Butler, S. (1998, November 23). Turning the tables in a very tawdry trial. *U.S. News and World Report,* p. 40.

Chidester, D. (1996). The church of baseball, the fetish of Coca-Cola and the potlatch of rock n' roll: Theoretical models for the study of religion in American popular culture. *Journal of the American Academy of Religion, 64,* 748–64.

Chomsky, N. (1968). *Language and the mind.* New York: Harcourt Brace.

Dichter, E. (1964). *Handbook of consumer motivations: The psychology of world objects.* New York: McGraw-Hill.

Dichter, E. (1971). *Motivating human behavior.* New York: McGraw-Hill.

Farrell, W. (1986). *Why men are the way they are.* New York: McGraw-Hill.

Fleischman, P. (1990). *The healing spirit.* New York: Paragon House.

Freud, S. (1963). Jokes and their relation to the unconscious. In J. Strachey (Trans.), *The standard edition of the complete works of Sigmund Freud.* New York: W. W. Norton.

Kuriansky, I. (1995). Sex simmers, still sells. *Advertising Age, 66,* 49.

MacLean, P. D. (1990). *The triune brain in evolution: Role in paleocerebral functions.* New York: Plenum Press.

Maddock, R. C., & Fulton, R. L. (1998). *Motivation, emotions and leadership: The silent side of management.* Westport, CT: Quorum Books.

Malmo, J. (1999, February 1). Many will pay extra to save more time. (Memphis) *Commercial Appeal.*

Maslow, A. H. (1970). *Motivation and personality* (2d ed.). New York: Harper & Row.

Miller, M. (1999, February 9). Study finds U.S. television overloaded with sex. *Yahoo News,* http//dailynews.yahoo.com/headlines/ts/s.

Ornstein, R. (1997). *The right mind: Making sense of the hemispheres.* Orlando, FL: Harcourt Brace.

Ramachandran, V. S., & Blakeslee, S. (1998). *Phantoms in the brain: Probing the mysteries of the human brain.* New York: William Morrow.

Romero, J. (1994). *Casino marketing.* New York: International Gaming and Wagering Business.

Time. (1998, March 30). Vol. 15, no. 12, Internet edition.

11

The Adaptation Motive

Diana Gonsalves

> We are all individuals.
> I'm not.
> —Monty Python's *Life of Brian*

BACKGROUND

Adaptation, the desire to be like everyone else, is one of the strongest motives in the building blocks. Marketers have capitalized on this ever since the Old West snake-oil days where testimonials from "cured" patients were used. The focus continued through the 1950s and 1960s, when keeping up with the Joneses was the order of the day and every household just had to have all the nifty new gadgets and mod cons (thank you, Ronald Reagan and the "Death Valley Days" TV commercials for GE). And it still abounds today, with celebrities or "professionals" extolling the virtues of products and the importance of being cool by wearing the fashionable brands and styles, owning the right gadgets and accessories, and living the accepted lifestyle. What self-respecting woman does not want to look like Cindy Crawford? What upwardly mobile man in his right mind does not want to own the sexiest vehicle, be it SUV, sports car, pickup truck, or Harley Davidson?

FROM THE WOMB

The Adaptation Motive is one that predates birth. The effects are seen in third-trimester ultrasound scans of unborn babies, where fetuses can be observed moving their hands to their faces as they try to adjust to the in-uterine environment. Appropriately enough, these movements are called *adaptors*. This continues after birth, which explains why babies need their nails trimmed and sometimes even require mittens to protect their faces. The reflex does go into remission shortly after birth, but is always present. It may emerge in times of stress and can be observed in thumb sucking, nail biting, compulsive eating, and even smoking, all hand to face motions—adaptors, in other words.

Soon after birth, neonates form a strong attachment with their mothers or other primary care givers. The adaptive behavior then abruptly converts to the innate tendency to follow the leader (imitation), which remains extremely strong throughout life. Other than the stress-related reflexes, there does not appear to be much of a connection between the two behaviors.

ADAPTATION BEGINS AT HOME

While young children do not imprint (fixate) upon their mothers as ducklings do, they do form a very strong bond with them or the primary care givers. It just takes a few hours of togetherness for the newborn to recognize his mother's voice and smell and, soon enough, face. With this fixation in place, the baby starts imitating the vocal noises, grimaces, and smiles of his mother.

Young children want to do what their parents and care givers do, which is why toys that are miniature imitations of appliances and fixtures around the house are perennially popular. Typically, one of the first toys a child is fond of is the toy telephone. They also want to "help" in cooking, cleaning, taking care of babies (dolls), mowing, shopping, and other grown-up activities, and in fact mimic what the adults around them are doing.

MONKEY SEE, MONKEY DO

Children are copycats. They learn through observation and imitation. Youngsters pick up habits and behaviors at a very young age that they will carry with them for life. Much of adult behavior is based on this imitative absorption during our childhood years. What we learn through observing—and imitating—our parents and care givers becomes an intrinsic part of ourselves, so much so that most of the time we do not realize that it is precisely this that drives our actions and behavior.

Research we have conducted for clients with cooking products shows that most women received subliminal cues about cooking and baking at a very young age, through observation of their parents, and carried these cues forward into their adult lives. They do not realize that they are imitating their mothers and what they had observed years before. If their mothers had found satisfaction in cooking and baking to nourish their families, the women would most likely find great satisfaction in cooking and baking as well, whether they have families or not.

New research findings bear this out, while finding a comfortable middle ground in the nature versus nurture question. A special report (Nash, 1997) indicated that researchers have found scientific support that neurological activity starts well before birth, and that the first few years of a child's life are the most important in creating a unique human being. This is when parental interaction and stimulation help hardwire nerve connections in the brain. If these connections are not reinforced, they will atrophy. And it isn't just emotional well-being that is involved. Sight and hearing faculties can be lost by lack of stimulation. This is the time that children take the greatest interest in copying their parents, and thus learn much from them through imitation.

Vocabulary is a prime example of learning by imitation. In the first years of life, children learn words voraciously. Language itself is innate (hardwired), like flying in birds or even walking in humans, but vocabulary and syntax are learned through imitation. Anyone with young children knows that profanities are immediately picked up by them, to be repeated, loudly, at the most embarrassing times! It is fortunate for parents' sanity that, soon enough, this imitative learning is directed outside the home.

ADAPTATION IN THE PLAYGROUND

In the toddler stages, children are so closely bonded with their closest adults that other children (and even pets) are seen as either toys or rivals in getting attention and affection. As they grow though, they realize that other children are people too, and then start interacting with them socially. This is when agemates (peers) gain in importance, and true adaptation kicks in.

Adaptation can be seen in the way children naturally segregate themselves by gender. They want to be like their friends, and they want to be surrounded by persons similar to themselves. Peer pressure becomes almost unbearable. Who doesn't remember whining,

"But everyone's doing it/has it/wearing it/going there?" Just as un-forgettable is the stock parental answer, "If everyone jumped off the bridge, would you?" Hugely popular sitcoms—from "Happy Days" through "The Wonder Years" to "Friends"—have celebrated conformity and normality. These are shows populated with charac-ters striving, sometimes desperately, to fit in with their peers. To not conform, to not be part of the group, would be tantamount to social suicide.

From around age eight, wearing the right clothes to school is of great importance, as is carrying the right book bag, pencil case, and lunch box. Even the nerds have their own style! In fact, social scientists have recognized the stress this competition places on young children, which is why school uniforms are gaining in popu-larity in the United States (Kessler, 1998). Instituting a school uniform in the Long Beach, California district appears to be di-rectly related to lowered crime levels in their public schools (Portner, 1998). Numerous other public school systems are also now initiat-ing uniform codes. There was some doubt about the direct correla-tion between uniforms and lowered crime, but, as President Clinton stated in his inaugural address in January 1996, "If it means that teenagers will stop killing each other over designer jackets, then our public schools should be able to require the students to wear school uniforms."

Uniforms remove all the stresses of peer pressure where dress is concerned. Wearing a uniform creates an instant group identity, thereby eliminating the possibility of becoming a social outcast (at least within school walls) by wearing the wrong fashions or brands. When clothing and dress codes are prescribed, children find it much easier to focus on learning and adapting themselves within what should be the more important facets of school life, such as academ-ics, sports, and social activities (Portner, 1996).

GET 'EM WHILE THEY'RE YOUNG

Our research has shown that a male child under the age of eighty months will wear any shoe put on him. However, after that age, he will only wear a brand name shoe. Ever since marketers discov-ered that you can sell to parents through their children they have been using and abusing children's needs to fit in. Though children are not buyers (yet), they are consumers. Children do have a say in a considerable proportion of household expenditures, such as gro-ceries, while also dictating what brand name clothes and shoes they wear, where they eat, and what toys they play with.

And how do they know what they want? Either through advertising or their friends (who have probably seen the advertising themselves). And how does this advertising usually work? It portrays racially diverse children of the same or slightly older age groups having lots of fun with the latest shiny new toy. The selling point is that these actors are clean, attractive, and, above all, normal (well adapted).

Viewers of children's shows on television are bombarded with messages to buy the latest dolls, remote control cars, action figures, and games that will last in popularity for a short while until the marketers come up with the next big attraction. Fads play a prominent role in this age group. A short-lived craze for a certain plaything (such as Tickle Me Elmo), fads appear to be an intrinsic component of the consumer world. Children have come to measure their social standing by their clothes and their possessions. As soon as something becomes fashionable, everyone has to have it. But once it loses favor (usually because a younger age group picks it up), it is immediately discarded for the next attraction.

Packard (1957) sets out a chilling account of the "psycho-seduction of children" by the marketing world in the 1950s. He cites numerous quotes from vaunted marketing and advertising persons, all driving home the point that instilling brand consciousness and loyalty at a very young age pays off, both by forcing parents to buy only their products *and* creating future buyers. This is still very much a part of the marketing scenario. The only change from Packard's time and today is the sophistication of the messages and media. An example is McDonald's restaurants, that attract the children and then the children bring the parents, by force if necessary. At the same time, the advertisers make it easier for the parents to accede by telling them it is good for the family to dine together (Spiritual Survival Motive, family values).

TEENAGE WASTELAND

The Adaptation Motive is extremely powerful, and can take precedence over most other motives. According to Maslow's (1970) hierarchy, physical survival is of utmost importance—the very foundation of his pyramid. To discredit his theory, consider the tobacco issue. The desire to be accepted by their peer group is so strong that many adolescents start smoking to look cool, all the while knowing (and being bombarded with messages) that smoking is a life-threatening habit. If not smoking, it could be drug abuse, vandalism, joining athletic teams, dressing similarly—the list is endless. Adolescents, by nature, are trying to learn who they are and what they want to be—looking for an identity, in fact. It is easy to fall in with a group of peers and take on a temporary identity from them and their behavior. The only threat to this adaptive behavior comes from the outside, when the "in" crowd turns out to be the wrong crowd and authority figures are forced to intervene.

The lasting popularity of gangs through the years attests to the inherent strength of the Adaptation Motive. It doesn't matter how difficult the initiations or how criminal the subsequent gang activities are, there always seems to be a steady flow of adolescents longing to be members. They can then identify themselves by this membership. They need to belong. Period. If they are lucky, the "gang" is a law-abiding one, such as a sporting team, computer club, or youth choir. If not, the members either die young or are forever marked by their activities. This marking can take many forms, be it physical (brandings, tattoos, scars), sociological (police records, prison sentences), or psychological, typified by the classic "us versus them" mentality.

Fraternities and sororities are the accepted form of gangs in universities. Some of these have very difficult initiation rites to weed out those who really don't belong. So tough are these ordeals that there are even a few deaths reported every so often. Initiations serve their purpose, though, by allowing entry to only those who would do practically anything to become a member. Hopeful entrants are accepted if they understand and agree with the abiding philosophy of the fraternity and are familiar with and liked by current members—which all adds up to them being the same type of person. Once accepted, members feel part of an elite group and can then relax, knowing they are surrounded (and protected) by their own type of people and that all the undesirables (those who are different) have been excluded. Such organizations do have their uses, providing adolescents with entry to groups with (mostly) legal activities and a strong feeling of belonging.

DISESTABLISHMENTARIANISM: REBELS WITH A CAUSE

Even when adolescents seek to rebel against the establishment, they tend to rebel as a pack, with a certain mode of dress, musical soundtrack, and lifestyle. The hippies of the 1960s were quintessentially antiestablishment. They forswore traditional jobs, normal clothing, mainstream music and traditional sexual behavior. They preached utopian ideals and were pacifists to the core in the era of the Vietnam War and social conservatism. And yet, despite these antiestablishment ideals and appearances, they quickly created their own establishment, with codes of conduct, dress, and behavior, albeit outside the norm at that time.

In the 1970s, punks took a more radical route to expressing their disenfranchisement, including their own atonal genre of music. Many dyed their hair rainbow colors and lacquered it into extreme coiffures, wore studded leather garments, and pierced their ears and noses, thus creating for themselves a uniform—colorful and strange, but a uniform nonetheless. Whereas hippie ideals were based on peace and love, punks practiced nihilism, a "live today, forget tomorrow" approach. Yet for both hippies and punks, their widespread adoption of a standard look and philosophy represented in itself a uniformity, an adaptation to a group mentality. Conformity rules, even amongst die-hard nonconformists.

HOW TO SUCCEED IN BUSINESS BY TRYING TOO HARD

Adaptation continues to dictate behavior in maturity, with adults conforming to corporate culture, neighborhood norms, and peer-group pressure. If an individual does not fit in, he or she is looked upon as eccentric and not a team player, ergo unsociable and undesirable. There was a very telling episode of the popular television show "Seinfeld," in which the character George Costanza is refused a job because he does not share in a piece of pie with his prospective teammates (only he knows it has been spiked by a vindictive chef). In other words, he seems to reject the corporate culture (does not adapt) and is thus rejected by his peers.

Maddock and Fulton (1998) relate an anecdote of an entire company copying the particular mannerisms of the CEO. Though it may seem bizarre, employees do adapt themselves to their work environments by imitating what their more successful colleagues do—be it mannerisms or dress styles, a habit of working late, or golf or skiing—whatever activity is enjoyed by the top executives. One of the most common factors in workplace culture is "corporate speak," a specialized coded language familiar only to employees on the inside. Whoever does not speak the language cannot succeed.

Whatever each particular corporate culture requires, an individual will adapt to it. He or she will learn to be like the others, to be a company person. In this day and age, when teamwork is seen as the optimal work policy, someone who doesn't fit in drastically minimizes his or her chances of success. He or she is seen as a maverick and a misfit. At this juncture, he or she will either be given a "shape up or ship out" lecture, be fired, or made so uncomfortable by isolation that he or she leaves of their own accord.

CLOTHES MAKE THE MAN (AND WOMAN AND CHILD)

Clothes are an obvious statement of the image we have of ourselves and what we want to project to the world. How else could "man of the cloth," "blue-collar worker," "old school tie," and the like become signifiers of a person's status and his or her background? Consider corporate dress styles, of which the IBM dark blue suit, white shirt, and red tie is a classic. Every corporate entity has its own set of expectations about what is acceptable in the workplace. Some companies have loosened their policies so far as to institute "casual dress" (mufti) rules, which are informal but still coded. Those who do not manage to pick up on the finer nuances, and therefore dress inappropriately, are summarily dispatched to the fringes of the "inside" group. It doesn't matter that "inappropriate" was never defined in the first place!

But it doesn't start in the workplace. The growing popularity of school uniforms reflects the self-same need to adapt to the group, at least in outward appearance. It could be postulated that adolescents suffer the most, as they see themselves as too old to have parents select their clothing, and yet are too young to be able to afford the clothes that are popular. The desperation to have it all can lead to shoplifting, assault, and even homicide, solely to gain possession of those expensive, hip sneakers or cool leather jacket.

Another example, which quite often extends from childhood till death, is advertising your affiliation to a certain sports team by wearing their licensed T-shirts, hats, and other emblems of membership. Some fanatics go so far as to confuse their own identities with that of the team—the team's competitors (and their followers) become the enemy. There are hockey games where there is more blood spilled on the stands than on the ice! European soccer fans have also carried this to ridiculous lengths, with heavy police contingents required to separate warring team supporters.

On the other hand, how often is the conferring of an honor paired with the donning of a garment (or a reasonable facsimile of a garment)? Graduation gowns and mortar boards, the green blazer of golf's U.S. Masters, medals on ribbons, sashes and tiaras for beauty pageants, belts for boxing, headdresses for State visits, religious vestments—the list goes on. All "uniforms" from school onward impart a distinct sense of belonging, of membership, made all the better if it is within a first-class, highly desirable organization.

So close is the association that, quite often, people take on spurious membership in a "tribe" by adopting the superficial look and stopping there. Returning to the punk-rock example, alienated midwestern American adolescents quite readily turned themselves into punks by copying the sartorial splendor, alienated attitude, and raucous music of Europe. All the while they never had a clue (and not bothering about it, either) that the punk movement was all about the rage felt by unemployed working-class youth in England faced with high inflation and no hope, or, as Johnny Rotten put it, "no future." Where was the parallel experience?

HIGH SOCIETY

It takes class(es) to be a snob. Not elegance, not grace, nothing but the division of society into distinct groups. As long as there is someone lower down the totem pole who can be sneered at, all will be fine in the world. The distinction could be wealth, residential neighborhood, ethnic origin, level of education, profession, or age. There is no getting around some sort of membership. The person who forswears society and its layers, boundaries, and rules then enters the group of "hermits, eccentrics, and outcasts."

Marketers have always known of these distinctions. From time immemorial, they could coax a reluctant prospect into purchasing goods (probably unnecessary) by promising a leg-up to the next rung on the social ladder. This is what status symbols are all about. No sooner does the customer settle into his or her new groove than the marketers change the rules and he or she has to start again.

An article in *New Yorker* magazine (Swartz, 1998) discussed the replacement of the trophy baby (who replaced the trophy wife) by the trophy lap dog. The young, gorgeous, bejeweled wives, worn practically as ornaments by much older, financially successful professionals, were replaced by infants dressed in the most expensive little outfits with the most expensive accessories. Now, probably due to babies' natural tendency to cry, spit up, and be generally messy, house-trained dogs are this season's rage. You know it's "in" when Gucci, Vuitton, Burberry, and Hermes offer pooch accessories such as collars, leashes, raincoats, beds, and dog carriers. It would probably not make a difference to the animal whether the collar is genuine hand-tooled Italian leather or a ragged bandana, but it has come to be seen as a reflection on the owner, whose standing in the eyes of his or her peers is now at stake.

Though this may seem extreme, it supports our observation that most people will follow the lead of those around them. Sometimes it just seems that socialites and celebrities take it to ridiculous lengths. But are "trophy lap dogs" as extreme as fraternity branding or gang initiation crimes? Those who don't follow the rules soon have to find themselves a new tribe, for the same reason that nonconforming employees quit. People everywhere are made uncomfortable by isolation and find themselves sidelined, devoid of peer acceptance.

Snobbery also rears its ugly head in the matter of participation in church activities. Leaving aside for the moment faith, religion, and creed, people who are active in a church community often come to loggerheads when issues such as construction, renovation, festive decorations, and social activities are at stake. With relatively easy access to churches of all religions and creeds, people have a choice as to where they worship, and they will attend where they feel most comfortable, among people like themselves. But if a project arises which involves a display or external symbol of any sort, there is a struggle to have control over the finished product. This is because people often identify themselves by the religion they belong to and the church they attend, and in turn want to impose their own tastes upon the church. They want to demonstrate to outsiders that their church is richer, classier, more beautiful, and more refined than any other church, and therefore they themselves are a step up from other churchgoers.

IN THE GHETTO

What would seem to be a direct contradiction to the strength of the Adaptation Motive is the presence of ethnic ghettos. Almost every major world city has a Chinatown, where the residents are Chinese, Chinese restaurants and stores abound, and even the street signs are in Chinese. Some cities have a Little Italy, or a Little India, or a recognized Hispanic or black neighborhood. One has to wonder why these residents do not adapt to their surroundings, be it New York, San Francisco, or whichever city they are in. They insist on retaining their original language and culture, customs, and clothing. Is it that their emotional makeup is different and therefore adaptation is not necessary?

The simple truth in these examples is that the people do not adapt because they do not need to—they and their predecessors have already adapted the surroundings to themselves. Theoretically, a lone foreigner landing in a new country will have to adapt soon enough, by learning the local language and customs, in order to survive. However, the presence of an ethnic enclave will provide him or her with all the comforts of home instantly, so that he or she will not need to change in any drastic way to fit in. It is so comfortable to be surrounded by familiarity that he or she will probably not want to adapt either.

It takes a critical mass of like-minded individuals with a desire to retain their own culture to create a racially segregated community with a self-sustaining economy and clearly demarcated limits. And it does not have to be ethnic origins that are the key difference with the natives. Other reasons could be sexual orientation (the Castro in San Francisco), religious belief (convents, monasteries, communes), or even wealth (Beverly Hills, Tuxedo Park).

Wherever people live, they will only be comfortable as long as they are surrounded by others like themselves. Why else would the word "suburbia" conjure up a distinct image? It may be a generalization that suburbanites are all of a type, but it does hold true to some extent: the minivan, the basketball hoop on the garage wall, the obsession with lawn care. Maybe "The Brady Bunch" wasn't fiction after all.

YOU ARE YOUR CAR

Since the first Model-T Ford rattled off the assembly line, Americans have been defining themselves by the vehicles they drive. Owning a certain vehicle is an overt statement about who you are and, more important, who you want the world to think you are. A vehicle is a portable symbol of personality and position. It even works with nonautomotive accessories emblazoned with vehicle logos—clothing, hats, shoulder bags, calendars, and so on. Harley Davidson has found a cash cow in its clothing and accessories line. What would you consider a vehicular symbol for hippies? A peace-sign-emblazoned VW van or Beetle, of course. How about men going through a midlife crisis? A convertible sports car is the standard. A young single woman? A zippy, two-door little number with a sunroof. A suburban housewife? Well, it used to be a minivan, but could now be an overpriced, overmuscled SUV. Or, conversely, who would you imagine is driving that Lincoln Town Car? Older, usually retired, conservative white couples. A red Jeep? A muscular, olive-skinned young man on his way to the beach.

Of course, such stereotyping seems overdone to some extent, but how wrong is it? Accountants and lawyers also ride big motorcycles, but probably not as their primary mode of transportation. They take on the Hog as a symbol of freedom, of being young at heart and an "easy rider." On the other hand, how many young folks would you see buying themselves a Town Car (assuming they could afford it)? Yet it is a comfortable car with all the accessories imaginable. The problem is it is seen as an older person's car. And this perception has everything to do with the manufacturers.

It is no surprise that most automobile manufacturers, although basically producing the same product (a metal box on wheels propelled by a combustion engine) for the same use (conveyance) have consistently managed to create a persona, a character, for each brand they sell. Part of this is the size of the car and engine, the accessories (or lack thereof), the colors available, and the price. But a large part is played by the image given to the car by the manufacturers in their advertising. Put a young, happy, attractive young woman in the commercials, and the car becomes a vehicle for that demographic group, or for other women who want to be young, attractive, and therefore happy. Use an older, distinguished gent, and it becomes a car for a self-respecting professional who wants to show his value to the world in an understated (usually expensive) way. The way the automobile companies create an image for their cars is by very careful selection of the person or persons who will be the "face" in the advertising. A minivan commercial will show a happy, active family with soccer-playing kids, camping equipment, and a large, tail-wagging dog. An SUV commercial, on the other hand, will depict attractive, fit, twenty-somethings off to the mountains or desert for mountain biking, kayaking, or some other strenuous activity.

IMAGE IS EVERYTHING

Contrary to a series of current commercials for Sprite, much of marketing is the creation and dissemination by marketers of a specific image associated with a product. Manufacturers of more middle-of-the-road cars know this well. They will usually hire a celebrity to be the face and sell the image. In these testimonials, the spokesperson will extol the virtues of the vehicle, but what he or she says is not as important as what image the buying public (the target demographic) has of him or her. It is likely that prospective buyers will want to emulate a highly credible person, and will want to do as he or she does. What better way to do so than by driving the car he or she endorses? These testimonials appeal directly to the Adaptation Motive, by using the desire of people to be like the others he or she knows, to keep up with them, or in some way have what they have. When branding a car for a certain demographic, the message works in two ways: First, members of the targeted demographic group obviously succumb to the advertising; second, people who do not belong to that group but desperately want to fit in, keep up with their peers, or climb the social ladder feel they need that particular brand or model to become the person they hope to be.

Cars are not the only product relying heavily on testimonials. Cosmetics, fragrances, and fashions are products that rely heavily on the face of the pitch woman. Women constantly monitor each other to learn how to dress and act appropriately in different situations. The image a woman presents to the world, in dress and makeup, is grounded in the Personal Orientation Motive, but takes form from the Adaptation Motive. Makeup literally creates the face a woman presents to the world, and where else would she learn what to wear and how to wear it unless she sees it on someone who looks the way she herself wants to look and wants to be? Every major cosmetics company has at least one beautiful model as its "image." One company branched out by using two spokespeople, a famous transvestite (RuPaul) and a minimal-makeup-wearing singer (k. d. lang). Perhaps the company's reasoning is that if its products can work on such seemingly diverse faces, it will surely work on yours!

Testimonials and endorsements are big business. It is accepted as par for the course that every major sports personality has a bevy of contracts. But it isn't just sports any more. Celebrities from other walks of life can also cash in, such as Dionne Warwick and the Psychic Network, or Sarah Ferguson and Weight Watchers. Whatever the faces are famous for, the endorsement game provides financial benefits to the endorser and a ready-made image to the marketer.

The other facet of endorsement is that of the peer group. Clothing is the most obvious example. The advertising works like this: Portray a group of young, trim, athletic people cavorting in mid-priced designer clothes, and those within that demographic group will buy in, as will those who want to belong. Along with this comes the brand names worn on the outside of the garments, to show that you do belong. The tag proves it.

THE MICHAEL JORDAN FACTOR

With his spectacular talent in basketball and his winning record, Michael Jordan has achieved fame throughout the world. In the June 22, 1998 cover story in *Time* magazine (Stein, 1998), it was mentioned that photographs of Jordan can actually be used for barter in Asia and Eastern Europe. And he can sell virtually anything. His big start came by promoting athletic shoes, but he has since branched out into sports drinks, apparel, sodas, fast food, and much more. It has gotten to the point where the product is becoming incidental to the endorsement. He is the ultimate pitch man. It will be interesting to see what effect his retirement from professional basketball will have on his selling power.

Why is he so popular? One reason is his exemplary record in basketball. At an age when most professional sports people have retired, Michael Jordan was still outscoring, outplaying, and outsmarting them all. When opponents invented strategies to keep him away from the basket, he improved other parts of his game to keep winning (Jordan, 1993). To his admirers, he is living proof that hypercompetitiveness, willpower, and a lot of hard work can take you to the top.

Or is it that he is so carefully bland off court that he gives everyone a chance to see in him whatever the viewer wants to see? Jordan was extremely aggressive during a game, so much so that he, rather than the coach, practically controlled the Bulls team on the court. But it was a different story at the end of a game. His media image is sanitized, deodorized, and G rated. He is aware of the constant attention and returns the favor by always being on role-model duty; well dressed and clean shaven, courteous and smiling. Even allegations about his gambling washed right off him, for he just seems too *nice* to be involved in any such dirty dealings. His fans are with him all the way, and will buy whatever he asks them to buy.

MISTAKEN IDENTITIES

People insist on projecting their own emotions and desires onto advertisements, which are necessarily made "one size fits most." Sometimes, though, the original message can be vague or open-ended enough to allow for the original message to get warped or even lost. A viewer will try to absorb the message being given to him or her by relating it to him or herself and his or her concerns (personalizing it), and when it works as intended by the marketers, the results can be astounding. For all the research and experience in the marketing and advertising world, though, surprises still abound.

As an example, in 1998 Volkswagen ran a series of TV commercials for their Golf line of cars. One of them portrayed two young men driving around aimlessly on a sunny day, stopping to pick up a trashed reclining chair, and then having to discard it due to its odor. There is absolutely no dialog, only background music. One way to understand the commercial would be to marvel at the amount of luggage space in the small car. But the homosexual community chose to see it as two young gay men driving around aimlessly on a sunny day. (Incidentally, the soundtrack to the commercial, "Dah-Dah-Dah," originally released in 1982 by the German band Trio, registered a sudden surge in popularity.)

The downside is much uglier, though. When the message is contorted a little too much, not only do sales suffer at that time, but so does the company's image. And, as bad reputations last far longer than good, this can be hard for a company to overcome. Calvin Klein fell foul of the general market when its series of commercials featuring young amateur models was perceived as imitation child pornography. Practically the entire nation was outraged, and the company had to pull all advertising material off the market immediately. The FBI investigated the matter, Calvin Klein had to make a public apology, and there was a lot of talk of boycotting his products. This is precisely the reason why major advertisers usually test drive their marketing efforts on a representative sample of the market before broadcast. The fallout from a misread message can be lethal.

HEALTH CARE ADVERTISING

For years, the Federal Communications Commission (FCC) disallowed hospital and medical advertising because of the possibility of undue influence in the very serious decision-making process of choosing doctors, hospitals, and other medical services. The average person is not knowledgeable enough to make this decision based on technical reasons. Accreditations and certificates not withstanding, it is the end result that is important. The cured and satisfied patient, the successful surgical procedure, or the pain-free dentistry are all that really count.

How likely is an individual to select a doctor from the phone book? Not very, as health is literally a life-or-death issue, and finding a good doctor is not to be taken lightly. Instead, many people will select a doctor or dentist by asking for referrals and suggestions from their families, friends, and neighbors. These word-of-mouth testimonials are free advertising for the professionals, who could not do any better by advertising commercially. This is the Adaptation Motive at its simplest.

For hospitals and other medical institutions who find this form of "spreading the good word" too small scale, commercial advertising focuses on exactly the same motivation. It is of no use to them to discuss the quality of services, as hospitals per se should have excellent service. After all, they deal with the spiritual issues of life and death, healing and survival. Marketers of medical services have to depict realistic situations and people so that potential patients can identify with them and thus personalize the information. By using a message that focuses on satisfied, fully recovered patients from all walks of life, hospitals try to convince viewers that they will be satisfied as well. An alternative is to use highly respected, credible celebrities. In the health area, endorsements and testimonials are the reigning form of marketing, all the way from witch doctors and Old West snake-oil dealers to modern medical professionals.

THE ADAPTATION MOTIVE: THE TRUE STORY

From the womb to the tomb, the Adaptation Motive is a controlling motivation. It dictates everything from how we dress and behave to who we perceive ourselves to be. It motivates our decisions every day, be it as trivial as what we eat for lunch to where we live, what we drive, who our friends are, and how we vote. Humans are social animals, and as such the need to conform to those around us is extremely strong. Marketers have always recognized and used the commercial potential of this innate desire to fit in, and will continue to use it to their advantage, as long as man needs society and society gauges acceptability by material possessions. No one wants to be left out in the cold.

REFERENCES

Jordan, M. (1993). *Rare air*. Chicago: Rare Air.

Kessler, B. (1998, March 25). N.Y.C. approves plan for uniforms in early grades. *Education Week, 17,* 3.

Maddock, R. C., & Fulton, R. L. (1998). *Motivation emotions and leadership: The silent side of management*. Westport, CT: Quorum Books.

Maslow, A. H. (1970). *Motivation and personality* (2d ed.). New York: Harper & Row.

Nash, J. M. (1997, February 3). Fertile minds. *Time,* pp. 48–56.

Packard, V. O. (1957). *The hidden persuaders*. New York: McKay.

Portner, J. (1996, February 14). Uniforms get credit for decrease in discipline problems. *Education Week, 15,* 1, 12–13.

Portner, J. (1998, January 21). California district points to uniforms for plunging crime rates. *Education Week, 17,* 6.

Stein, J. (1998, June 22). The one and only. *Time*.

Swartz, M. (1998, December–January). Rag trade: Don't even think about giving a dog a bone in Manhattan. *New Yorker,* p. 40.

12

The Expectation/
Resolution Motive

Achievement is the process of steadily raising one's levels of
aspiration and expectation.

—Jack Nicklaus

We never live; we are always in the expectation of living.

—Voltaire

EXPECTATION IN LIFE AND IN DEATH

Hopefully we live a long and a healthy life, and then we die. Voltaire
should have added that we also live in expectation of dying. Newspaper research that we have done has found that the obituaries are
one of the best-read sections in the newspaper, but the people who
read them can't tell you why they read them. Usually they respond,
"I'm looking for somebody that I know." But when they don't find
that somebody, day after day, they still go on looking. What are
they looking for?

We introduced the notion of a paradigm or a framework in Chapter 7 and showed how it was related to what people personalize.
What the perusers of the obituaries could not tell us is that they
are reading about the paradigms that other people had in their
lives, up until the time that they died. And then they compare their
own paradigm with those of others. It's a way of saying, "Am I good
enough?" "Will I make it?" Fleischman (1990) says that one of the

crucial elements of every religion is to die a meaningful death, but it's pretty hard to have a meaningful death if you haven't had a meaningful life. People scan and peruse the obituaries in the same way that they examine the classified advertisements. Most of them are not even interested in buying a car or getting a new job. They just want to know what they are missing out on, if anything, and what other people are doing.

EXPECTATION AND RESOLUTION

The Expectation Motive is one of the most heavily researched motives in psychology. In fact, it is the only motive that we have introduced in this book that has been heavily researched in psychology. Although most of the research carried out in expectation is with rats who run mazes with the expectation that there will be some cheese at the end, there are also any number of studies by social psychologists whose research tends to support this very important motive in humans (Kelly, 1955; Vroom, 1964; Rosenthal, 1966; Festinger, 1957; Lewin, 1951). Interestingly, very little if any research has been done on the overwhelming human motivation to complete or resolve open-ended and ambiguous issues. Resolution, by definition, is expectation, since it occurs in the future.

Our own casual and unpublished research on the resolution issue provides some interesting findings. In newspaper research, an "info" line was installed so that people could call a central telephone number that was published in the newspaper and receive sports scores, stock market quotes, household and gardening tips, and a myriad of other pieces of information. At the time this was installed they did not have this information available to them on computers or the Internet. Interestingly, our finding in reviewing the records was that 43 percent of the calls on the info line were for soap opera updates. This research may be considered casual and nonscientific, but the results speak for themselves. Resolution is obviously a burning issue and one that demands fulfillment.

There are many other examples of the high priority that is placed upon resolution. Television resolves hundreds of debacles and tragedies every day and every evening. These resolutions may involve professional or college sports, wrestling, dramas, or soap operas. Recently, shows in which individuals bring their own personal problems into the TV studio and wash their dirty laundry before millions of viewers have become enormously successful. Why would someone want to listen to the problems of someone that they don't even know? The answer is that they really don't care much about the problems. What they are looking for is the paradigm (everyone has one) in these people's lives and, if it involved conflict, how it was resolved.

The Expectation/Resolution Motive deals with our attempts to handle the future. Often this is seen in terms of how we have dealt with the past. The past is the best predictor of the future, but not always. The results obtained in our empirical research on the Expectation/Resolution Motive indicated that this motive was not as vibrant as the others. However there is enough evidence from the neurosciences, from previous psychological research, and from marketing and advertising to presume the endurance of this very strong and vibrant motive. People are involved in resolution every day.

THE NEUROLOGICAL BASIS FOR EXPECTATION AND RESOLUTION AS A MOTIVE

MacLean (1990) refers to a very important aspect of the Expectation/Resolution Motive when he talks about the "memory of the future." He reviews the case of a man with bilateral vacuities in the prefrontal region of the brain who was accused of murder. He states that the argument before the court was that it would be impossible for him to commit murder through premeditation, for premeditation required not only the ability to plan but also the step-by-step memory of what *was* planned, or a "memory of the future." This is because expectation and planning require a blueprint of a paradigm:

When the expression "memory of the future" is used, it may be asked, "How can there be a memory of something that has not yet happened? Wasn't it the intention to say *planning* instead of *memory*?" Planning, however, represents a developing, ongoing process. It is the blueprint in the *drawing stage*, not the blueprint itself. In a competitive sport such as football, it would generally be self-defeating to plan a play while the game is in progress. What is important is to remember the "blueprint" already available that provides a foreknowledge of where each player is supposed to be. This requires, one might say, a frontocerebellar "mind set" of the number and direction of turns and running distances. Accordingly, it has been implicit in all of the illustrations previously given that it is not only the planning, calculations and predictions involved, but also the memory of what is planned, as, say, the restrictions in a will, the conditions of national trust, and the like. (p. 561)

For Ramachandran and Blakeslee (1998), this "memory of the future" is a collection in the brain of a representation of all the various possibilities and systems. These systems that do the planning are located in the cingulate and in supplementary motor areas in the frontal lobes. Damage to the anterior cingulate gyrus of the brain results in a condition where the patient merely lies in bed, unable or unwilling to do anything, even though he or she is fully aware of his or her surroundings. Alzheimer's patients and patients suffering from senile dementia often go through a phase like this within the progressive stages of senility and organic psychosis. Ramachandran refers to this as "a total absence of free will."

One of the notable anomalies that befell Phineas Gage when the tamping rod pierced the ventromedial region of his frontal lobe was that he lost the ability to plan his future. According to Damasio (1994), "Gage's example indicated that something in the brain was concerned specifically with unique human properties, among them the ability to anticipate the future and plan accordingly within a complex social environment; the sense of responsibility toward the self and others; and the ability to orchestrate one's survival deliberately, at the command of one's free will" (p. 10).

There is clearly evidence, beginning with Gage in 1848, that the expectation function is found in the frontal lobes, and when damage occurs, as in a prefrontal lobotomy, there can be drastic changes, as there were for him. Not only did he lose the uniquely human ability to plan for the future, but he also became disoriented to time and place, wandering off from his job without any regard for others. The disorientation phenomenon has been presented by us as a motive and is found in Chapter 9. The fact that Gage lost the functions of both orientation and expectation suggests that there is a close relationship, behaviorally and neuroanatomically, between what we have referred to as the Orientation Motives and what we are now seeing as the Expectation/Resolution Motive.

THE EXPECTATION/RESOLUTION MOTIVE
IN EVERYDAY BEHAVIOR

There are numerous examples of the occurrence of the Expectation/Resolution Motive in everyday behavior. We plan not only what we will be doing tomorrow or next week, but many also make plans for the hereafter. Men and women have been doing this since the dawn of time. There are four areas where expectation and resolution play a major role and from which we can learn. They are

1. Casino gaming.
2. Health care.
3. Banking.
4. Entertainment.

The first three areas involve illustrations of the Expectation Motive and the last one is concerned primarily with resolution.

Casino Gaming

We offered what we think is a fairly conclusive argument in Chapter 9 for the involvement of the four Orientation Motives in casino gambling, which we also stated is one area of the fastest growing industry in America (O'Brien, 1998). One reason why we believe that it is growing so fast is because it gives people exactly what they want: disorientation and disconnection from their everyday lives in the four spheres of person, place, time, and circumstances. We offer further support for this observation in Chapter 15 from interviews that have been conducted in casinos. We cannot overlook the importance of this motive in the overall picture of casinos or in any other kind of gambling, including sports betting, parimutuel betting, and so on. There is an expectancy on the part of the player that he or she will win. Where do they get this information, or this insight?

The majority of players, and particularly the "low rollers" that Bennett and Pennington brought to the party, do not feel that they have any special quality that allows them to beat the odds. They come to the casino strictly for the purpose of disconnecting from whatever they are connected to in the outside world. They are motivated by the four Orientation Motives. They decide ahead of time how much money they want to lose and they stick with that figure. If they come out ahead they put that money into a sugar bowl, and that money guarantees them yet one more day of disorientation and disconnection. Disorientation is the primary motive and expectation is secondary in this case. There is always more than one motive involved in any activity.

But there is also a much smaller number of players, usually local, who do believe that they have a special quality, which they refer to as "luck." They may not believe that they have it every day, but they do believe that it comes and goes, and they believe that they can tell when it comes and when it goes. Whenever they are in doubt about this they will either stay home or consult a psychic.

Luck is a lot like love. You can't measure it, weigh it, hold it, or cut it up into little pieces. It is a construct and an abstraction. But the paradox is that many of the people who hold this belief about luck don't have the kind of intelligence which allows them to handle constructs and abstractions. This is because, in general, their thinking and thought processes are concrete and not abstract. This is not meant to imply that they are unintelligent, because they are not. However, they are concrete and very practical and down-to-earth in their style of thinking. This style of thinking does not entertain theoretical concepts and impressions. When asked what luck really is, they point to the pit of their stomach and say, "It's something down here. I know it's there. I can feel it. That's all I can tell you right now." This is referred to as a "gut feeling." The gut feeling is about as far as this group can go in dealing with abstract thought.

Both groups—low rollers and regulars—operate on the basis of the Expectation Motive, but the regulars operate almost entirely on expectation/resolution. This is what brings them back, day after day, to the casino. Some get into card counting and other nefarious methods of winning, but many of them don't. They merely play until their luck runs out, and when that happens, they somehow find a way to get back into the game and start the whole process over again. They are very unrealistic and will often mortgage their homes in order to "stay in the game." They are counting on their luck to "turn."

Note that the different segments within the gaming community are defined in terms of motives. For the recreational gambler, the major motivation is disorientation, with less emphasis on expectation. For the local who goes to the casino at least once a week, the Expectation/Resolution Motive is a lot stronger and disorientation motives are in the background. For the more frequent and serious gambler, spiritual survival is also a motive, combining with expectation/resolution and with the orientation group. The purpose of Motigraphics is to break down the extent to which each of these motives contributes to each of these different segments of gamblers.

I was struck by an example that was given to me by an elderly lady in Tunica, Mississippi not long after the casinos had settled in. I noted that the used car lot in Tunica, which normally had fifteen or twenty cars, had expanded its boundaries and had fifty to seventy-five cars on the lot. She said that I probably thought that people got into trouble at the slots or tables and then would have to sell their car. I agreed, but she told me that I was wrong. What happens, she said, is that they wake up in the morning and sell the car before they go to the casino. When asked how this worked, she said, "They wake up and they say, 'This is my lucky day! I can feel it in my gut. Today I'm going to win the door prize and possibly the jackpot.'" They then take their car title out to the man at the casino, get the money, and start to play. She added that she had never known of anyone who ever got their car back again.

There are a lot of people for whom the Expectation/Resolution Motive can be very destructive because it gives them a sense of false hope. People have lost not only their cars in Mississippi, Iowa, and other states, but they have lost their homes, their land, and their life's savings, not to speak of the loss of their families. The Expectation/Resolution Motive is a positive motive because it pushes people in a positive direction. However, it can certainly have negative results.

The Expectation/Resolution Motive works this way in other contexts also. In 1996 we wrote about the 90–10–10–90 reversal theory which is often seen in the workplace. According to this theory, ninety workers out of one hundred take their full-time job less seriously than they ought to because they believe that they will either inherit big money from a rich uncle, win big in the lottery or at the casino, or will be "discovered." The fact is, however, that only ten out of one hundred, if that, will actually cash in on a treasure hunt, and the rest of us will have to work for a living until we die or retire, whatever comes first.

Health Care

It seems paradoxical to many people that the same motive that is involved in casino gaming is also involved in the act of choosing a physician. This is because most of us who are not licensed physicians or dentists have no idea what it really takes to be a conscientious, reliable, and competent health care professional. We don't know the criteria and we don't know the rules. Therefore, we either take it on faith or we rely on a good friend to tell us who is a competent physician and who isn't. If we go the route of relying on a friend, then we are following the Adaptation Motive, in which we ask our peers what to do and they tell us. The problem here is that most of them don't know a whole lot more than we do about what makes a good doctor and what doesn't.

The Expectation Motive is intimately involved in choosing a physician because all that we can realistically do is make a choice and then sit back and trust the person to whom we have entrusted our health and our well-being. Hopefully we have made the right choice, but this rather simple approach becomes increasingly more difficult as managed care companies take over the whole health care picture.

In testing applicants for Emergency Medical Technician (EMT) positions, I was told by some of the ambulance attendants a story which I thought illustrated quite well the strength of the Expectation Motive in health care. In routine runs to a retirement community, most of their calls, not surprisingly, regarded heart failure. After the pick up it was only twelve miles to a local hospital, where the emergency room physician could administer lifesaving techniques. Beyond the local hospital—across the Mississippi River bridge and thirty more miles of travel—was the medical center, where most of these heart victims were being treated by their own personal physician. EMTs on the ambulance strongly suggested that they stop at the local hospital because of the serious nature of the illness, rather than trying to go another thirty miles to the medical center. But they were never successful in selling this idea to any of their patients. The patients all insisted on going the additional forty-five to sixty minutes to the medical center and to "my doctor." So strong was this tie between the patients and their doctors that they were willing to risk their lives, and many of them did just that. The problem of patients expiring during the extra forty-five minute excursion forced attendants to put releases in the ambulances. This is a testimonial to the absolute strength of the Expectation Motive. It was their doctor or no one.

According to a survey that is regularly conducted by the *Wall Street Journal*, physicians are among one of the most trusted groups in America. But at the other end of this survey—the lowest end—are the managed care organizations. And many if not most physicians today work within a managed care framework. So here lies a great chasm that needs to be bridged. The consumer knows about physicians and how trustworthy they are, but what about managed care organizations? In Chapter 16 we illustrate how this bridge was built, successfully, appealing to the motives of the Silent Side. But the important element here is trust. Trust is a major element of the Expectation/Resolution Motive. Once the advertising agency knew that trust was the issue, it became possible to build all kinds of bridges between the physician and the managed care organization.

In Chapter 8, where the motives were introduced in detail, it was noted that health, well-being, and health care were elements of the Physical Survival Motive. This makes common sense. So where does the Expectation/Resolution Motive fit in? There is always more than one motive involved in a product or service, and usually there are three or four, or more. This is the case in health care. Whereas health care in and of itself is related to the Physical Survival Motive, the choice of a physician—which is not the same as health care—is associated with the Expectation/Resolution Motive. This is because the choice of a physician is an issue that involves trust, belief, and faith, all of which are concepts that assist us in dealing with the future and in planning. So the choice of a health care provider is an issue within the Expectation Motive, whereas physical health and wellness is obviously an issue within the Physical Survival Motive.

Banking

The foundation of banking is trust. This is why once a customer has established an account it is very hard to get them to change banks. Trust is at the heart of banking and also at the heart of the Expectation Motive.

Most banking studies that we have done on an annual basis indicate that there are two reasons why people say that they go to a particular bank. The first is friendly tellers, and the second is convenience. These are rational, left brain responses and do not include any of the emotional or motivational reasons why people choose a bank, or why they may choose to remain a customer or become a loyal customer.

One of the best ways to promote the Expectation Motive, which is the key to customer loyalty in banks, is to promote some of the elements that are associated with spiritual survival. The promotion of the top two or three elements in Fleischman's hierarchy of motives will promote trust. This includes witness significance and membership, or the feeling that one belongs and has a place in the organization. Eastman Corporation, Federal Express, and others have all used these factors to promote peace, harmony, and excellence within their organizations. Each of them has gone on to win the coveted Malcolm Baldridge Award (Milliken, 1996).

The first and most important factor is witness significance. Borrowed from religion, this means that many people believe (and have believed for millenniums) that a higher power listens and is aware of them, no matter how small or insignificant they may think that they are. In organizations, this transfers to key-person leadership, and if the key person is charismatic, the leadership works even better. Dave Thomas has built an enormous business by doing his own advertising and talking directly to the customer. How many banks do you know that do this? How many bank executives—even if it's not the CEO—can you drop by and chat with when you visit the bank?

Rick Fulton, my coauthor for two other books, has turned at least four plants from losers to winners. As plant manager, he is out on the floor at least twice a day, talking when he can, and when the noise prohibits conversation, he has a big smile and two thumbs up for whoever he sees. He is a charismatic leader.

We cited a significant number of references in Chapter 3 to show that behavior modification and strictly rational methods of management are on their way out. Ashforth and Humphrey (1995) have presented the background for this liaison among motivations, emotions, and leadership: "Leaders may persuade with logic, but they motivate through emotion. Leaders must come to grips with the challenges of emotion, a key driver of productivity, quality and other factors that lead to business success. The words 'motivation,' 'emotion,' and 'motion' all derive from the same Latin root meaning 'to move.' When you want to motivate people to take action, engage their emotions" (p. 97). The same thing goes for motivating customers.

The second manner in which the Expectation Motive can be promoted to new prospects is through membership. People—particularly those who are younger—have a hunger and a thirst to belong to something. In surveys we have done, this element of membership often comes out on top. They like to be around people who believe the same way they do. Professional and trade organizations, churches, and societies make attempts to do this, but they do not always fill the gap.

This is not to say that banks can do this. However, they can do a lot more to make customers feel like they belong and that there is something very special about the bank that the customers have chosen. The best way to do this is to start with the employees. Once the employees believe that they are members of something special and unique, that emotion will spill over to the customers in a virtual waterfall of enthusiasm. The message, "I wouldn't even think about working anywhere else," will be the subliminal cue that bank customers get, and the word will spread. The bank executive needs to ask himself or herself, "What subliminal cues do I want my customers to have about this bank?"

Bank personnel have always shied away from emotion and particularly the expression of emotion. But as Ashforth and Humphrey (1995) have commented, when you "neutralize, buffer, prescribe or normalize" emotion it usually comes out in spite of your attempts, and under these conditions it comes out as a negative rather than a positive; as destructive rather than constructive.

The third element of the Spiritual Survival Motive which applies here is lawful order. This is what people expect in banking. They feel much more secure when they know that their bank is operated in an orderly, systematic, and methodical manner. This may seem like it is so obvious that it does not even have to be repeated, but it does. We have done research in supermarket banks and in drive-in parking lot banks that people did not take seriously and therefore did not do serious banking. In some cases where they were asked to visualize or draw a bank, they made a joke out of it. They had a problem with younger tellers who came to work on Friday in jeans and pocket t-shirts. They had a problem with noise and confusion and, in some cases, with a party atmosphere and people eating at their work stations. They had many other problems that undermined the key motive that we know is involved in banking, and that is the Expectation Motive.

Witness significance, membership, and lawful order are three key elements in spiritual survival that will bring back the trust, belief, and faith that are the key elements in the Expectation Motive.

Entertainment

The entertainment business is the resolution business. Each night hundreds of crises are resolved on TV. Some are rivalries between competitive sports teams. Some are dramatic presentations. Others consist of political infighting and outfighting, as seen on MSNBC or C-Span. Still others involve trials and judicial proceedings. What all these things have in common are that they work toward some type of a resolution.

In 1995, there was overwhelming interest in the "trial of the century" when O. J. Simpson went on trial for the murder of his wife. People not only in America but around the world held on to their seats, waiting for the entertainment, but it never came. Instead of being treated to a courtroom drama such as appears on television every night, they were bored to tears. It didn't take long before most of the audience was gone, but when the resolution was about to take place—the pronouncement by the jury as to guilty or not guilty—everyone was back at ringside, waiting with intense and passionate anticipation. Resolution is a fundamental human motive.

The brain is wired for closure. Whether it's in artwork, in drama, or in the day-to-day crises that arise, resolution is a must and it is essential. We have included it here as part of the Expectation Motive because resolution is a futuristic activity. It takes place in the future, and in most cases involves extensive planning, timing, and execution. The kinds of activities that bring about resolution seem to be a function of age, gender, and social class. Young children prefer emphases on the physical resolution of conflicts, particularly the type that is dispensed by Steven Seagal, where eight or ten challengers are taken on and defeated by him. This occurs at least six or eight times in a movie. Movie critics apparently don't appreciate this, for Seagal has been nominated for six or eight Razzie Awards (Worst Picture, Worst Actor, etc.) (www.razzies.com). If more pre-teen and teenagers were on the panel, Seagal's ratings might improve dramatically.

The pursuit of resolution in terms of physical methods (fighting, yelling, shooting, chasing, etc.) is popular with young children because they don't have the ability to think or reason in terms of intent, motive, or implication (Piaget, 1932). This is a well-developed and universally accepted finding. Their reasoning is said to be concrete rather than abstract, and Piaget and Inhelder (1956) have given us sufficient evidence which supports the notion that this is true and factual. When a child reaches the stage of formal operational thinking at around the age of eleven or twelve, much of this changes. Thinking and reasoning then occur in terms of abstractions. Resolution, which is a major issue throughout life, can be achieved by reading books and novels and watching television shows, where resolution may take place in the bar room, or in the court room, or at many different places in-between.

Unfortunately there is very little in the psychological literature concerning resolution, even though it is an extremely important issue that is intimately related to motives and motivation. In our own research with clients, much of which is unpublished for reasons of confidentiality, we have found that one of the problems with newspapers and the current steep decline in subscriptions that they are experiencing is the fact that they don't resolve issues that have been discussed in previous news items. Much of this is not their fault. In real life, not everything gets resolved. Murderers and rapists do escape and don't get caught or punished. People go bankrupt, or die, or get divorced. Horrible automobile accidents occur where the perpetrator is uninsured, leaves the scene, and makes no reparations. This is the kind of news that newspapers print. But if resolution and closure are as important as we believe that they are, it is not at all surprising that there is a generalized apathy and disinterest on the part of many, many Americans toward the news. Cal Thomas (1998) with the *Commercial Appeal* summarizes this apathy toward everything that is happening today and particularly toward the news: "We are richer than ever, yet more impoverished than ever. We don't care about much of anything, but pretend that by not caring we are not being 'judgmental' (an even worse sin, if we believed in sin, which we don't). Those who would blame Bill Clinton for this mess are looking at the wrong man. He's not the cause of our decadence but the result" (p. B4).

SUMMARY: EXPECTATION AND RESOLUTION

Human behavior is controlled primarily by subliminal cues. Furthermore, the earlier in life that these subliminal cues are received by the child, the more permanent they become. This was introduced in Chapter 3, and in Chapter 15 we show that it is important that respondents be regressed to an earlier age so that we can understand and catalog some of the feelings and emotions that are associated with the product that is being researched.

Bettleheim (1989) has hinted at this in his treatment of fairy tales, which are many children's first exposure to life and the way life is lived by other people. For Bettleheim, the deep internal conflicts that the child experiences are never dealt with in most children's literature and no one ever discusses these conflicts with the child. Therefore, it only follows that the child experiences desperation, isolation, and loneliness as he or she develops over the first five years, feeling that no one has ever shared these feelings with him or her and that he or she is totally alone. In fairy tales, there is the reassurance that others have shared these feelings and conflicts, and that they have resolved them. Bettleheim says that unlike the Bible, fairy tales are not about morality, but instead they present the reassuring theme that, in spite of adversity, one can and will succeed. The child meets heroes in fairy tales who enter into the darkness and grope their way through, convincing him or her that even though he or she may feel lost in the deep woods, he or she will get through and succeed. He or she will find the help when it is needed. And if that is not enough, each fairy tale ends with the assurance and the confidence that "they lived happily ever after." That's resolution.

After thousands of interviews in clinical evaluation and consumer settings, we remain convinced that there are substantial differences between those who were exposed to fairy tales in the first three years of life and those who were not. These differences are measured in terms of success much later in life. We also feel, although we have no evidence for this, that those children who are exposed to fairy tales when they are very young have a much stronger sense of expectation and resolution, simply because of the strength of the subliminal cues that have been inlaid early in life.

REFERENCES

Ashforth, B. E., & Humphrey, R. H. (1995). Emotion in the workplace: A reappraisal. *Human Relations, 48,* 97–126.

Bettleheim, B. (1989). *The uses of enchantment: The meaning and importance of fairy tales.* New York: Vantage Books.

Damasio, A. (1994). *Descartes' error: Emotion, reason and the human brain.* New York: Avon Books.

Festinger, L. (1957). *A theory of cognitive dissonance.* Evanston, IL: Row-Peterson.

Fleischman, P. (1990). *The healing spirit.* New York: Paragon House.

Kelly, G. A. (1955). *A psychology of personal constructs.* New York: Norton.

Lewin, K. (1951). *Field theory and social science.* New York: Harper.

MacLean, P. D. (1990). *The triune brain in evolution: Role in paleocerebral functions.* New York: Plenum Press.

Milliken, W. F. (1996, October). The Eastman way. *Quality Progress,* pp. 57–62.

O'Brien, T. L. (1998). *Bad bet: The inside story of the glamour, glitz and danger of America's gambling industry.* New York: Time Books.

Piaget, J. (1932). *The moral development of the child.* New York: Harcourt Brace.

Piaget, J., & Inhelder, B. (1956). *The child's conception of space* (F. J. Langon & E. L. Lunzer, Trans.). London: Routledge & Kegan Paul.

Ramachandran, V. S., & Blakeslee, S. (1998). *Phantoms in the brain: Probing the mysteries of the human brain.* New York: William Morrow.

Rosenthal, R. (1966). Teacher's expectancies: Determinants of pupils' IQ gains. *Psychological Reports, 19,* 115–18.

Thomas, C. (1998, November 29). Ignorance and apathy. *Commercial Appeal* (Memphis), p. B4.

Vroom, V. H. (1964). *Work and motivation.* New York: Wiley.

13

The Play Motive and Laughter

Humanity has advanced, when it has advanced, not because it has been sober, responsible, and cautious, but because it has been playful, rebellious, and immature.

—Tom Robbins

The place of the father in the modern suburban family is a very small one, particularly if he plays golf.

—Bertrand Russell

THE UNIQUE ROLE OF PLAY IN MAMMALIAN BEHAVIOR

MacLean (1990) has addressed the role of play and indicated that it is a uniquely mammalian trait, the origin of which is unknown. From MacLean's description we have added play to the building blocks of human motivation as an additional motive. This was the last motive to be discovered and was not included in our factor analysis or in other empirical investigations. However, it has been encountered a number of times in our research and it explains behavior that is unexplained by other motives.

For example, in a study on why women sew, it was clear that very few women engage in this activity and those who do experience a unique and different kind of satisfaction. The two words used most often in this study were "creative" and "enjoyment." They also spoke of fulfillment and satisfaction, and the impulse that they would have to go and make a dress or a blouse, or perhaps to make slip covers or drapes for the home. The impulse was expressed as a sudden desire or arousal, such as, "I would take a notion to sew."

In a study we conducted on why women sew, it was found that in 1895, 95 percent of the women in America sewed, making clothing for their families. In 1995, that ratio was completely reversed, and only 5 percent sewed. Sewing, in this context, is defined as actually making a dress or a set of drapes for the home and not just attaching buttons or repairing tears or seams. Most of this reversal in the number of women who sew is due to the fact that there are limitless quantities of clothing available in the marketplace for prices that are much lower than what it would cost to purchase and follow a pattern, especially if one counted or added up the time involved in doing this. So there is very little reason that can be given today for making a dress or making a child's clothing, other than the satisfaction, enjoyment, and creativity that one experiences in the process of making it and then again when one sees the completed product.

Another similar finding was seen in a study of why women cook. This was a study that was completed for an evaporated milk product that was used primarily in scratch cooking. Scratch cooking and baking are almost lost arts, since ready mixes have been around since the 1950s and today a person can buy the whole cake or pie without going to any trouble or making any kind of a mess. Our client wanted to know if there was any equity left in the brand. According to him, many companies with older products have merely "abandoned the brand."

Like sewing, cooking—and especially scratch baking—are impulse activities and many women in the study said that they cooked "when I take a notion to." Like sewing, cooking is an example of the "good impulse" as it is seen and embedded in the Play Motive. Many packagers of quick and easy products and purveyors of gourmet foods that can be served at home feel that their product takes advantage of the time and the mess that is involved in scratch cooking, not realizing that time and effort are the reward and the payoff. The resolution involved is satisfaction and completion, which is much stronger and more fulfilling than the resolution that would be achieved when simply opening a box of cake mix.

Many years ago, when cake mixes were first introduced, all that was necessary was to add water. The concept failed. Then a creative director suggested that they at least require the cook to add an egg or two, so the cook could feel like he or she had a hand in the baking. It worked like a charm, and some cake mixes still require that the cook add a couple of eggs or some butter, when in fact the cook could make the mix without that requirement. Cake mixes are made for people who want to play and create and have fun, but who don't have quite as much time as the scratch cook does.

Another example of play is golf, which is of course a game. However, we showed in Chapter 10 that what begins as play can often move up the building blocks of human motivation to another higher level. In golf, that level would be territorial. As the golfer becomes more serious about his or her game, starts to wager on it, and takes more and more time to improve the game, it moves from the Play Motive to the Territorial Survival Motive. This may occur quickly or it may occur over a more gradual period of time.

WHEN THE PLAY MOTIVE SHIFTS INTO A MORE SERIOUS AND COMPELLING LEVEL

How do we know whether a game, such as golf, is simple play or whether it has evolved to a higher level; that is, to the territorial survival level or perhaps even to the spiritual survival level (at which point golf becomes a passion)? MacLean (1990) addresses this "fine line": "Even in the case of international games, there appears to be a primitive, childlike and fine line between enjoying fun at play and getting mad and fighting. Hence we have seen international games become a political means of displaying national will at showdown situations" (p. 560).

This insight perfectly describes the situation that we referred to in Chapter 10 where there can be a confusing transposition of motives from one level to the next. Play, in its typical format, is defined as not having a stated outcome or purpose other than "winning" and filling in time that would otherwise not be utilized. Play also aids in helping people disconnect or disorient from their daily activities. As an activity, play is satisfying in and of itself and there are no other stated or expressed goals. Often it takes place not alone or in a vacuum but in concert with other activities, such as feeding or at festivals and picnics.

When other goals are established, as in tournaments, contests, and competitions, the activity that was once considered play has a tendency to move up to the territorial level. It may then move from that level up to the spiritual survival level, and that is seen in terms of the time that the person devotes to the game, the passion with which he or she plays the game, and the overall expectations that the individual has regarding outcomes.

This is quite clear in casino gaming. We have presented this activity as being associated with disorientation (Chapter 9) and expectation (Chapter 12), and in this chapter as play. Keep in mind that all human activities have multiple causes when it comes to motives, and so there will always be more than a single motive that is involved in any activity. For a small segment of gamblers who are referred to as "sweats," casino gaming is not play; it is very serious business. It is a spiritual endeavor. These individuals engage in card counting and other activities. We saw in Chapter 10 that in spiritual survival activities any means is usually justified by the end. Hence, these players will consider any method of cheating in order to gain an advantage over the house. They usually quit their job and spend full time in the casino. Since they are unwelcome in the casino they are often evicted and casinos share their identity with competitors, but in some cases they even go so far as to have plastic surgery so that they can reenter the casino and continue their obsession. When engaged in serious gaming pursuits, they rarely eat, drink, or have sex. Formally, they are known as compulsive gamblers, but in the casino they are known as "sweats" because they literally sweat at the table. They make other players very uncomfortable and uneasy and often drive business away for that reason. This is an example of how simple play can be elevated to the level of the Spiritual Survival Motive and become an obsession. We have presented the Spiritual Survival Motive as one that is desirable and preferable and which accounts for the highest level of functioning in advertising, marketing, and individual behavior. However, we have also shown how that motive has two sides. Since the Spiritual Survival Motive involves passion, and passion itself has two sides, the Spiritual Survival Motive can be responsible for overwhelming goodness or overwhelming evil.

When an executive has a miniature golf green in his office we might determine that he has elevated his golf game to at least the level of territorial survival (mixing golf and work) and possibly to the level of spiritual survival. We may or may not be correct, but one thing is certain, and that is that he has confused two levels of the building blocks of human motivation: the level of the Play Motive and the level of the Territorial Survival Motive. Golf is play and work is territorial. Generally, when two levels are confused like this, complications soon begin to develop.

NEUROLOGICAL BASIS FOR PLAY AND LAUGHTER

Although we have not drawn our conclusions on the Play Motive from empirical investigations, there is neurological support for the existence of this motive and we have seen this in studies that we have done with consumers. MacLean (1990) has observed that play is a uniquely mammalian trait and that it does not exist in birds or in reptiles. He suggested that the function of play was originally related to the effort to relieve the tension that is caused by over-crowding in the nest. He quotes studies that show that play is also identified with "the most recently evolved division of the limbic sys-tem—the thalamocingulate division" (p. 559). The fact that laughter is centered in a very recently evolved structure of the brain would explain why people laugh, but animals don't. MacLean also says that it is important to consider the role of the frontal lobes in the regula-tion of play and laughter. However, there is very little evidence on the role of the frontal lobes in play. Two studies, Bianchi (1895) and Franzen and Myers (1973) report reduced play in two- to three-year-old monkeys following a frontal lobotomy on the right side.

Koestler (1964) has clarified the role of humor and laughter by comparing it to creativity and defining it as "perceiving a situation or event in two habitually incompatible associative contexts." We have defined it in a similar fashion in Chapter 6 where we dis-cussed absurdities. However, we can go further and define the con-texts which are generally incompatible with each other, such as the association between sexual survival and spiritual survival (sex in the Oval Office of the White House); territorial survival and sexual survival (sex in the workplace); and, in the present context, play and territorial survival (putting greens in the office). These and other situations that involve the meeting of two incompatible con-texts (or motives) can be a culture or breeding ground for humor but can also create a setting for potential disaster and catastrophe.

Ramachandran and Blakeslee (1998) have cited two very inter-esting but very rare cases of people who literally died from laugh-ing. In each case, they said, "The abnormal activity that started the laughter was always located in portions of the limbic system in a set of structures including the hypothalamus, the mammilary bodies and the cingulate gyrus that are involved in the emotions. I find it intriguing that a relatively small cluster of brain structures is behind the phenomenon—a sort of 'laughter circuit'" (p. 201). In these cases, Ramachandran and Blakeslee indicated that a post-mortem in one revealed a hemorrhage involving the floor of the thalamus which compressed several adjacent structures. The other was caused by a large ruptured aneurysm in an artery at the base of the brain which compressed part of the hypothalamus, the mammilary bodies, and other structures on the floor of the brain.

Obviously, these cases are very rare, but in studying this kind of pathology we are able to determine, from compression damage, just what structures are involved in the various functions that we present here and particularly the motives that are presented and their elements. Empirical investigation alone is not enough, nor is neurologic probing. These methods, along with extensive observations of what kinds of things really work, taken together have helped us to arrive at the definitions and descriptions of why people do what they do.

There is one additional observation regarding laughter. We noted in Chapter 6 that laughter is an antidote or remedy for anxiety. We base this observation on our own studies of nonverbal behavior (Maddock & Fulton, 1995) in people who appear somewhat insecure and unsettled. When these people make a statement they will often chuckle at the end of the statement in a way that is often barely noticeable. This chuckle usually negates whatever the person said, or at least gives the message that what they just said is not to be taken very seriously.

The fact that laughter is intimately associated with anxiety and fear gives further support to the notion that the limbic system is intimately involved in the mediation of laughter, since the limbic system is the control center of the brain for the emotions. It also helps to illustrate that there is a very thin line between what can be very funny and what can be extremely catastrophic.

REFERENCES

Bianchi, I. (1895). The function of the frontal lobes. *Brain, 18,* 497–522.

Franzen, E., & Myers, R. (1973). Age effects of social behavior deficits following prefrontal lesions in monkeys. *Brain Research, 54,* 277–86.

Koestler, A. (1964). *The act of creation.* New York: Macmillan.

MacLean, P. D. (1990). *The triune brain in evolution: Role in paleocerebral functions.* New York: Plenum Press.

Maddock, R. C., & Fulton, R. L. (1995). *The silent side of communication.* Des Moines, IA: American Media (video and workbook).

Ramachandran, V. S., & Blakeslee, S. (1998). *Phantoms in the brain: Probing the mysteries of the human mind.* New York: William Morrow.

PART III

SILENT SIDE METHODOLOGY AND MEASUREMENT OF MOTIVES AND DESIRES

14

The Basic Building Blocks of Human Behavior

FROM QUALITATIVE TO QUANTITATIVE

There is a considerable gulf that exists in market research between those who do quantitative research and those who do qualitative research, and at times it appears that "never the twain shall meet." It is unfortunate. Quantitative research has a number of flaws and impairments, and so does qualitative research. Quantitative research lacks depth. It also lacks the power to explain, since all it can really do is describe. Another critical flaw is that it is usually based upon behavioristic principles, which means that it is strictly limited to describing consumer behavior and is unable to explain it. Quantitative research also requires people to respond to an artificial, synthetic, and often awkward questionnaire that has been designed for the convenience of the person who is scoring it rather than the respondent who is taking it. Perhaps the biggest complaint with quantitative research is that it doesn't tell us anything that we didn't already know. This is the so-called and well-named "so what?" phenomenon.

However, quantitative research provides us with numbers. And numbers do a lot more than weigh and measure things. Numbers give us a way to organize and synthesize our findings and to present them in a format that is logical and rational. This makes the research presentation very attractive to the left side of the brain, since the presenter will be giving facts and figures. However, there is also a "something missing" syndrome that leaves the audience saying, "But isn't there more to it than that?"

FILL DIRT

What is missing is the emotional, affective, and subjective side of the data. This is what we have been referring to as the Silent Side. It is also missing from psychology and psychiatry, and we have covered that topic in this book. But for many, even if what they have read makes intuitive sense, they will reject it. They will reject it because of the influence of behaviorism, which denies the influence or even the existence of the unconscious, and they will also deny it because it is, by definition, qualitative and not quantitative and therefore cannot be expressed in terms of numbers. And everyone wants to see the numbers.

When we started our research, this is exactly where we were. We felt, and we believed, that anything associated with the unconscious mind had to be, by definition, qualitative. But at the same time we were saying something that was almost contradictory, and that was that the unconscious mind is very simple, and not complex. If it is simple, then measurement should also be simple and straightforward. And this is exactly how Motigraphics was developed.

An effective quantitative scoring system will evolve from a valid qualitative system. We emphasize this basic principle simply because most consultants and researchers believe that the two kinds of systems are mutually exclusive from one another. In stark contrast, we are saying that they are not mutually exclusive; they are mutually dependent.

A VALID SYSTEM

The eleven-tier inverted building blocks of human motivation is a valid system. We know that it is, for several reasons:

- When judges take statements that were made at random they can easily sort them into the eleven motivational categories that we have presented throughout this book.
- When judges place these statements into their appropriate categories, the correlation between where they put the statements and the criterion is high (r = .86). The percentage of agreement between judges and the criterion is reported in Chapter 15.
- People actually talk in the categories that make up the inverted building blocks: orientation, survival, play, adaptation, and expectation.

- Factor analysis carried out by us supports these categories and motives.
- Advertising and marketing efforts have been using these categories and motives, by intuition, for a long time.
- There is neurological support for these categories and motives, backing the notion that they are hardwired into the brain.

To summarize, the system that we have developed and expanded upon in this book which leads to Motigraphics is a valid one. As a result, what appears to be a qualitative system can now be expanded into a quantitative one, and motives can be measured and weighed in terms of their importance in the overall scheme of things. Up until this point, anything that was written or said about motivation was analogous to politics and politicians: It was strictly limited to discourse and rhetoric.

Another very important point, in addition to the validity of these motives, is the fact that they express what is really important to people, and this is expressed in their own ideas, phrases, and beliefs. For example, we have shown that academic and professional psychology, in their quest to become a science, have ruled out spiritual survival (passion) as an issue in human behavior. But as any seasoned salesperson knows, if you are going into a person's office and expect to make a sale, you need to spend some time talking to him or her about what his or her spiritual survival consists of. By ruling out passion, emotions are ruled out. Then, and as seen in cognitive psychology, emotions are elevated to the level of thoughts instead of passions. When this occurs, everything is handled and treated on a rational basis.

At times we have been criticized for going in the other direction; that is, ruling out rational thinking. But this is not true. What we are doing is trying to bring the irrational into perspective, but not to make it rational or reasonable. The woman who sits at home and burns her arm with a lit cigarette is not engaging in rational behavior, but it's not enough to say that what she is doing is irrational. She already knows that. The solution to her problem is to deal directly with the spiritual pain that is the issue, and not to try to run away from it by using techniques of distraction that are harmful, painful, and leave scars for a lifetime.

We believe that rational behaviors have to be weighed in with irrational behaviors in the marketplace, but we have left it to someone else to work with and factor in these rational behaviors. We believe that when it comes to assessing the cadre of people who deal with the rational side of motivation, there are plenty of experts and a plethora of consultants. After all, this is primarily what attorneys do for a living.

MAKING THE TRANSITION

The successful move from qualitative to quantitative is completely dependent upon valid categories. As subliminal cues are added up and placed in the appropriate categories, they add weight (or in the case of negative motives, subtract weight) from each motive. Motives may then be used to assess larger samples, as in Extended Motigraphics. Motives may be used to define different groups of consumers as described and defined by their motives (e.g., loyal customers, at-risk customers, etc.). Motives may be entered into regression equations and/or covaried with other measures, such as demographics and psychographics. Also, motivational profiles of individuals or of entire consumer or employee groups may be developed using this system.

VISUALIZATION

One the things that we have to do in order to get to the Silent Side is get people to visualize rather than just verbalize their preferences and beliefs. This is based upon a recognition that the left side of the brain, which is more factual, logical, and rational, is also more verbal. In order to reduce (we can never eliminate) left side interference, we use visualization. The right hemisphere of the brain thinks in pictures, not in words. Therefore, we have incorporated a number of different visualization methods into our research that we feel allow us to derive information from the more intuitive, feeling, and emotional side of the brain. We get our respondents to "think" or express themselves in pictures, not in words. This procedure is fully described in Chapter 15.

WHY WE DO THIS

Motives are the single most important determinant of human behavior in the marketplace or anywhere else. Motives lead directly to decisions. Motives that are expressed today, to do or not to do something, can lead directly to predictions of future success or failure.

Wolfe (1999) has traced the search to define human motivation back at least 200 years. He says that at first the "social physicists" of the eighteenth century believed that the same Newtonian laws of physics could eventually be applied to defining human motivation. Freud thought that the key to human motivation was in the libido, or sex drive. B. F. Skinner thought that it was all tied up in rewards and reinforcement. We have already discussed Maslow. For Wolfe, Carl Jung had the most credible and viable theory of human motivation, saying that it originated in the roots of childhood that remained active in the unconscious. This is similar to the approach that we are taking in this book.

For Wolfe (1999), the reason that psychologists and marketers have never dealt effectively with motivation is because of the issue of free will:

Free will limits attempts to project consumer behavior in the classical scientific format of cause-and-effect. Researchers and marketers can be fairly accurate projecting what masses of consumers might do, but free will makes projections of what one consumer will do mere speculation. That didn't matter in the heyday of mass marketing, but it matters a lot in relationship and in one-to-one marketing.

Interestingly, what Wolfe (1999) proposes as a solution to this dilemma is that we become familiar with the basic building blocks of behavior:

[There is] a basic set of building blocks from which all behavior emerges, much as all organic life emerge from four nucleotides, which are the basic building blocks of DNA. The basic building blocks of DNA are identical in all creatures, from the lowliest bacterium to homo sapiens. How useful it would be in marketing to have the behavioral equivalent of DNA to guide inquiries into consumer behavior.

Indeed, what we have in this structure of human motivation is "the basic building blocks of human motivation." Beyond that, we have the basic building blocks of all human behavior.

People often ask if they can apply Silent Side methods to focus groups. When you are working with the basic building blocks of human behavior you can apply this methodology to all human behavior in any context. In the Appendix we show where it has been effectively applied to issues in law enforcement, management, and leadership. We have done some work in the area of attention deficit hyperactivity disorder (ADHD), but we are not in a position to say that it has been that effective. And, of course, the whole methodology originated in a clinical setting, where it was very effective in reversing a large number of psychological problems that at the time were considered intractable.

METHODOLOGY

The visualization method, which gives the interviewer considerable control and authority over the respondent, also gives the interviewer considerable responsibilities. The method that we are about to describe is not "fun" and it is not necessarily entertaining to the client. It is generally much easier to sit back, enjoy, and savor the camaraderie and fellowship of a friendly focus group, as opposed to spending time frantically searching for results. But it is not nearly as productive. Silent Side one-on-one interviewing is a results-oriented method, and clients are never reluctant to pay for a procedure that brings them results.

REFERENCE

Wolfe, D. (1999). Solving the riddle of consumer motivation. Available e-mail: dbwolfe@ix.netcom.com.

15

Interviewing on the Right Side of the Brain

BACKGROUND

The interview is critical to the success of the right brain research methodology. It is different from any other interview that is conducted in consumer research. The major difference, which is not unheard of but is rare, is that it takes data that are collected in a qualitative setting and transforms them into ordinal data that are quantified. The advantage of quantified data is that they can be entered into equations with other research, can be used to present graphic representations of motives, can be used to support marketing and management programs, and can be entered into Extended Motigraphics when larger sample sizes are required.

There are four cornerstones of right brain research:

- Visualization
- Relaxation
- Repetition
- Direction

These four techniques are administered in a one-on-one setting that lasts for about one hour. Each one is critical to the main issues, which are to (1) break through the resistance that all consumers have and (2) enter the unconscious mind of the consumer to uncover the real reasons why people do the things that they do, as opposed to the fancy and whimsical reasons that they make up in order to impress others. These separate procedures, which make up the body of the right brain interview, will expose the subliminal cues that were described in Chapter 3 as well as the motives which are involved in consumer buying behavior.

THE NEED TO GET BEHIND THE CONSUMER FACADE

Martin (1995) has discussed the failure of focus groups to deliver information that is useful to management in many cases. For example, Martin lists the products that would have never made it to the marketplace if marketers had listened to their customers in focus groups. Included in this group that would have never made it are the Chrysler minivan (the car of the 1980s), the microwave oven, fax machines, cellular telephones, VCRs, and Federal Express. In each case, the focus groups turned thumbs down on the product, but management turned thumbs down on the focus groups.

When medical advertising was new and novel, a focus group turned down a video spot which showed an individual unstrapping his artificial foot before he went to bed. The accompanying voiceover said, "Diabetes: give it an inch and it will take a foot." One opinion leader in the group was highly offended and he persuaded all other members of the group to go along with him. We were then asked to conduct right brain research on the same group members, plus a few more. The results were totally contradictory to the first group, and the agency took this as a green light to go ahead. Today, fifteen years later, the ad is still running and doing its job, and it has collected one Clio award and several other awards since that time.

There are many reasons why people can't (or won't) tell researchers the real reasons why they do what they do. Perhaps the most important reason is the fact that they don't know themselves. For example, when people are asked why they bungee jump or travel half way around the world to find a killer wave for surfing, they come up with rationalizations rather than real reasons. We can think of many different emotional reasons why they might do these things: to feel better about themselves, for sense of pride, to build self-esteem, to impress their friends, and so on. But their own answers are usually not related to this. This is because they are uncertain of why they do what they do, and as a result they provide rationalizations that don't really respond to the actual question: "I do it because it makes me feel better," or "Once I conquer a killer wave, I'm walking on top of the world." Conversely, right brain research has shown that one of the real reasons is because these kinds of activities (thrill seeking) build self-control and self-image, which the surfer or the bungee jumper may or may not know, and may or may not tell you, the interviewer.

One problem with most consumer research is that the researcher asks the customer to respond to a questionnaire or an interview format that is unnatural and generally removed from real life. For example, real people don't generally think in terms of five-, six-, or seven-point scales. Cognition is more fluid and liquified than that. It is not that rigid. This is another area where marketers have been lured into a false trap by psychologists; the trap being the oversimplification of human behavior and the *reductio ad absurdam* when it comes to explaining human motivation.

Another problem with standard market-research methodologies is that they involve contexts in which other people are around, and things being the way that they are most people like to impress others; particularly those they have never seen before and know that they may never see again. Schindler (1998) has shown that when a person receives a price break that they will experience what he calls "smart shopper feelings," and so the smart shopper phenomenon may be the focus of a lot of individual and group research even though it was not the original reason for the purchase. The motivation here would be to impress others who are in the focus group.

Still another problem is that motivation has never really been seriously studied by psychologists or marketers and we don't really know the categories that are important and significant when it comes to cataloging information. This is kind of like going about fifty miles out into the Gulf of Mexico and dropping a fishline over the side of the boat. This procedure may net a few fish. However, the smart fishermen, who are netting more than a few fish and a lot of big ones, use Loran and Global Positioning Finders (GPF). They mark the fishing holes (where the fish are) and return to the same place day after day, and that way there are no surprises. The parallel to this procedure in market research is asking questions to which we don't really know what the answers will be. Any first-year law student knows that this is an ill-advised procedure. The attorney who asks questions to which he does not already know the answer had better be prepared for a lot of surprises, and the courtroom is no place for surprises. Marketers should heed these lessons from fishermen and attorneys: Don't tread in areas where surprises may be looming. This advice may seem to be a little circular, but it is a basic tenant to right brain research. Since people can't tell you why they do what they do, we never ask why. We do ask who, what, when, where, and how. When we do, the why emerges. But not without the fish finder or a lie detector.

SUBLIMINAL CUES

In Chapter 3, we discussed subliminal cues, which form the basis for research into the unconscious mind. These subliminal cues are discovered in right brain research and are then grouped into the various motivational categories that were introduced earlier (Maddock & Fulton, 1996) and were discussed in more detail in Part II. The key to effective right brain research is the collection of subliminal cues and their subsequent classification into the right brain motives. This is what Motigraphics is all about.

One thing that right brain research allows us to do is to talk to people on their own terms, instead of some stilted and structured research format that is unfamiliar to them. People really talk in terms of the eleven motivational categories that we introduced in *Marketing to the Mind* (Maddock & Fulton, 1996) and which are further elaborated upon in this book. Therefore, we don't have to ask them questions and talk to them in terms that they don't really feel comfortable with.

The second advantage of right brain research is that we know what we are going after. Like the fisherman with a GPF, we know where the fishing holes are.

The most important consideration, however, when it comes to subliminal cues, is that for the right brain researcher they constitute the universe. Statisticians always talk about universes, and when they do they are talking about the bigger picture. When we say that subliminal cues are the universe what we are getting at is that, even though we do our research with people, our real concern and interest is with the subliminal cues that they already have in their heads. Marketers need to know this, and they need to know that people already have cues in their heads about their products and their services. The job of right brain research is to get them out and categorize them.

In a study of why women cook we interviewed twenty-one women. Would you, as a marketing manager, want to base your national marketing strategy on twenty-one women? Our client was frightened at this prospect. However, when it was explained to him that twenty-one women yielded a universe of 241 cues, he took a deep breath and relaxed. From that point on he felt perfectly comfortable with right brain research. His exact words were, "241 cues. That's quite a respectable sample!" The universe is subliminal cues.

In right brain research the actual multiplier appears to be between ten and twelve. In other words, a sample of eight will yield around 96 to 110 cues, which is also a respectable sample. So what may seem to be small samples ends up being fairly large and respectable. The number of subliminal cues in any one study is finite. This means that by the time we interview thirty or forty respondents in one demographic group we have just about reached a point of diminishing returns. We will most likely not find any additional subliminal cues. The only reason for interviewing more respondents in a project would be if the client wanted more demographic groups represented, since right brain research is sensitive to geography, sex, race, gender, and other standard demographics that are used in traditional research formats.[1]

RESPONDENTS FOR RESEARCH

Respondents are recruited in much the same way that they would be recruited for one-on-one research. We may want to consider demographics, psychographics, and other variables such as geographical product preferences and users versus nonusers. The difference is that we recruit far fewer respondents because we have the confidence that we are getting the same reliability and validity, since our universe is subliminal cues and not people. This not only lowers the overall cost of the project but also enables us to complete the project a lot quicker, since most marketers want their results yesterday. It also simplifies recruiting, which also lowers the overall cost of the project. Finally, when Motigraphics is added to the package, we end up not only with quality but with quantity.

INTERVIEWERS AND INTERVIEWER TRAINING

Respondents are seen in a one-on-one interview with a trained interviewer. The interviewer knows not only what questions to ask and, more importantly, what questions not to ask (no surprises!), but also knows how to catalog and categorize the motives. In other words, the interviewer can put the subliminal suggestions into the proper categories while he or she is conducting the interview. A computer program aids and assists with this task.

We are often asked how difficult it is to train interviewers. The answer lies not in an opinion but in the data. Anytime that qualitative data are being turned into quantitative data, there needs to be some kind of agreement, among judges or interviewers, as to which subliminal cues go into which motivational slots. In order to establish agreement, studies in interjudge agreement or reliability are normally conducted.

For right brain purposes, fifteen judges were given one hour of training in right brain motives and elements, and basic definitions were given. Then each judge received a preshuffled deck of seventy-six cards with statements on them. Each statement was numbered, from one to seventy-six. Judges were then given a list of the motives and told to match the statement number with each motive. Statements consisted of common, everyday cues that are often uttered by people who are in focus groups or seen in popular advertising. Some examples were as follows:

- I feel like my life is moving much too fast and I can't keep up (OR:[2] Circumstances).
- Delta Airlines gives you what you have the least of: time (OR: Time).
- I like to drive a hot, fast car (Sexual Survival: Impulse).

Other examples came from subliminal cues that were articulated by famous people, such as presidents, and which are almost universal in that they are widely remembered, whereas other statements of famous people are not remembered: Some of these examples were the following:

- I hate broccoli (George Bush, 1989, Physical Survival: Food).
- I'm not afraid of dying; I just don't want to be there when it happens (Woody Allen, Expectation/Resolution).
- I did not have sex with that woman, Monica Lewinsky (Bill Clinton, June 1998, Sexual Survival).
- I am not a crook (Richard Nixon, August 1974, OR: Person).
- Ask not what your country can do for you, but what you can do for your country (John F. Kennedy, Inaugural Address, January 1961, Spiritual Survival).

Studies in interjudge reliability are generally reported in terms of correlational studies. In this case, the correlation describes the linear relationship between the placement of the statements that were defined by an experienced interviewer and the statements placed in the same categories by inexperienced interviewers who received a one-hour review of the system and how it worked. These percentages of interjudge agreement are seen in Table 15.1.

Interjudge reliability is the measure of agreement between each judge and the criterion measure, which was established by the author. The overall percentage of agreement between each judge and the criterion measure was 83 percent. This is high, and the only disappointment was that two of the motivational categories were below 75 percent. One was expectation/resolution, which appeared to be a little difficult for some of the judges, and the other was physical survival. These two categories were confounded, since

Table 15.1
Percentage of Agreement with Motivational Categories Using
Fifteen Judges

Motives	Selected Elements	% Agreement
Personal Orientation	Self-control	86
Place Orientation	Location, facility, locale, area, residence	92
Time Orientation	Time, timing, urgency, beat (music)	78
Circumstances Orientation	Pace, circumstances	88
Spiritual Survival	Love, Patriotism, passion, commitment, family values	91
Physical Survival	Food, air, water, taste	60
Territorial Survial	Career, assets, income, greed, money	77
Sexual Survival	Impulse (bad), inhibition and impotence, gender	89
Adaptation	!mitation (of others), learning	98
Expectation/ Resolution	Future, trust, belief, death, resolution	71
Play	Enjoyment, impulse (good), fun, creativity	91

health care is an element of the Physical Survival Motive, and seeking out, finding, and trusting a physician or a surgeon is an element of the Expectation/Resolution Motive. This is an area that can be easily ironed out with just a little more training. In this study the group of judges had only one hour of exposure to the right brain system, and the results that were achieved are nothing short of remarkable and strongly support the simplicity of the overall system of motivations. The consequence of this is that interviewers can be trained easily and put to work, and their results, when correlated with other judges and interviewers, will be about 83-percent reliable when computed across categories and across judges who have learned the same system.

In addition to the reported percentages of agreement, convention dictates that such interjudge agreements should be reported in terms of correlation coefficients. In this case a chi-square statistic was computed for agreement and nonagreement, and the resulting chi-square was 30.33 ($p < 0.00076$). The results of this chi-square were then entered into the coefficient of contingency and the resulting correlation was $r = 0.86$. This correlation is very respectable and indicates that the overall system is clear, concise, and easy to learn. It is also consistent with the percentages of agreement that were reported.

Once an interviewer learns to do the interview, he or she must also be capable of identifying the cues, categorizing the statements, and matching them with the appropriate motivational category, with the assistance of a computer program. This computer program is currently being developed and is basically a contextual analysis program for analyzing verbal statements rather than numerical data. With a correlation coefficient of 0.86, it is anticipated that it will not be difficult to develop a program that is both reliable and valid.

THE FOUR DIMENSIONS OF RIGHT BRAIN INTERVIEWING

Visualization

We have already presented many of the basics in visualization. Visualization is used in order to get the respondent to relate to "pictures" in his or her mind's eye that the interviewer "paints" for him or her. A blindfold is used to expedite visualization and focusing, and it is very effective. If respondents are claustrophobic they are simply asked to close their eyes in order to visualize and this often works just as well. Interviewers who are just beginning feel rather strange about talking to someone with a blindfold on and they will often demonstrate that strange feeling by being rigid, reluctant, and intimidated. But they should not feel intimidated, since they are the ones who are in control. It can take a while to adjust to this.

Another problem with interviewers is that they are afraid that they will run into the individual—and there are a few of them—who cannot visualize, or who won't. This is generally seen in the person who says, "It's just all black. I don't see anything." The problem here is not that the person can't visualize; the problem is the same one that we meet over and over again: resistance. We get around the resistance with reassuring cues: "You will be able to see it clearly in a few seconds, so just relax and it will come." Or, "It will come into your mind's eye in just a minute or two, so just relax and let it come." Occasionally and very rarely a respondent will still not be able to see anything. The next step, if this occurs, is to tell him or her to "just pretend that they can see it." For example

R: I don't see a thing. It's all black.

I: Well, just pretend that you see it.

R: How do I do that?

I: You know, like when you were a kid. You pretended that you went some place, even though your parents told you that you couldn't go.

R: Oh yeah. Well, I see the boardwalk and the sand, and there are a lot of people on the beach.

I: Where are you? Are you on the beach? (Note use of present tense, addressing the respondent as if he is right there at this time.)

R: No, I'm on the boardwalk looking at the beach. (Note he is still somewhat resistant, since the interviewer wants him to be on the beach and he is on the boardwalk. However, he is moving in the right direction.)

I: Good. What does the beach look like from the boardwalk?

R: It looks inviting.

Only very occasionally and rarely will the interviewer encounter the individual who is totally resistant and defensive, and this person will have to be dismissed and let go from the interview. This is often seen in people who are clinically depressed. They respond in one- and two-word sentences. They are distant, affect (emotion) is flat, and at times they will even begin to cry. Depressed people need to be dismissed from the research and paid for their attempt to participate, and then replaced with a floater.

The other kind of defensive and resistant behavior is seen in people who come only for the money and have no interest in the interview at all. These people will usually be identified by the fact that they do not respond to cues and suggestions on the part of the interviewer. They are easily identified because they have no interest in the interview. These respondents are also rare, since those who are contacted are usually at least tangentially involved in the product or attraction and will therefore become involved and interested in the interview. These two kinds of individuals are rare, but the interviewer needs to be prepared for them. Remember, no surprises!

Relaxation

In right brain interviewing we are primarily interested in accessing the emotional, feeling, and intuitive part of the brain rather than the rational and logical side. We are interested in real reasons and not in rationalizations and justifications. Research tells us that these characteristics and capabilities are located primarily in the right prefrontal lobe of the human brain. This part of the brain thinks in pictures and not in words, since language is housed

in the left prefrontal lobe along with logic and analytical and rational thinking. Relaxation is a way to get into the right brain. When
an individual is relaxed they are much more likely to be intuitive
and emotional than rational and analytical. However, this is not always the case, and we need to remember at this point that everyone is
different and everyone has a different threshold at which they become
relaxed and more compliant. Therefore, each respondent has to be
treated differently in terms of where they are on a scale of relaxation. Nevertheless, it is our finding over the last twenty-five years
that regardless of how relaxed they are, they will generate subliminal suggestions when the interview is conducted properly.

A respondent is relaxed in a reclining chair. This encourages and
facilitates maximum relaxation. Before the respondent is put in a reclining position it is explained to him or her that this is a special kind
of interview. Most respondents who come in are expecting a focus group
because they have been to one or more focus groups in the past. What
is explained at this point is that the interview requires relaxation,
and that in order to help them to relax they will be blindfolded. A
standard sleep mask is used, the kind that is used by day-sleepers
and available in any department or drug store. After the interview
procedure is explained, the respondent is put in a reclining position in the chair with feet elevated, and then the mask is applied.

The first exercise directs respondents back to where they came
from, assuming it is their home. They are asked to imagine that
they are sitting in their favorite chair in their den, living room,
patio, or the like. Generally, we ask where their favorite chair is.
There are two reasons for this exercise. First, this is a strange procedure to most respondents, and they need to be reassured from
the very beginning. To do that, we take them to a place that is very
familiar to them, their own home. Then we ask them to describe
the room and everything around them in detail. This exercise usually takes up to about ten minutes. Respondents who are less verbal and/or less visual will tend to give a bleak and barren description
of the room and they need to be encouraged. Encouragement comes
in the form of "tell me more," or "you can see the walls now, the
paintings, the furniture, etc." The phrase, "you can see," is used
quite often as a way of encouraging respondents to keep responding and giving information. It is a reassuring method that is nonthreatening and noninvasive. The last thing that we want to do is
heighten their defenses. The whole idea behind relaxation is to lower
defenses so that we can access the right brain, in pictures rather
than in words. To accomplish this, the interviewer encourages the
respondent to "think" in pictures rather than words.

The second reason for this introductory procedure is that it gives
the respondent an introduction to visualization. For many this may

be the first opportunity that they have had to visualize on a formalized basis. Today more and more teachers, coaches, and memory trainers are making use of visualization in many different areas, particularly in sports (Van Kampen, 1992). Visualization is a valuable and necessary tool when attempting to enter the right brain and expose much of the material that we refer to as unconscious.

A third reason for visualization is that it gives the interviewer more control over the whole interviewing process. The major mistake that was made by marketers was that they took the basic concepts of humanistic psychology and incorporated them into focus groups. Humanistic psychology promotes the idea that everyone is equal and, given a relatively unstructured environment with nondirective leadership, everyone will put their best foot forward and exhibit positive motivations. There are many problems with humanistic psychology, but one of the most serious ones is that groups often bypass the designated leader and end up looking to the loudest mouth or the most opinionated person for leadership. Anyone who has been in a poorly managed focus group knows this and recognizes humanistic psychology for what it is. The leader must be in control. Consumer probing must be invasive, controlling, and directive in order to get results. This means that the focus group leader must be trained in getting the information from respondents that he or she is looking for and not the information the respondents want to give him or her. This is what leadership is all about.

Once the respondent is relaxed it is necessary for the interviewer to give him or her cues, on a timely basis, to continue to relax or that "you will feel more and more relaxed as we progress through this interview." At other times it may become necessary to cue the respondent to relax a specific part of his or her body. For example, respondents will often cross their arms, sometimes out of force of habit, but crossed arms are a sign of left brain resistance (Maddock & Fulton, 1995) and we try to undo that as soon as possible. The way this is done is to give the simple cue, "You may relax your arms now." Generally, the respondent gets the message immediately and will undo the defensive behavior. Believe it or not, a person who has his or her arms crossed is not listening to what you have to say. Some people make it a habit to stop talking to anyone with crossed arms until he or she agrees to uncross them.

Repetition

Repetition deals directly with the issue of going beyond what respondents tell us and into what they really mean. The importance of taking this rather circuitous route is clearly seen in the depositions and testimony of President Bill Clinton and others before the

independent counsel during the summer of 1998. Indeed, this repetition is the key to any courtroom testimony and also to a deposition. The attorney never takes the first response, but goes beyond
it. A simplified version of this is seen in marketing and is referred
to as *laddering*.

In Clinton's (1998) testimony, the principle of repetition is seen
when he is asked by the Special Counsel if he was ever "alone" in
the White House with Monica Lewinsky. This would seem to be a
very simple question, on the surface, requiring either a "yes" or
"no" response. Instead, the president went into a long description
of the Oval Office and the layout of various adjoining rooms, including a hallway, a service kitchen, stairs, and so on. An example
of how the principle of repetition applies is shown in this small
portion of a right brain interview:

Question: Where are you in your mind's eye?

Visualization: I am standing in front of the detergents in the Kroger store.

In this clip, we are attempting to take the woman through the decision-making process and we begin at the supermarket.

Question: What do you see?

Visualization: It's confusing . . . to say the least. There are all kinds of sizes, colors, boxes.

Question: What do you tell yourself about all of this confusion?

Visualization: It's hard to make a decision.

"What do you tell yourself" is typically used by interviewers in this kind of interviewing to get at auto-cues, or cues that the respondents give to themselves.

Question: What are you going to do?

Visualization: I think about it. I really don't think there is much of a difference between any of them.

Question: What makes you say that there is very little difference?

Visualization: It's just hype. Advertising. I don't pay much attention to advertising.

Question: What is it about adver-tising that you don't pay much attention?

Visualization: It's just hype; that's all.

This is an example of consumer resistance. Respondents want you to think that they are

Question: So what are you going to do?

Visualization: I just pick the Tide.

Question: What about the Tide makes you pick it?

Visualization: Well, I've seen this ad on TV where the kids are playing football and they come home and they're filthy. That's my kids. Then the lady shows the stuff after it comes out of the dryer.

rational people and they are not influenced by hype or by advertising of any kind. Everyone is influenced by advertising or else the industry would not exist.

She has already told us that she doesn't pay attention to TV or other advertising, but as it turns out, this is probably the number-one reason why she buys one detergent over another. It is also probably the number-one reason why she makes other purchase decisions.

Another brief clip illustrates this process. This one was in an interview that was done on front doors. In this case, management had committed itself to selling front doors to builders and to building supply houses. However, right brain research found out that the primary customer is the woman who buys the home, since she makes the decision. As a result, the company found a new customer, expanded its market, and set up "door stores" in affluent neighborhoods to cater to these customers.

Question: Did you tell me that you had a lot to say about the choice of the front door on your home?

Visualization: Absolutely.

Question: OK. You're right there now, talking with the builder. I want you to go back in your mind's eye, three years ago, when you built your home. You are talking with the builder. Where are you?

Visualization: I'm in the living room. It's just a skeleton. The walls aren't even in. The windows are leaning against the studs that will become walls.

Question: And what is the builder telling you?

Visualization: He said that these plain doors without windows are more serviceable.

This is regression, which is handled in the next section after this one. We attempt to take her back to the very scene where she made the decision and get her to visualize it. We encourage her to see a lot of details.

Question: What do you tell yourself about what he is saying?

Visualization: I don't like it.

Question: What about it don't you like?

Note "What about it don't you like," as opposed to "Why don't you like it." The interviewer never asks why.

Visualization: I want a window. It's my house. If you walk up and down this street and look at the homes, almost all of them have stained glass windows. I don't know why he is telling me this.

"Walk up and down the street and see how everyone has a window in their front door." This is the Adaptation Motive, which is doing what other people do.

Question: What do you tell yourself?

Visualization: It's my house. If there is no window, it makes the whole house appear uninviting. What would people say about me if my house was the only one on the street where there was no window in the front door?

"What would people say about me?" She is referring to herself, the person who lives in the house. This is the Orientation to Person Motive and is very important in helping her to make a purchase decision.

Question: What would they say?

Visualization: They would think that I was unfriendly, inhospitable, and that I did not want anything to do with them. They would not want to visit me. They would think that I was trying to exclude them.

In this response, she talks about the kind of person that other people would think that she was if she didn't have a window.

Question: What makes you say that?

Visualization: The door is the very center of the house. It expresses the personality of the house. At Christmas, Halloween, and other times, the front door lets people know that you are "in the spirit." It's the front door that sends a message to the whole neighborhood.

For many women, their home has a personality. The front door expresses this personality.

The repetition involved pursues every salient statement in order to find the underlying subliminal cue. For the lady buying a front door, there were a number of subliminal cues exposed.

- I can't be the only person without a window.
- They (neighbors and others) judge me by my front door.

- The front door sets the personality of the house.
- The front door sends a bold message to neighbors and others about the kind of person that lives there.
- The presence or absence of windows in the door sends a similar message.

The interviewer asks certain kinds of questions and makes certain kinds of statements in order to get to the subliminal cues or else to induce further relaxation so that more subliminal cues will surface. Some examples are the following:

Procedure	Interviewer Probe
Clarification and enhancing visualization	You are right there and you can see everything very clearly in your mind's eye. Do you feel as if you are right there?
Help respondent define reality. Reality for this person is not the field facility or the room he or she is in. Reality is where you say he or she is. Interviewer must continually reinforce this.	
Clarification and enhancing visualization	What color is it?
Find source of auto-cue	What are you telling yourself about it?
Find source of external cues	What are others telling you about it?
Expose feelings about the product	What do you like about (product)?
Enhance visualization and reality	What about it don't you like?
	What about it makes it different from the others?
	Tell me what you see.
	Tell me what you hear.
Enhance relaxation	You will relax even more, and feel even more relaxed in a few minutes.
	You are feeling so relaxed now.
Enhance regression	Go back to when you felt that way.
	Go back to when you first saw one of them.
Rule out or block out any background noise or interference.	Nothing bothers you and nothing disturbs you.

It is extremely important that the interviewer understand that reality for the respondent is not the present situation (field facility, reclining chair, etc.). Reality for one hour is wherever the interviewer takes this person and "what they see in their mind's eye." When conducting interviews for recreational facilities and retirement communities or other attractions, people often felt so good about what they saw that when it was over they refused to take the money (honorarium). They would walk out with a feeling of being uplifted and renewed.

Whenever the interviewer finds a subliminal cue it is recorded using a laptop computer and then printed on a 3 × 5 card. The constant repetition that occurs in these interviews is how we get to the bottom line in right brain interviewing. However, it also makes these interviews very difficult to watch, because they are so tedious and repetitious. Many people thought, when they found out that the O. J. Simpson trial in 1996 would be televised, that they would see a real-life drama comparable to what is seen on television every night, with disclosures, resolutions, and theatrical embellishments. Instead, what they saw was a repetitious and boring performance on the part of the attorneys and the judge, some of whom were competent and others who were not. As attorneys often will do (never on TV) they read from notes that they had jotted down on legal pads. All of this led to a very disappointing and monotonous exhibition which generated little interest until the very last days of the trial. Right brain interviews are similar. They are also hard work for the interviewer. They are different, but the work that goes into a right brain interview pays off in the end in terms of marketable recommendations and increased sales. This is because most people are influenced by the Silent Side; that is, the right temporal lobe, in making buying decisions. This is especially true when that decision involves spending a lot of money, as on a big ticket item that will supposedly last for a long, long time.

There are two other examples of interviews later in this chapter. One of them deals with a person's first automobile, and the other deals with casino visitation.

Direction

Direction is the fourth cornerstone to the right brain research methodology. In order to understand the emotions and the feelings that people have about a particular product, service, or anything else, it is necessary to take a person back to certain times in their life and get them to visualize their first experience with the product. This is because subliminal cues originate at many different "plot points" in a person's lifetime.

In work done with a newspaper, respondents were directed to the first experience that they had with the newspaper. It was predicted that they would regress to the first or second grade, after they had learned to read. Surprisingly, they went back beyond that, sometimes as far back as four years old, before they had learned to read. What we found out was that many of them spontaneously regressed to a time when they could not read but were able to enjoy the pictures, particularly those that are in the Sunday newspapers. Subsequent research with other newspapers and also with other products supported this and showed that the best readers often get started with graphic formats, long before they learn to read words and sentences (McKay & Neale, 1985; Cipielewski & Stanovich, 1992).

Direction from one place to the other can be enhanced by getting the respondent to visualize a clock on which the hands go backward instead of forward, or by visualizing a calendar in which the pages go backward in time. When this is done, the interviewer needs to make sure that the visualization is clear, and it is the interviewer's job to "paint the picture" of the clock or calendar as clearly as possible so that it seems real to the respondent. This further enhances the direction.

Keep in mind that we are looking for the emotion that is attached to the product. People usually form emotional attachments at many major points in their lives. For example, with car buyers we found that the earliest attachments were formed before the age of five. This is not surprising, since toy cars and trucks make up a very large part of the toy market. We need to go back to that point in order to describe and understand the emotions that are involved in the product. Why do we need to understand the emotions involved in the product? Simply because emotions are an important part of brand equity. Feig (1997) says that the emotional investment that customers have in a brand is an important part of a brand's equity. Our own unpublished research has shown that, in terms of Motigraphics scores, the emotion involved in a product is at least 50 percent of that product's brand equity. The reason why you don't hear about brand equity anymore is because so much of any brand's equity involves the emotional investment that the customers have in the brand and that has built up over the years, and no one has figured out, until now, how to measure it.

In 1989, one of the most revered names in U.S. history was sold on the steps of the U.S. District Court in Tampa. That name was Chris-Craft. To many boaters and nonboaters alike, this name ranks right up there with Ford, GM, and IBM. Since the company had experienced, in the 1980s, a series of owners who cut corners and turned out defective products, the bankruptcy judge felt that there was nothing left but the name, and the bidding would not reach $20 million. But he underestimated the equity involved in the brand!

There were two bidders, Hatteras Yachts and Outboard Marine Corporation. Outboard Marine eventually topped the bidding at $53 million and now owns the company (Rodengen, 1998).

During the previous decade, in which Chris-Craft was floundering, there were a number of cracked and blistered hulls which resulted from defective fiberglass layup processes, and these defective hulls brought on lawsuits by the boat owners. For this reason, the judge underestimated the equity in the brand. What was the equity? Almost a century of emotion and name recognition. To many, Chris-Craft is still the only name in boating. This is why Motigraphics measures emotion.

Up to this point we have discussed in some detail the methodology of right brain research. This methodology involves four strategic dimensions: visualization, relaxation, repetition, and direction. It is now time to move away from straight methodology and look at the content of the interview and the method of sorting statements into content categories or motives. This is the unique part of right brain research and to date, what no other research offers.

CONTENT AND THE SORT

Background

We have researched and established the categories that we refer to as motives that allow us to convert qualitative data to quantitative data that are meaningful and lead to recommendations and suggestions. The interviewer attends to the needs of the respondent (need to be more relaxed, need to visualize, need to regress further, etc.) and each time a subliminal cue is identified it is recorded and later printed on a 3 × 5 card. Although at one time the interviewer did the sort as he or she was interviewing, this can be rather difficult for some people. With the interviewer concentrating upon the respondent and the questions, as well as writing down the subliminal cues, he or she has enough to do. Also, it was found that when cues are sorted after all of the interviews have been concluded the whole process of sorting goes very quickly. Subliminal cues are quickly and readily assigned to motives.

The criteria for the identification of subliminal cues does not include opinions, attitudes, prejudices, biases, or other rational categories. We said at the beginning of this chapter that this is not our major interest. The criteria for the identification of a subliminal cue is whether it fits into a motivational category. This is not a problem. Our judges had less than one hour of training and within that time they mastered the task. Here, for purposes of illustration, we have listed some statements and the categories that they fit into. A few will be seen to fit into two categories. In most cases, the element associated with the motive is identified also, since elements are more concrete and therefore easier to identify and recognize.

Now is the time for all good men to come to the aid of their country.	OR: Time and Spiritual Survival (patriotism)
I love to eat.	Physical Survival: food
I trust my doctor to do the right thing.	Expectation: health care
I look forward to the future and whatever it will bring.	Expectation: future
I look after my territory and protect it with everything that I have.	Territorial Survival
A person's home is their castle.	Territorial Survival
I like sex.	Sexual Survival: impulse
I like a hot, fast car.	Sexual Survival: impulse
I keep careful track of all of my assets, income, and expenses.	Territorial Survival
I am not the kind of woman that goes to bars and picks up men.	OR: Person
I like to go someplace different on vacation, just for a change of place and scenery.	OR: Place
I listen to people when they tell me what to buy, and I often do what they say.	Adaptation Motive: testimonial
I love to play.	Play Motive
I always eat all my vegetables.	Physical Survival: food
I want everyone to know the kind of person that I am.	OR: Person
A woman is what a woman wears.	OR: Person
I am passionate about Jesus.	Spiritual Survival: passion
I am passionate about golf.	Spiritual Survival: passion
When I look into the future I see all kinds of opportunities.	Expectation Motive: future
I work at my job eighteen hours a day.	Territorial Survival: career
I want a sensuous woman.	Sexual Survival: impulse
Revlon is sensuous spices.	Sexual Survival: impulse
I like my play time.	Play Motive

To me, cooking is fun and enjoyment. It's like playtime for me.	Play Motive: fun
December 7, 1941. A day that will live in infamy (Franklin D. Roosevelt, December 7, 1941).	OR: Time
Everybody wants to get where they ain't, and then when they get there they want to get back home again (Henry Ford, 1919).	OR: Place
When I am in the casino I lose all track of time.	OR: Time
I want to be the type of woman that everyone looks up to.	OR: Person
For everything there is a season; a time to live and a time to die.	OR: Time
In the future I know that I will do better.	Expectation Motive: future
I worry a lot about my health and physical problems.	Physical Survival: health
Follow the leader. Do what he tells you to do.	Adaptation Motive
If a man in a white coat on TV tells me what medicine to take, I usually try it.	Adaptation Motive
I often lose track of time.	OR: Time
I was taught to clean my plate and I still do it.	Physical Survival: food
I would give up watching the Superbowl for good sex.	Sexual Survival: impulse
I bought a Honda because everyone says that's the best.	Adaptation Motive: testimonial
The teacher said that I should read this book, so I did.	Adaptation Motive
I consider myself to be an understanding and caring person.	OR: Person
I am passionate about my family and I put them first in my life.	Spiritual Survival: family values
I am looking for some fun and some play time in my life.	Play Motive
The circumstances of my life are often just too much for me to cope with.	OR: Circumstances
I am sometimes overwhelmed by the pace of my lifestyle.	OR: Circumstances

Federal Express sells you what you have the least of, time.	OR: Time
Read my lips: No new taxes (George Bush, 1987).	Territorial Survival: money
I am the kind of person who always tells the truth.	OR: Person
Cooking a good meal is a way that I can show my family that I love them.	Spiritual Survival: family values and love
Because you care about what's riding on your tires (Michelin Tire).	Spiritual Survival: family values and love
A diamond is the best way that a man can show his love to a woman.	Spiritual Survival: love
When I buy a car I am influenced by what my friends have told me and by the cars that they drive.	Adaptation Motive: testimonial
When I go to my doctor I expect absolute quality of care; nothing but the best.	Expectation Motive: health care
Life moves too fast for me.	OR: Circumstances: pace
A drink at the end of the day helps me to forget all of the circumstances of the day.	OR: Circumstances
When I look at travel brochures I dream of being in a different place.	OR: Place
The times that we live in are depressing because of all the crime.	OR: Time
I like to wear sensuous gowns and dresses that turn men's heads.	OR: Person and Sexual Survival: impulse
When I am driving my four-wheel-drive truck (with big tires) it makes me feel more like a man.	Sexual Survival: gender
I love springtime.	OR: Time
Sometimes I feel as if circumstances are crowding in on me.	OR: Circumstances: pace
Although I know better, at times I dream that Ed McMahon will come knocking on my front door.	Expectation Motive: resolution
Whenever I go to the casino I plan on winning big bucks.	Expectation Motive: resolution
I need to bring some closure to my life.	Expectation Motive: resolution
When I grow up I plan to be a nurse.	Expectation Motive: future
I am not the kind of person who wears their feelings on their sleeve.	OR: Person

Every time I position myself where the president can see me, I get a call from him soon afterward (Monica Lewinsky, *Starr Report*).	OR: Place Sexual Survival: impulse
I let time escape me, at times.	OR: Time
In the last few weeks, the stock market has become a roller coaster. I fear for my personal assets.	Territorial Survival: assets
My career means almost everything to me.	Territorial Survival: career
Lifting weights and measuring my biceps makes me feel more like a man.	Sexual Survival: gender
Is it possible for a man to be sexually harassed?	Sexual Survival: gender

SETUP

Generally, the interviewer works from a preestablished format, much like a focus group format. Such a format may be designed as follows:

Explain difference between Silent Side interview, focus group, one-on-one interview

Explain visualization and access to the right brain

Introductory exercise

> Take respondents through their home, favorite chair, and so on

First age regression

> First time respondent had experience with the product

Second age regression

> Another time respondent had experience with the product

Third age regression

> A third time the respondent had experience with the product

Fourth age regression

> Last time that respondent had experience with the product

Visualization

> Take respondent to supermarket and through the steps of decision making, picking the product off the shelf, and so on

An outline is made up differently for each client, depending upon the needs and special requirements of the client. Once the client has approved the interview guide, the same guide is used in all of the interviews.

ACTUAL INTERVIEW EXCERPTS

Two excerpts from interviews are included at this point so that the interviewer can get some idea as to how the interview proceeds. The first is on automobiles, and the lady has been instructed to go back to when her parents were purchasing her very first car. This tells us what a person first attends to when they purchase a car and what features and benefits are important to them. The reason this is important in right brain research is because, although needs change over the years, some things remain sacred and fixed. Also, as people grow older they seek to satisfy the needs they had when they were younger that went unfulfilled. Take, for example, the number of old people who belong to motorcycle clubs and who are doing things that they never got to do when they were younger.

Visualization: I want a Triumph Spitfire. They were convertibles, had a black convertible top. I think it was a 1965. It had to be bright red and green.

Interviewer puts her in the situation where she was selecting her first car, and speaks in the present tense.

Question: What about that is important?

Visualization: That was a hot color. That was the color I had to have.

What's important about bright red and green?

Question: What about that color is hot?

Visualization: It was just popular. It was cool. It was *the* color.

Question: Tell me what it is about the car that's so great.

"It's cool and hot." Hot refers to Sexual Survival—Impulse Motive, cool refers to the Adaptation Motive; that is, what everyone else has.

Visualization: Well, it was a lot of fun to drive. I drove it pretty fast. I used to pile a lot of people in that car; three in front and two in the little tiny place in the back. We were kind of wild in those days.

"Fun to drive." Play Motive.

"We were wild." Sexual Survival—Impulse.

Question: What makes it so fun to drive?

Visualization: It's small. You can just zip in and out.

Question: What's important about small?

Visualization: It was a sports car. Small is comparable to a sports car. It was just sporty.

Small equals sporty equals young. This is the Orientation to Person Motive since she is talking about herself, her youth, her needs. She wants her car to reflect her and her personality.

Question: What's important about it being sporty?

Visualization: I was young. It was great
to be young and drive a sporty car.

Question: What do you tell yourself
about having a car like that?

Visualization: That I was lucky to have   "A car that other people wish
a car that other people wish they had.   they had." This is the
                                                 Adaptation Motive. It's
                                                 what everyone else wants.

In this interview, almost everything she says can be retrieved by
the interviewer and written down as a subliminal cue. Many of
these are in terms of belief systems that she has.

- It had to be bright red and green.
- That was a hot color. That was the color I had to have.
- It was just popular. It was cool. It was *the* color.
- Well, it was a lot of fun to drive.
- We were kind of wild in those days.
- It's small. You can just zip in and out.
- It was a sports car. Small is comparable to a sports car. It was just
  sporty.
- I was young. It was great to be young and drive a sporty car.
- I was lucky to have a car that other people wish they had.

Although right brain interviewing may appear difficult at first,
the interviewer has to realize that people really talk in these terms.
They talk about themselves, what they want, time, place, their territory, sex, what they think is fun, sports, and so on. When they do
this they are not just filling in time. They are talking about what is
really important to them and, more important, about what really
motivates them.

The second interview is an excerpt from one that was done on
casino visitation. We have included only that part of the interview
that represents a breakthrough. The first part of the interview is
repetitious and consists mostly of rational, left brain material. This
does not mean that it is void of subliminal cues. However, what we
want to illustrate here is the breakthrough, where the lady real-
izes that it is not winning that attracts her, but instead the orientation issues and also peace of mind (spiritual survival).

Question: Visualize being in a casino.
You're playing with the quarters.

Visualization: I put in a quarter and push that button and see those things spin around. I'm anticipating some kind of win.

"Anticipating some kind of win." This is the Expectation Motive. It is well-known to casino management, but it is usually a rationalization.

Question: Well, what do you tell yourself about that?

Visualization: I'm real excited.

More Expectation.

Question: You're excited. What else?

Visualization: Yeah. I keep thinking if I don't win, then I'll put another quarter in. Maybe this time.

More Expectation.

Question: As you keep telling yourself "maybe the next one," what do you feel inside?

Visualization: It's exciting.

More excitement.

Question: It's exciting and what else?

Visualization: It's exciting and fun to me. Now, this may sound crazy, but it's relaxing too!

"This may sound crazy, but it's relaxing too!" Here's the breakthrough. The interviewer must get her to clarify what she means by "relaxing."

Question: It's relaxing? OK. Now you're feeling relaxed too, aren't you?

Visualization: It's like when I go down there and I'm playing slot machines, I'm totally relaxed. I noticed that the very first time I went down there. When I was plunking those quarters into those machines, I thought of nothing else. It was like it consumed me. I forgot about all of my problems at home, all my work I needed to be doing. It was just me and that machine!

She now refers to the real reason that she goes to the casinos: Disorientation. In this case she said that she is "consumed," which means that she is disoriented in all four spheres: person, place, time and circumstances.

Question: What is it about the cards that is so difficult for you?

Visualization: I don't know because I've never really been taught. I've never really had an interest in card games.

Question: What is it about the cards that doesn't interest you?

Visualization: You know, I really don't know.

The interviewer moves on to table games. In this case, she is telling us that she does not want to look stupid in front of other people. However, O'Brien (1998) says that the slots were "mindless," and if disorientation is the issue, we are strongly inclined to

Question: Well what do you think it is?

Visualization: It's just too complicated for me.

Question: It's too complicated?

Visualization: It *seems* complicated. I do know how to play blackjack. That's the only one that I do know how to play. But I do not know how to bet. That's the problem.

Question: What's the problem?

Visualization: I don't know how to bet.

agree. He says Bennett literally "took an axe to the baccarat tables, declaring that casino gaming was no longer a "Frank Sinatra business" (p. 39).

She is saying that even though she knows how to play, she would not play and comes up with another excuse. Clearly, she would have to remain oriented if she was going to move up to table games, which would undo the whole experience for her and defeat the purpose of her visit.

Management has responded to people not knowing how to bet by offering courses in various table games. This is a rational approach to an irrational situation. Clearly, this interview shows that the respondent comes to the casino to be disconnected, and she engages in a mindless activity, which is watching the windows rotate as she pulls the lever. Table games would reintroduce the need to be connected and oriented, which is just what she wants to escape from.

The interviewer may feel that at times he or she is performing some kind of a juggling act, for he or she has to keep the respondent on task at all times. Several different functions are being performed at the same time:

- The interviewer keeps the respondent relaxed.
- The interviewer keeps the respondent regressed, until such time as it is appropriate to bring the respondent back to the present time.
- The interviewer continually reassures the respondent that he or she is relaxed and comfortable, is not disturbed by any kind of outside noises or other interferences, can visualize and see very clearly what the interviewer wants him or her to see, feels as if he or she is right there at the time when it is happening, and undoes any competing behaviors, such as crossed arms or legs, or the like.
- The interviewer needs to remember that he or she has complete control over the respondent, and that almost any cue or suggestion given by the interviewer will have an impact. Therefore, the interviewer needs to be very careful about what cues are given and what suggestions are made.

CONCLUSION

At the end of the interview, something very important happens: The respondent needs to be brought back to reality. Reality, in this case, is the room in which the interview is taking place, the purpose, and the reason. An interviewer may mistakingly assume that since he or she is in tune with reality that the respondent is also. This is not the case. The respondent may have gone back twenty years, or may be in their garden or in a supermarket standing in front of a shelf. Therefore, at the end of the interview it is important and incumbent upon the interviewer to bring the respondent back to reality. This is done by a simple command: "We have now completed our interview. I am going to count to three, and when I do you will remove the face mask and blink your eyes, since you will find that it is very bright in this room. At the count of three you will take off the face mask and blink your eyes and look over at me."

NOTES

1. The relationship between the number of respondents in a study and the number of subliminal cues that are generated is best illustrated by a curvilinear relationship like this:

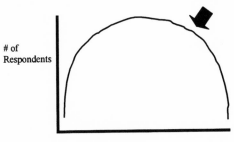

Subliminal Cues

This curvilinear relationship between the number of respondents and subliminal cues indicates that the more respondents there are in a study the more subliminal cues—up to a point. After that point, which is located at the position of the arrow, diminishing returns are to be expected. From that point on, there is considerable repetition of the subliminal cues, and there is no appreciable gain from adding more respondents.

Subliminal cues are collected during the interviews. They are defined and identified in terms of the Silent Side Motives that were introduced and reviewed in Part II. People actually talk in terms of orientation to person, place, and time; in terms of adaptation and expectation; and in terms of the various Survival Motives. This means that these motive are easily defined and placed in categories just by listening to ordinary, everyday conversation and writing down what people say. It is effective in any context, not just that of marketing.

2. OR refers to the Person, Place, Time, and Circumstances categories that fall under the Orientation Motive.

REFERENCES

Cipielewski, J., & Stanovich, K. E. (1992). Predicting growth in reading ability from children's exposure to print. *Journal of Experimental Child Psychology, 54,* 748.

Clinton, W. J., President of the United States. (1998). Testimony before the Grand Jury empaneled for Independent Counsel Kenneth Starr (released September 21). *Jurist: The Law Professors' Network* [online]. Available: http://jurist.law.pitt.edu/.

Feig, B. (1997). *Marketing straight to the heart: From product to positioning to advertising—how smart companies use the power of emotion to win loyal customers.* New York: American Management Association.

Maddock, R. C., & Fulton, R. L. (1995). *The silent side of communication.* Des Moines, IA: American Media (video and workbook).

Maddock, R. C., & Fulton, R. L. (1996). *Marketing to the mind: Right brain strategies in advertising and marketing.* Westport, CT: Quorum Books.

Martin, J. (1995). Ignore your customer. *Fortune, 131,* 8, 121 (4).

McKay, M. F., & Neale, M. D. (1985). Predicting early school achievement in reading and hand writing using major "error" categories from the Bender-Gestalt Test for young children. *Perceptual and Motor Skills, 60,* 634–47.

O'Brien, T. L. (1998). *Bad bet: The inside story of the glamour, glitz and the danger of America's gambling industry.* New York: Times Books.

Rodengen, J. (1998). *The Legend Chris-Craft.* Ft. Lauderdale, FL: Write-Stuff Syndicate, Inc.

Schindler, R. (1998). Consequences of perceiving oneself responsible for obtaining a discount: Evidence for smart-shopper feelings. *Journal of Consumer Psychology, 7,* 371–92.

Van Kampen, K. (1992). *Visual golf.* New York: Simon & Schuster.

————————— 16

Motigraphics

Until you've measured something, you don't know what you're talking about.

—Lord Baron Kelvin

WHY EMOTIONS AND MOTIVATION HAVE NOT BEEN MEASURED

The measurement of motives is something that was long ago placed on the back burner and never brought to the front. There are probably several reasons for this:

- Motives are situational, and therefore illusive. They vary from one situation to another.
- Motives are associated closely with emotion, and emotion is difficult to study and even more difficult to contain or measure.
- Motives originate in the unconscious and the unconscious has never been measured.
- People can't tell you why they do what they do. Some other method of investigation must evolve before we can grasp the whole notion of motivation.
- There was no adequate definition of motives.

As a result of this postponement and the failure to study motives and motivation, the richness and abundance that students of psychology expect to see is absent. Instead, there is a vacant quality about the descriptions of behavior that we get from psychologists, since there is no depth or dimension to the explanations. It is sterile and dull and colorless. Students in introductory psychology can come away from the course with a feeling of disappointment because they sometimes feel like something has been overlooked, or left out.

What we get in marketing today is descriptive and not explanatory. We are told how, what, where, and when, but never why. And what is amazing is that students of marketing and management don't see this critical flaw until it is pointed out to them, and then it's like a ray of light begins to shine: "I never noticed that before."

Law enforcement personnel notice. So do salespersons and people who have to deal with motivation on a day-to-day basis. When law enforcement officials have a perplexing and difficult crime, they sometimes call psychics, not psychologists. Salespeople often call in self-appointed sales trainers, who have very little formal education but usually do a great job at what they say that they can do: training people to sell and to recognize and take advantage of the hot buttons in sales and marketing situations. But usually it is very difficult to assess motivation, and the marketer often has to do a lot of guessing in his or her attempts to write a marketing plan or to make meaningful changes in a business plan.

How would a casino manager know to throw out tables and put in more slots? How would a restaurant owner know to open for breakfast, as well as lunch and dinner? How would an air express carrier know to expand into foreign markets? Typically, when you ask people if they would like to have more services or expanded facilities they always agree that they would. But too many marketers have believed what people told them and then when they tried it things did not work out.

Motigraphics is the recognition, classification, and measurement of motives. When motives are measured, we are able to know not only what people want and what they expect, but how strongly they want it. We can also get people to respond to an idea or to a product or service that does not exist, through visualization, and then measure the motives and design that product around the emotions and motivations that are expressed. This is called *projection*, and it is the best way to get customers to design a new and novel concept that they have never seen or encountered before.

MEASURING CONSUMER RESPONSE

When Federal Express started out in 1972, they started in Little Rock, not Memphis, which is where they are now. Prior to opening they sent out salesmen who asked people, primarily those in business, if they would use an overnight express company that delivered documents and small packages the next day—guaranteed. The response was beyond enthusiastic. However, when the company actually started flying, the results were very disappointing. They closed down their Little Rock operation in about a week. The company became successful when consultants examined passenger and freight manifest records from the Federal Aviation Administration and from other sources. These same consultants also urged management to move to a more central location and to start out with cities that had heavy traffic. When this was accomplished, Federal Express opened with a bang instead of a whimper.

Generally, when you ask people if they would like a new product they will say yes, but that doesn't mean that they will use it. Even if they say they will use it, the results of many surveys are suspect. Often the questions are not asked in the proper manner. We have asked people to describe and draw a "real bank." We have asked them, "Where are the real Ozarks?" and "Where is the real seashore?" The point is that they will respond to any question that is asked. No one ever stopped us and said, "What do you mean, the real seashore? What kind of a question is that?"

In focus groups, we have already looked at the fact that participants may be negative or they may be positive, and much of this depends upon the opinion leader in the group. Similarly, we have found that when people watch a videotape of a news anchor or of some politician and are told to press a button when he says something that is annoying or agitating, they will do it. But where is the reliability check? We have also found that the same thing occurs on a Likert-type instrument with five, seven, or nine choices. They will circle one and only one of the categories on each question. But how do you know if what you are getting is reliable and valid?

Most of these methods are valid in situations that simply want an opinion of certain features of a product or service. For example, the little survey that you see on the television when you check out of a motel is a quick way of gathering opinions about services and attempting to determine whether the customer was happy or unhappy. Sometimes these kinds of surveys will even focus on a glaring weakness in service delivery. The fact that they lack reliability and validity is not a real issue in these situations. They yield a "quick and dirty" assessment of the level of customer service that is being measured.

But there are places where the marketer does not want to use instruments that are not valid and reliable, and which do not go into depth in their assessment of a service or product. This is the case in launching a new product where big dollars are about to be spent, or perhaps when moving into foreign markets. It is absolutely the case when money has already been spent on a product, service, or advertising message, or where it is about to be spent. It is the case when an older brand is about to be either abandoned or resurrected. There are many other situations where reliability and validity are essential.

WHAT MOTIGRAPHICS MEASURES THAT OTHER PROCEDURES DON'T MEASURE

Brand Equity

With Motigraphics, we are capable of measuring the equity that is contained in a brand, since the equity that a brand holds within it is usually about 50 percent emotion. The story of Chris-Craft, detailed in Chapter 15, strongly supports this observation. This is why, in measuring motives, we always attempt to go back to the beginning of the brand's life. This is often accomplished by going back to the beginning of the customer's life, or as far back as we can get. We have worked with many old products that have been long abandoned and where management had no idea what emotions were still involved in the brand when they abandoned it. Many of these emotions were from childhood and from the first time that the brand was ever introduced. Even if there are no plans to reintroduce the product, if the product or trademark is sold, Motigraphics will assess the emotion that is involved in the brand and this can be factored into the brand's selling price. Failure to do this results in leaving money on the table. Hence, the use of Motigraphics with a brand generally results in found new money.

Customer Benefits

Motigraphics measures brand benefits. Focus groups, surveys, and most of the electronic methods usually measure brand features. Brand features are what the customer wants and, for the most part, he or she is able to tell us what he or she wants. Brand benefits consist of what the product does for the customer, and for the most part the customer cannot tell us about what the product does for him or her. This information is "extracted" using Silent Side research. Of the two kinds of brand information, benefits (to the consumer) are more important than features (of the product). This is because most consumer decisions are made on the basis of emotion and not reason. Silent Side research is the only process available today that taps pure emotion.

Subliminal Cues

The foundation for this whole procedure is subliminal cues. This was seen in Chapter 15. We will also see, in the Appendix, where attempts to define and describe criminal and other pathological behaviors fall short of the mark because subliminal cues are not recognized. When this happens, motivation is not recognized and what results is a description of the phenomenon but not explanation. This is why law enforcement personnel call on psychics rather than psychologists.

The importance of subliminal cues in customer services lies in the fact that customers already have subliminal cues in their minds about products. We have done research on products in markets where the product did not even exist. However, the respondents still had subliminal cues in their minds about the product. If these cues did not relate directly to the brand that was being researched, they did relate directly to the generic of the brand.

If people already have subliminal cues in their minds about you and your product, then you need to know what they are. If they are negative and adverse they can't be dispensed with, but they can be replaced! If they are not replaced they will continue to grow, ulcerate, and become inflamed, infecting other people who are in touch with the person who is the carrier of these negative cues. In other words, negative subliminal cues spread like a communicable disease.

Customer Motivation

What motivates your customer, and why is motivation important? Since we have gotten along so well without any knowledge of motivation or emotion, the question often encountered is, "Why do we need to know about motivation?" Motives are what move your customer toward action. Your customer is motivated to buy or not to buy. He or she is motivated to bank at your bank, rather than at your competitor's bank. Motives lead directly to decisions and decisions lead to action. Motives are important because they are only one step removed from action. The only thing that lies between a motive and "buy–no buy" action is the decision.

Customer Loyalty

Customer and brand loyalty are often difficult to get a handle on and very hard to measure. It has been our experience that these qualities are best measured and described with Motigraphics. This is because both customer loyalty to a service and loyalty to a brand

are heavily based in emotion and motivation and what the customer feels about a brand but either cannot or will not express. For
example, a customer may feel very loyal to Pillsbury brands of baking provisions because of the Pillsbury Doughboy (a graphic subliminal cue), but embarrassed to say this, particularly in a focus
group. However, this will inevitably come out in Silent Side interviewing and then can be measured in Motigraphics.

In research that we have carried out for clients we almost always
find a group of motives that account for customer and/or brand loyalty. These are the motives which, as a group, account for customers who are fiercely and intently loyal to the product and to a
particular brand. These are the customers who keep coming back,
over and over again, in spite of the competition's attempts to pull
them away. We refer to the motives that characterize this group as
"the loyalty group" of motives.

Usually, the loyalty group of motives includes elements from both
the Personal Orientation Motive and the Spiritual Survival Motive.
For example, in a study on choice of a location in real estate and in
another study on beer drinking, elements from both of these motives
were prominent. These motives are shown in Figures 16.1 and 16.2.

Customer loyalty is always defined in terms of motives and motivation because it is the only way to define it. The elements that define a
loyal and devoted customer have always been illusive because motives have never been clearly defined. Motigraphics allows us not only
to define but also to measure the motives that are involved in customer and brand loyalty, brand equity, and customer dependability.

Customer Tracking

Motives change with time. For example, in the last four years
women's shoes have taken on a more masculine appearance. More
women are wearing boots and shoes that are very comparable to
what men are wearing. Similarly, more men are wearing sandals,
which at one time was considered to be appropriate only for women.
Since motives are only one step removed from decisions and action,
tracking studies can be carried out which track the change in customer motives and overall motivation. Using Motigraphics to do
this would add one more dimension to the customer profile, and
with three, four, or five tracking studies we would be able to make
some very valid predictions of what is going to happen in the future. For example, let us suppose that white women prefer athletic
shoes and heavy boots more than black women, who prefer foot-
wear that is more feminine and less restrictive. Will the one group
influence the other group? Will this kind of demographic difference

Figure 16.1
The Loyalty Group of Beer Drinking

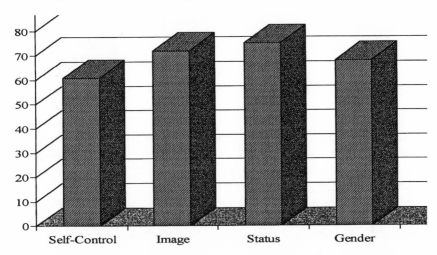

Numbers on the left axis are T-scores, with a mean of 50 and a standard deviation of 10.

Figure 16.2
The Loyalty Group of Real Estate Location

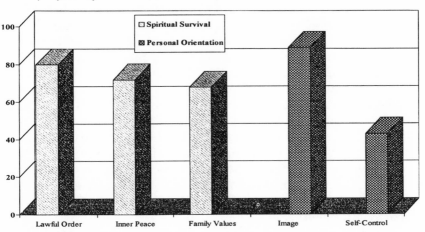

Numbers on the left axis are expressed in T-scores, which have a mean of 50 and a standard deviation of 10.

effect motivational differences? Most tracking studies will also look at interactions between demographics, psychographics, and Motigraphics, and changes over time in these interactions.

THE METHOD OF MOTIGRAPHICS

Subliminal Cues

As described in Chapter 15, we start with subliminal cues. Subliminal cues are collected by the interviewer during the process of conducting the interview. They are printed on 3 × 5 cards, using a program that generates these cards. On Windows NT, 95, or 98, *FileMaker Pro* can be modified to do this, as can some word processing programs.

How do you uncover a subliminal cue? In Chapter 15 we showed that this procedure is not difficult, and that is because we have a very simple and straightforward structure. The structure is the eleven-motive inverted building blocks. Subliminal cues are uncovered mainly through repetition. Seventy or eighty subliminal cues were paired with motives in Chapter 15, so that the reader could see the match between the categories and the cues.

Sorting Subliminal Cues

This involves converting qualitative data to quantitative data which lie on an ordinal scale. What allows us to do this is the comprehensive system that has been described in Part II, and which is shown in Figure 1.1, the building blocks of human motivation. This framework is believed to be complete. People really talk and communicate to one another in these terms. They talk about orientation, survival, expectation, adaptation, and play. Every subliminal cue can be fitted into one of these categories. At times one subliminal cue may fit into two categories, but this is the exception and not the rule. Take the following statement, which is a subliminal cue: "Now is the time for all good men to come to the aid of their country." This statement should be placed in the spiritual survival category because of patriotism, which is a form of human love (i.e., love of country). But it also speaks of time, so it needs to be placed in the time orientation category. In this unusual case, both time orientation and spiritual survival apply. Neither is weighted more heavily than the other.

There is one step missing here, and this step is essential. It involves the elements of the motives. It was stated earlier that elements are a lot easier to identify than motives, since motives represent abstractions and many people do not think in terms of abstractions. An example of an element which appears often in Motigraphics is family values. The family values element was one of only two elements added by us to the category of spiritual survival. The other ten were provided by Fleischman (1990). When an individual says, "Well, I don't have much use for the magazine, but I buy it for my children," this is a reference to the element of family values.

WHY PEOPLE SUBSCRIBE TO AND READ A FASHION MAGAZINE

As an example, here is a typical grouping for a project done with a fashion magazine. In this project, we interviewed fifteen women. We could interview more respondents, but in every project we have done over the last twenty-five years, by the time fifteen are interviewed it is quite clear that a point of diminishing returns has been reached. In fact, we usually reach this point after ten or twelve respondents have been interviewed. Interviews last for exactly one hour. The population in this study consisted of 176 subliminal cues. Most marketers would feel very secure with the size of this universe.

To make the sort simpler, it helps to identify each subliminal cue by its element. In simpler analyses we group only motives, but in more complex analyses we group motives by elements within motives. For purposes of illustration we will do only the simple analysis, looking at the motives but not at the elements.

The Arithmetic

In this classification we have listed about ten subliminal cues under each motive so that the reader can get a feeling of how the classification scheme works. In parentheses following the motive itself you will find the actual number of subliminal cues that were assigned to that motive. In some cases we also identify the element associated with the motive, for clarity and simplicity and for quicker identification.

The number of cues in each category are counted in a simple frequency count. Let us imagine, for purposes of illustration, that the number of subliminal cues were added up in each category and appear as follows:

Personal Orientation (67)
- Wearing the right thing helps me to feel more in control of myself (self-control)
- I feel better when I am wearing something new (self-image)
- What I wear is what I am
- I feel more respectable when I am dressed up (self-image)
- I am more likely to speak up and be heard when I am dressed appropriately

- What I wear gives me an "ego boost" (self-image)
- I feel like a unique person when I am dressed appropriately
- I try it on and know almost immediately from a gut feeling if it is right for me (self-control)
- I choose my clothing knowing what feels right or wrong for me
- Wearing the right dress or suit increases my own self-respect
- Dress right and feel right

Spiritual Survival (31)

- I wear what I think will make my family proud of me (family values)
- It is important to me that my family likes what I wear (family values)
- There are things you can wear and things you shouldn't wear and these rules cannot be broken (lawful order)
- Clothes aren't everything, but they certainly bring self-assurance and peace of mind when you are dressed right (peace of mind)
- I would probably stay in my housecoat all day long, but would not want my children to see me that way (family values)
- When I arrive and know I am wearing the right thing I feel an inner peace (peace of mind)
- I would not want to embarrass my family by what I was wearing (family values)
- Clothes won't buy you love but they sure help (human love)
- I would have a lot more in my wardrobe than I do, but I am a mother and my first obligation is to my children (family values)

Place Orientation (33)

- Where I am going determines what I am going to wear
- The background (in magazine ads) determines, to a large extent, what clothing I buy and where I choose to wear it
- There is nothing worse than wearing the wrong thing in the wrong place
- I find out where we are going before I decide what I will buy
- I would feel very uncomfortable in a strange place, not knowing what to wear
- I would like to have at least one outfit in my closet for every different place that I go
- I enjoy looking through the magazine and shopping for clothing more if I am looking forward to going to a very special place
- What I wear is determined by where I am going to wear it

Time Orientation (33)

- The magazine tells me what people are currently wearing (timing)
- When it comes to clothing I want to be in tune with the times

- Fashions change every season and often in between; it pays to keep my subscription current (holiday and seasonal)
- Fashions are always changing; I don't want to miss out (timing)
- People who are out of style or out of date are out of it
- When something is in it's in and when it's out it's out
- Timing is everything when it comes to what I wear (timing)
- I always give clothing for Christmas and birthdays because you can't go wrong and it is always appreciated (holiday and seasonal)
- I like to dress up and go to parties on the holidays; that's why I especially like the holiday fashion edition (holidays and seasonal)

Adaptation (21)
- I could keep up with the styles just by watching television; I really don't need to subscribe to the magazine
- I want people to walk up to me and ask me where I got it
- The magazine shows me what other people are wearing and that's how I'll decide what I will wear
- People watch people
- Others will walk up and ask me where it came from
- I watch very closely what others are wearing
- I feel like I have more class and I want others to know it
- I want to wear something exquisite so that others will notice
- People can tell by your appearance whether or not you have "arrived"

Sexual Survival (12)
- I like wearing something that brings out the feminine qualities in me (gender)
- I don't want to wear something that is too revealing or the men that I work with might get the wrong idea (inhibition)
- I like feeling feminine (gender)
- I like wearing clothing that is sensuous when the occasion calls for it (impulse)
- Sexy is what sexy does (impulse)
- Given a choice I would rather be sexy than brilliant; when it comes to what I wear or anything else (impulse)
- I always choose bathing suits that are revealing and divulging (impulse)
- I am not happy with unisex fashions, where the girls dress up like boys (gender)
- Some fashions reveal too much for me (inhibition)
- When it comes to sensuous gowns and sleepwear, I say the least is the best (impulse)

The total number of subliminal cues for each category is equal to the total number of subliminal suggestions that were collected in the fifteen interviews that comprised this project. Keep in mind that this is not a project on fashion, but instead a project that measures the motivation to continue subscribing to a magazine on fashion. The demographic shown included only those who said that they were subscribers and readers.[1] If the client had been interested in why people cancel the magazine we would have added another demographic: people who cancel. This would increase the number of interviews to thirty and consequently increase the cost of the project.

Data Conversion

The key to Motigraphics is in normalizing the data. Normalizing allows us to compare one motive with another, and the motives in one study with the motives in another study. For example, we may want to look at women's motivation in fashion and compare that to another study that has examined women's motivation in cosmetics, since both are similar. Normalizing would also allow us to compare motives toward certain products or services at the beginning of the year versus the same products or services at the end of the year (tracking). Normalization and conversion of data also allow us to force those data into a normal distribution so that the most important motives are given the most attention. Finally, conversion of the data allows us to analyze motives in many other formats: cluster analysis, factor analysis, and analysis of variance, and also allows us to apply correlational and nonparametric procedures.

z-Scores

The first step in conversion is to take the raw data that were seen previously and convert them into z-scores. z-scores or standard scores allow us to take raw data, which in this case consisted of a frequency count, and place each motive or each element of each motive at its respective position on a bell curve, which is the normal distribution. The formula for z-scores is as follows:

$$z = \frac{X - \mu}{\sigma}$$

where

X = individual score (from example)

μ = mean of the distribution

σ = standard deviation of the distribution

The formula for working out the standard deviation is as follows:

$$s = \sqrt{\frac{n\Sigma x^2 - (\Sigma x)^2}{n^2}}$$

where

X = scores in each category
n = total number of categories

This formula and the procedures for working out the standard deviation using a calculator can be found in any basic statistics book. Many hand calculators will compute a standard deviation with the depression of just one key.

In this case, we are deriving z-scores for motives only. It would also be possible to derive z-scores for the elements within motives, so that we could make a comparison of the elements within motives and see how the elements compare with one another.

Using the formulas and procedures illustrated, the z-scores for each motivational category are as follows:

Motive	z-score
Personal Orientation	2.01
Spiritual Survival	0.009
Place Orientation	0.197
Time Orientation	−0.924
Adaptation Motive	−0.443
Sexual Survival	−0.924

These numbers are meaningless as far as comparisons are concerned and their only purpose is to indicate the relative position of each motive under a normal or bell curve. This is what is meant by normalizing. The next and final step is to transform these numbers into T-scores.

Actually, at this point any ordinal scale could be used to transform the numbers. However, we have chosen T-scores as the easiest to use, for purposes of computation and for presentations. This is because there are no negative T-scores and also because T-scores have a mean of fifty and a standard deviation of ten, therefore lending themselves to simple interpretation. The formula for converting from z-scores to T-scores is as follows:

$$z = 50 + (z)(10)$$

Where 50 is the desired mean in this case and 10 is the desired
standard deviation. The result of this transformation is as follows:

Motive	T-score
Personal Orientation	70
Spiritual Survival	51
Place Orientation	52
Time Orientation	41
Adaptation Motive	46
Sexual Survival	41

The data are shown in graphic format in Figure 16.3.

How Data Might Be Used

Since motives represent the one consumer activity that is closest
to the final buy–no buy decision that we can measure, they are
probably the most important consumer activity that can be measured. The output of this study tells us that personal orientation is
by far the most important motive in fashion. A woman buys clothing first and foremost to satisfy herself, and she will only buy what
she feels good in and looks good in. Women's fashions, above all,
should instill and imbue confidence, confidence in herself and confidence in what she is wearing. This is the major benefit, and as
seen in Figure 16.3 it is two standard deviations above the mean.

Two other categories that are above the mean are place orientation and spiritual survival. These two categories are also related to
confidence, for as can be seen from some of the responses, clothing
and the right fashions provide a woman with "peace of mind," which
is one of Fleischman's (1990) elements that we have included under spiritual survival. The other elements of spiritual survival refer to lawful order (rules of fashion and dress) and to family values.
These elements have powerful implications for marketing and advertising, if only because they are the bottom-line motivators in
fashion. Many women never get tired of hearing about peace of
mind, self-confidence, self-control, dressing for the occasion, and
wearing the right thing in the right place. These categories stand
out in Figure 16.3. They tell us where to direct our advertising, our
marketing, our sales training, and all our efforts.

Even the categories that are below fifty but above zero are important for decision making. For example, if we had probed further
we may have found that territorial survival is a big factor in the
"dress for success" crowd, but this limited study did not probe in

Figure 16.3
Motives in Fashion Magazine Subscribers

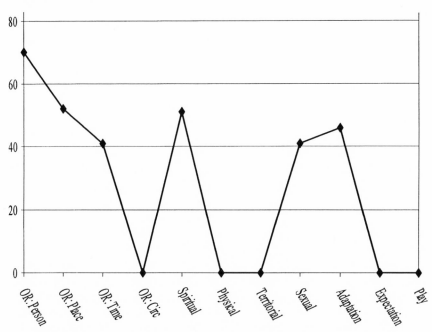

this area, nor did we probe into the areas of play and casual clothing. The magazine for whom this work was directed was not interested in these areas.

The importance of Figure 16.3 is that it highlights and spotlights the major motivational issues in clothing. Typically, we would go beyond this analysis and include a number of subanalyses which compared motivational elements with one another, and more recommendations would have arisen from this.

When Motigraphics is combined with data that are already available to the marketer, powerful new insights appear in the form of new information. Often these insights offer solutions to problems that were illusive before, because they were at the unconscious or motivational level.

Other Applications

Motigraphics represents a new dimension in tracking studies and in follow-up analyses of consumer behavior. Motives are very close to emotions, and since consumer loyalty and brand loyalty are about 50-percent emotion, they are useful for tracking these qualities.

Motivational analysis and Motigraphics may also be used in premeasures and post-measures of advertising copy. In studies such as these we usually have the respondent examine the copy before the interview starts, then visualize the copy in the interview, and then look at it again after the formal part of the interview after the blindfold is removed, in order to get any additional comments. Removing the blindfold is a signal to the respondent that the interview is over, and often under these conditions we will get additional useful information and more subliminal cues, since the respondent thinks that the interview has "officially ended" and therefore is more relaxed and feels like he or she has more freedom to say what he or she wants to say.

Motigraphics can be used in many different ways other than those mentioned. This is because motives, which up to now have been so illusive, can be subjected to measurement.

FURTHER BENEFITS OF A MOTIVATIONAL ANALYSIS

Probably the most important benefit of all in using Motigraphics is that we get around, behind, and under the problem of people telling us what they think we want to hear. By using visualization and minimizing verbalization we believe that we are getting very close to real motives. Advertising works very, very hard to give people subliminal cues, such as the ones that we elaborated upon in Chapter 3. Doesn't it follow, then, that these subliminal cues are genuine and authentic motivators that constitute the real reasons why people do what they do?

In carrying out Motigraphics research we also encounter the rational reasons why people do what they do. Rational issues include price, discounts, convenience (which is also emotional), and other rationalizations that consumers usually give. We put these rational reasons in a special category when they are requested. However, our whole effort and approach is to uncover the irrational reasons, which factor analysis has indicated to us account for about 70 percent of the sale. Also, the larger the item, the more important the irrational and the less important the rational and logical.

EXTENDED MOTIGRAPHICS:
MOTIGRAPHICS WITH LARGE SAMPLES

Traditionally, the universe for Motigraphics has been defined as the subliminal cues, and this is appropriate. However, there are some marketers who prefer a larger sample than what has been traditionally used in the classic motivational approach. This is because the classic motivational approach has always done an in-depth analysis rather than "skimming the surface." Many marketers want to base their judgments on a larger number of people. When this is important, Motigraphics can be carried out with an additional 600 to 1,200 people in what we call an Extended Motigraphics analysis.

To do this, we start out with the traditional eight to fifteen in-depth interviews and collect all of the subliminal cues that come from these respondents. As indicated, there will probably be anywhere from 100 to 180 subliminal cues that result from this initial analysis. The next step is to take the motives that have arisen from this in-depth analysis and to construct questions which measure these motives, which are then administered in large-scale telephone or mall-intercept interviews. It is very unlikely that we will encounter any additional subliminal cues after doing an in-depth analysis on eight to fifteen individuals, and so we can content ourselves with the fact that the complete and total universe of cues is available to us, which then allows us to construct a questionnaire which is subsequently administered to a larger group of respondents. Extended Motigraphics analysis provides the assurance that most marketers need to draw their conclusions, but it is not a necessary step toward reliability. This is because Motigraphics, in extracting subliminal cues, has reliability and validity already built into it.

The quantification of motives in Motigraphics allows us to look at the consumer from a whole new dimension: the emotional, which has been ignored for such a long time. When covaried with other dimensions, or entered into a regression equation or cluster analysis, consumer behavior begins to take on a whole new look. This is particularly true when there is an ongoing phenomenon that cannot be readily explained, such as customers slowly moving away from you and toward your competitor. In this situation, they usually won't tell you the truth about why they left, but Motigraphics will.

MOTIVATIONAL PROFILES

A motivational profile is an overall assessment tool that can be used in many different situations. The profile consists of the five motives and eleven motivational categories and, in a way, this outline serves as a structured interview guide. It is filled out by an interviewer, who follows the outline that is seen in the inverted building blocks.

In most cases it would not be appropriate to ask questions about sexual survival, including gender preference and particularly questions related to impulse. Surely it would not be appropriate in an employment situation. However, in a criminal assessment, which is an area where these motivational profiles have been used, questions about sex and sexuality would be entirely appropriate.

The interviewer can feel secure that when this profile is completed, with the exception of questions on sexual survival, he or she will have a complete and comprehensive picture of the individual's level(s) of motivation. We are currently developing a questionnaire that will serve as a checklist for the motivational profile, and which may be objectively scored.

MEASURING BRAND EQUITY AND BRAND LOYALTY

A large number of marketers have given up on trying to measure either brand equity or brand loyalty. They feel that it is too elusive. But again, what makes it elusive is the fact that most of what makes up brand equity is the consumer emotion that is involved in the product. The same thing goes for brand loyalty. Our guess is that both of these issues are about 75 percent emotion. This seems to be supported by the example of Chris-Craft, and it is also consistent with observations Feig (1997) has made. But Feig makes another statement which is unfortunate; he says that emotion is just one more thing that cannot be "graphed or measured." We take issue with that statement, since this is what Motigraphics is all about.

We have shown that, in Motigraphics, subliminal cues are the bottom-line unit of measurement. As such, they may be compared with standard units of measurement in other areas of science. We have already stated that consumers have ideas, beliefs, and opinions about you and your services, before they even attempt to use them. These ideas and opinions and beliefs stem from subliminal cues. The more (positive) subliminal cues that individuals have in their minds about a product or service, the stronger the brand equity. Quite naturally, negative subliminal cues would be subtracted from the positives in any frequency count.

The good news is that brand equity and brand loyalty may be measured using the subliminal cue as the standard unit of measurement. Pretests and post-tests may be given before and after exposure to a product or service. The effectiveness of advertising can be measured directly after consumer exposure to a particular campaign. The effectiveness of a public-relations campaign or an advertising agency's effort may be measured in terms of subliminal cues. There is finally a way to measure and get a response to the age-old question, "Does advertising really work?"

If you haven't taken into account the emotion invested in your brand by your customers, then you may be grossly underpricing the true value of your product or service.

EXTENDED MOTIGRAPHICS: A WORD OF CAUTION

One problem that arises in Extended Motigraphics is the use of standard Likert-type scales that are very popular in psychology and in marketing. But they will not work in this case. The reason is based upon a commonsense understanding and interpretation of motives.

The motives that arise out of Silent Side in-depth interviews are homogenous. That is, everyone who is interviewed experiences these motives in relation to the individual products that are being investigated. To put these motives into a Likert format in order to do Extended Motigraphics would yield substantial agreement and very little disagreement. This is more support for the fact that these motives are related to the product that is being investigated, and more support for the fact that these motives do exist. However, when applied to Extended Motigraphics, there will be very little variability.

The solution to this problem is seen in using a forced-choice or a semantic-differential format. In this way, each motive can be paired with every other motive for all permutations of combinations. This method will not only support the motives that were originally extracted in the one-on-one interviews, but will also give the marketer extensive information on the importance or the weight of each motive, their hierarchical placement, and their contribution to the overall consumer decision-making process.

NOTE

1. Depending upon the client's need for information, what we have presented here could easily be split into two categories: readers and subscribers. Because of the vagaries and unique aspects of magazine and newspaper readership, many readers are "pass alongs" and are not necessarily subscribers. The example used here was kept simple, for purposes of illustration.

REFERENCES

Feig, B. (1997). *Marketing straight to the heart: From product to positioning to advertising—how smart companies use the power of emotion to win loyal customers.* New York: American Management Association.

Fleischman, P. (1990). *The healing spirit.* New York: Paragon House.

PART **IV**

APPLICATIONS TO ADVERTISING AND MARKETING

17

Specialized Applications

WHAT BUSINESS ARE YOU IN ANYWAY?

When we look in depth at the person as we have in this book, you may want to reconsider the business that you are in. When people talk about what they have gained or acquired from a product or service, this is known as a *benefit*. However, when marketers talk about their products, this is done in terms of features. There may or may not be a match here. Product features do not always ensure consumer benefits.

For example, we have looked at health care as an industry. Quite often, a provider, like a hospital, will promote quality, cleanliness, excellence, superiority, or leadership. But in our research we have found that this is really not what the customer is looking for. In health care the customer is looking for some person or institution that he or she can trust, believe, and have confidence in. We have done any number of health care projects in which the hospital contradicts itself in this area and gives off a double message. Hospitals often address issues of physical survival, when what the prospective patient wants to hear about is issues of expectation resolution and spiritual survival (caring).

In a project involving refrigerators, we found that empty-nesters, who had no one at home except themselves, would often order one of the largest appliances on the floor; twenty-six or twenty-eight cubic feet. When research was carried out on this group, the underlying issue was spiritual survival. How did spiritual survival ever creep into refrigerators? Remember family values? The first consideration on the part of the woman was that the box would be big enough to accommodate that family dinner, even if it only occurred once or twice a year. Interestingly, the men did not even have a clue to this and for the most part they were baffled. The woman, who made the final decision when it came to large appliances, made that decision on the basis of the size of the box, and Motigraphics revealed that most of the other appliance features were virtually insignificant.

Newspapers in particular and the news in general has a very hard way to go today. This was discussed in Chapter 8 in terms of the lack of interest and apathy that is pervasive today when it comes to the news in any form. People just aren't interested. There is a pervasive narcissism or self-centeredness that theologians refer to as "contented worldliness." Our own research showed that what people really want is to be entertained. More research needs to be done, and in our opinion, the only research that will turn up anything is that which looks directly at subliminal clues. Anything short of that will end up dealing with rationalizations and not with reality.

The business that you think you are in may not be the business that you are really in. The public demands entertainment in the news, and eventually they will get it. The ratings and sweeps will see to that. In fact, some say that it is already happening. We have shown that there is a gulf between what the professional marketer thinks that he or she is offering and what the general public is demanding. Casinos offer excitement and prizes, but what people are looking for is disorientation and disconnection. Restaurants offer glitzy menus and boast about their food, but what people are looking for is escape and, again, disconnection from the world that they have been living in all day long. Banks offer more interest and friendly people, but what customers really want is the elements of the Expectation Motive: trust and faith, belief and security.

CHANGING COURSE

One example of a business that was on the wrong track and saw the light during the last decade of the twentieth century is academic institutions. Most of the administrative types in these institutions were guided and influenced by the professors and teachers, who felt that what drove people to the university was a quest and a thirst for knowledge. Therefore, great importance and significance was placed upon what they already knew, and tests were given to assess their knowledge base. Often applicants were asked to write letters so that they could verify the purity of their motives for wanting to get into a graduate program.

All that began to change in the early 1970s. Pepperdine University was one of the first to go to where the students were instead of making the students come to them. They picked an easy target, and set up classrooms on every available military base in the United States and eventually on many that were overseas. Other universities and colleges followed suit. Universities had made an earthshaking discovery: People did not come to college for knowledge; they came for degrees and qualifications. Graduate programs proliferated. There had always been diploma mills, but starting in the 1970s and 1980s, top-rated universities and eventually even state-owned institutions began to advertise and publicize the fact that their doors were now open to everyone. Entrance standards were lowered. Some believe that today an MBA has the status that a high school diploma had in the 1960s.

Our research had a leading role in the initial changes that took place in some graduate institutions and we were able to make recommendations for getting more students without lowering standards. We did this through a whole variety of methods: changing names, increasing visibility, emphasizing environment, emphasizing personalized attention in small private schools (personalization), and directly focusing on the Territorial Survival Motive, which is why people go to school in the first place. They want to make more money and they want to have a more meaningful life. Academic and professorial types were somewhat slow to accept this change, but administrators jumped on board immediately. It is quite clear that many institutions now realize that the student is their customer, and thinking within that particular framework, most schools have changed their whole approach to adult education. Without students, they would not be in business, and education and learning is business, big business!

SOME CONSULTANTS BORROW YOUR WATCH TO TELL YOU WHAT TIME IT IS

In the practice of psychology and psychiatry we agreed that for what we charged we should be able to give our patients and our clients more information on their condition than they could get from their neighbors across the backyard fence. This was because it cost a lot more to come to our office than it did to talk with a neighbor. The same thing is true in consulting. A consultant should be able to give you new and novel information, not something that you have heard over and over again. The complaint most often heard is that consultants came in and "told me what I already knew." Price-Waterhouse said, "If your consultant comes in with a BB gun, you need to be talking to the people with the big guns." We believe they are right; consultants should be giving you more, not more of the same.

Silent Side research goes beyond the obvious and excavates the subtle and the imperceptible; that which is below the surface, that which makes the eventual difference. By getting new information from a different source—the unconscious mind—and by verifying that information with Motigraphics, recommendations begin to flow in from areas that you may have never even imagined.

CASINO GAMING

We have referred to casino gaming over and over again since it is a strictly emotional, nonrational activity and there is a considerable abyss between what the customer wants and what management thinks the customer wants. Casinos are also highly regulated and for that reason are commodity businesses. It is difficult for the customer to distinguish one from the other. It is also one of the fastest growing industries in America, so they must be giving people what they want.

Casinos are the best example that we know of that addresses the customer's need to disorient. They disorient people in all four spheres: person, place, time, and circumstances. Customers are disoriented from the time that they enter until they leave, and some of them even after they leave. To some extent, casino management knows this. They have no clocks, no windows, and so on. Most of this is by tradition. But some of their attempts to disorient their customers have caused distractions rather than attractions and have sent people in the other direction; that is, toward the competition. One example of this was Circus Circus, where they had a live elephant in the casino who would have frequent bowel movements on the carpet. According to O'Brien (1998), the clowns, jugglers, tightrope walkers, and other performers were a distraction to the games and to the players in Las Vegas, even though the families and the children liked it. But children don't gamble, and eventually the Circus Circus in Tunica, which lasted only a short time, closed to make way for its replacement, Gold Strike Casino.

In one study we asked casino customers what their ideal was when it came to a vacation or a place to go when they got away from work and from home. Since all of them lived inland, they said that the thing that they missed the most was the beach. They missed the seashore: the smells, the sounds, the sights, and the moonlit beaches at night. They missed the surf and the seafood. Most of the people in the area that were interviewed preferred the seashore over any other escape route that they could take for their vacation. So why not bring the seashore to the casino? From a boardwalk to seafood restaurants and perhaps even a wave pool with a surf and sand, lovers of the seaside domain would only have to drive a few miles and could go to the beach year round. Would the seaside be a distraction rather than an attraction for gamblers? Perhaps it would, but its popularity in that area, which was halfway between two oceans, would certainly pull in more people than any other casino had succeeded in doing. Other casinos had museums and themes of one kind or another, some of which were exquisite and very tasteful. However, they did not reflect the passion of the majority of their customers, which is what the seashore theme would be able to do.

How do we know that a seashore, including a beach and an ocean, would be successful in a casino? We know because of the blueprint that we have developed for human motivation. The motives involved here include disorientation to person, place, time, and circumstances as well as spiritual survival in the form of peace of mind. Expectation, of course, is a given, and is already built into the total casino picture. But look how much the seashore, beach, and boardwalk would add to the total picture. When the casino installs such a theme, it appeals directly to what customers really want and in that way it distinguishes itself among a group of competitors that are indistinguishable, at least to the consumer.

In another set of recommendations made to casino management it was recognized that the Orientation to Person Motive and indeed all of the orientation categories were instrumental in getting visitors to casinos. This is particularly true when dealing with recreational gamblers, who have relatively low expectations about winning but high expectations regarding escape, special treatment, perks, and personal recognition. This "motivational mix" can be seen in the Motigraphics printout in Chapter 16.

Since recreational players have these expectations, and since motives play a major role in determining which casino they will prefer over others, the recommendation was made, on the basis of the Orientation to Person Motive, that casino employees take the "mega memory" course. This course trains them to recognize players who are regulars in the casino and to refer to them by name whenever this is possible and feasible. Although it was not possible to train all of the dealers (because of costs and other reasons) it was possible to train greeters and floor persons along with some other high-profile personnel in the casino for facial recognition. This turned out to be more than just a public-relations program; it was a direct appeal to motivation and what recreational players wanted—but did not necessarily expect—when they returned to the casino. They wanted to be recognized, appreciated, acknowledged, and treated in a special, individualized, and personalized way. This motivational blueprint was consistent not only with the universal need to personalize the service, but with the Orientation to Person Motive which intensified the need to be treated as "special." In other words, like a big shot, which is to some extent what casino visitation is all about.

HEALTH CARE

Bridging the White Coat and the Green Eye Shade

We have already mentioned results that were reported in the *Wall Street Journal* on the considerable gulf between consumers of health care and the managed care companies. Doctors are the most trusted group in America and managed care organizations are the least trusted. Hospitals are also close to the bottom of the list.

Overcoming this gap was a matter of positioning. Since the FCC has instituted the white coat regulation it is not legal to put an ordinary person in a white coat, since the viewing public immediately assumes that the person is a physician. And this is as it should be. However, in any and all health care advertising, a fundamental principle is that the professional person himself or herself needs to be seen. This is another variation on the spiritual survival element of witness significance, which we have already seen in Chapters 8 and 10 is a critical determinant in what people do and how they do it. In the case of health care, witness significance applies to the fact that the professional must be seen in any and all marketing and advertising attempts. The presence of the doctor with his or her words of reassurance is the only way that managed care can raise their image up from where it is now.

Our recommendations to a major managed care organization were to do just that. The doctor involved was a young and attractive woman who was a pediatrician. That allowed us to appeal not only to witness significance—the presence of the physician—but to another very important element of spiritual survival, and that was family values. Putting the doctor, young patients, and the managed care organization together in advertising was the answer to the managed care organization's prayer. The public's belief in managed care changed markedly, as measured. This illustration also confirms the fact that the more different motivations are involved and combined, the more effective and powerful the advertising will become.

Some hospitals in smaller towns have difficulty in getting their patients to stay home for their health care needs, rather than going off to a nearby city where there are more specialists and better facilities. We have worked on this problem since 1982, when medical specialists began to advertise their services. The answer again is the appeal to the emotional elements; in this case, the doctor, not the hospital, has to give the reassurance and build the trust that the patients need: witness significance. When in doubt, consult Silent Side Motives and their elements to see what you should be doing. It is a blueprint for human motivation.

HEALTH CARE: HOSPITAL ADVERTISING AND MARKETING

Steve Puckett, in St. Louis, has been a steadfast enthusiast of Silent Side research for the last twenty years and has applied it to many areas, but particularly in health care. In a hospital commercial for a major children's hospital, he focused on the nursing staff, who in turn were focused on a four-year-old patient and his teddy bear. They told of his incapacitating illness and how they had used a number of technological breakthroughs in order to treat him. They talked of the long road to recovery and how around-the-clock nursing was often required. They talked of all that they did, medically, to bring him back to health. But isn't that what people expect of hospitals? Good story, but nothing new here.

Then Puckett added the clincher. The nurses state that in every way they acted professionally and capably, except in one area. That area was in dealing with their own feelings after their little patient went home. They just weren't quite certain how they were going to deal with the fact that they would miss him, terribly, and their little patient's departure would leave an empty spot in their hearts and in their guts.

From Puckett's lengthy experience with Silent Side research, he knew that even though health care is an issue in physical survival, for him that's never been enough. The next step or two from physical survival is spiritual survival, and that's where he always goes. In health care advertising, that's the payoff. Hospitals and health care facilities like to talk about their equipment and their eminently qualified staff of physicians, surgeons, and nurses. But that's just what everyone expects. However, the hospitals that go beyond this are the ones that attract patients, because they know that physical survival is not the bottom line in health care.

HARDWARE AND NEW HOME CONSTRUCTION

Through our research, we know a number of hardware stores have had problems because they have so may items in stock that their customers become disoriented. Again, this shows how disorientation is a major factor in human behavior, but in this case it is a negative, not a positive. People do not want to be disoriented while they are trying to make major purchase decisions or when they are dealing with their money. Indeed, under these conditions they want to remain as alert and oriented as is possible. We have already said that this was found to be the case in supermarket banking, where the banks were located too close to the center of confusion and commotion, interfering with major banking transactions.

Our research made some recommendations to a major hardware chain to lower the disorientation factor. Recommendations included sinage, lighting, counter height, traffic patterns, and other forms of "customer overload." What was happening was that the customers were leaving without having made their purchase, claiming that they were confused and "dizzy." Some even said that the store gave them a headache. These were references to overload that resulted in disorientation.

Doors

A hardware supplier of doors and windows felt that his major audience was builders and do-it-yourselfers. Silent Side research found, and Motigraphics confirmed, that there was another whole customer base that the supplier had ignored, and that was the retail customer, primarily women, who made most of the major decisions in home building, including decisions about doors and windows.

New Home Construction

A project was carried out on new home construction which verified a number of wants that new home buyers looked for in their home. Among the most popular was a home that had an office, which many of them do, and which was wired for a computer network, which most of them are not. The client started his own business, prewiring homes for computer networks. This is an interesting variation on a business that is already very successful, but is restricted to wiring offices. The recommendations that were made on home computer network wiring were based upon the needs of customers expressed by the Territorial Survival Motive.

OLD PRODUCTS

Silent Side research is often used to revive old products, such as products for scratch baking and for sewing. These kinds of activities have all but been abandoned by women whose lifestyles have drastically changed. Our research took women back to their very first experiences with products that were associated with baking and sewing, recapturing the emotion that was associated with these activities. This emotion was easy to capture, since all of the respondents were very young and impressionable when they had their first experiences with these products. As a result of this research, three things were accomplished. First, the emotion was recaptured and built back into the product for use in marketing and advertising. Second, the emotion associated with the product which was found in Silent Side research and then confirmed with Motigraphics was an important determinant in measuring brand equity. Third, the emotion in the product was captured, built back into the product, and then used in order to instill new customer loyalty and allegiance.

SMOKING AND THE USE OF SUBLIMINAL CUES

Government-funded antismoking campaigns had considerable success under the Clinton administration, except with high school dropouts and adolescent girls. These populations were deemed unreachable. Although no work was done on this project, Silent Side research strongly recommended the avenue of product placement as the only way that messages would be effective. A product placement is when a sponsor or advertiser pays to have his product included in a TV show, even though the name of the product is never mentioned. For example, Dodge may pay to have one of their pickups involved in a high-speed chase, even though no direct advertising of the vehicle takes place on the show.

Product placements are much more effective than regular advertising. Product placements work because they go directly into the unconscious mind as subliminal cues. Furthermore, they are indirect and so they bypass the usual consumer and customer resistance. Any other form of advertising or marketing, including outdoor, radio, TV, newspapers, and so on is direct, and is therefore subject to the resistance that was described and defined in Chapter 5. The antismoking methods that the government was using had been successful in getting through to groups in higher socioeconomic levels, but not to the high school dropouts and adolescent girls. And the two things that we know about these two groups is that they have a lot of resistance to taking advice from adults and they watch a lot of television, since they don't have anything else to occupy their time.

What is important here is that the recommendation involves working directly with subliminal cues. In our opinion and experience, this is the only way that we can effectively change human behavior. This phenomenon; that is, the way television can address major changes by working with subliminal cues, was addressed in Chapter 3.

NEW PRODUCTS

The Silent Side research method is very effective in the design of new products and has been used successfully in turning out new food products, innovations and fragrances. One fragrance after only one year was in the top twenty in the world, which is quite remarkable when measured against hundreds that are available worldwide. The reason is simple: In each research project we find the appropriate emotions with which the product needs to be positioned.

Silent Side research takes a person back to the first time that they used a product or had experience with it. The pleasant emotions are identified and used to build the new product. Under conditions of relaxation and being blindfolded, the respondents' senses become very acute, and taste, hearing, smell, and visualization are all very sharp. Furthermore, the procedure is totally projective, which means that the respondent projects all of his or her available subliminal cues onto the product. If fifteen to twenty respondents are interviewed, this means that over 200 subliminal cues that are relevant to the product will be used to build the new product, or a variation of the old product.

PACKAGING

Not only is the product designed but the package is also invented. In a project for aluminum can manufacturers, respondents were relaxed and taken, in slow motion, completely through the drinking and swallowing process. This is a fairly complex procedure that we generally take for granted because we do it every day. It involves the lips, tongue, teeth, tonsils, and those muscles involved in swallowing, as well as the entire digestive system. Twenty-five respondents were taken through this process in slow motion and under blindfolded conditions, and videotapes were then viewed with the client. The unmistakable conclusion was to widen the mouth on the can, so that cans would be more competitive with bottles. The deciding factor was the Physical Survival Motive and the related element of taste. The wide-mouthed can has now been adopted by almost all of the juice, soft drink, and beer manufacturers worldwide.

CONSUMER SERVICES

This is an amusing pet project which was done at no cost to the client but which had some interesting results, supporting the strength of the Expectation Motive.

Do people spend money on personal services and other things when they go to the casinos? The answer is a resounding no, with the exception of jewelry and souvenirs and food that is purchased in the casino itself. However, a beauty operator heard that they were going to build a shopping center near the casinos, and wanted to know if it would be possible to make a living there. She knew that people did not spend any money outside of the casino, but she just thought that there may be some exceptions.

In a small project we found considerable exceptions. Our advice to her was to put a psychic in the beauty shop, who would more than earn her keep and at the same time bring business to the beauty shop. An added benefit would be that the customers would not mind waiting to have their hair done because they would be preoccupied talking to the psychic about their "luck." The results in this project were excellent, all because of the Expectation Motive. With Motigraphics we were able to project her first year's earnings and she exceeded that by a wide margin.

RESORT MANAGEMENT

A very old resort had been known for its thermal baths and hot springs. In the late 1800s, many came from distant cities by train to take the baths, believed at that time to be a cure for arthritis. Although there is no cure for arthritis today, there are many medical remedies that render the trip to the spa a thing of the past. Hotels had been built around the baths and other tourist attractions, but the old town was mostly a ghost town except for a few months in the fall and winter when elderly people would travel through in motor homes.

One of our research projects found that a very high priority among our present generation is stress and more particularly, how to get rid of it. Whereas arthritis was of some concern fifty years ago, today it is stress. The chamber of commerce was presented with this information and took considerable interest in it. The results are at this point unknown. However, if this repositioning of the town is successful, and an increase in tourism is seen, it will be based upon the strength of the Physical Survival Motive and the Orientation Motives, which urge us to escape the factors that cause stress and go to a place where we can deal with stress.

READING

Since 1994, all television sets manufactured include closed captioning for the hearing impaired. This is required under the Americans with Disabilities Act of 1989, so that hearing-impaired people can enjoy television. But closed captioning has another feature. Our research has shown that it is used by many to learn English as a second language. But there is another benefit that many don't know of and which is even more valuable. Closed captions can be used to teach people to read, making use of the very friendly medium of television.

Although some people might object to captions because they cover some aspects of the picture on the screen, when the volume is cut and the TV set is muted they are forced to use the captions to see what the characters on television or on the videotape are saying to each other. This encourages reading among nonreaders and speed reading among those who are already reading. Research carried out by us on this point will not involve Silent Side research methods. In this case, we will be relying on a standard research format, using an experimental and control group, to see how much closed captions can actually increase a nonreader's ability to read. Preliminary results are very encouraging.

REFERENCE

O'Brien, T. L. (1998). *Bad bet: The inside story of the glamour, glitz and the danger of America's gambling industry.* New York: Times Books.

A Blueprint for
Human Motivation

OVERVIEW

The purpose of the Silent Side approach to motivation is to look at the internal, enclosed, and secret "drivers" of the individual. It is to see how the person "processes" what they experience in the world around them. Psychologists refer to this as cognitive psychology, but we resist using this term because, as we have seen, it is just another term for behavioristic psychology and learning.

The most important contributions that have been made in psychology in the last 100 years were made not by psychologists but by those outside of the field: Freud and Piaget. Freud was a neurologist and a medical doctor, and Piaget was a biologist. Interestingly, neither one of them employed the "scientific method" as we understand it today. At the time that they were doing their investigations there was no such thing as scientific sampling. They looked at individuals, not groups, and they looked at individuals in depth, not superficially. They did something that, if a psychologist or marketer did it today, would be held in contempt of ethics violations, and that is they made observations on their own family members. By doing this they were able to make longitudinal observations; that is, they were able to observe growth and development over a period of years.

Although Freud made many major errors and was unpopular in his time, his great contribution to the history of man was the discovery of the unconscious. If we focus only upon this and none of his other theories we can see why his theory is positioned, along with those of Copernicus and Darwin, as one which changed the way that we see our world and ourselves in relation to our world. We are not in complete control of all of our own mental faculties. Because this is a very unpopular hypothesis, there are many today who still flatly reject it.

Piaget was also unpopular because he showed that children go through stages of development, and that there are certain kinds of tasks that a child cannot do until he or she reaches that stage. This is why we don't teach children algebra when they are in the first or second grade, and don't try to teach them the calculus until they are at least in high school. Piaget's approach to child development was unpopular in America because he showed, by implication, that there was nothing that a parent could do to hasten or accelerate what a child is capable of learning. Americans had been led to believe, by behaviorists, that they could "shape" their child into becoming anything that they wanted him or her to become, through that magical and all-inclusive process called *learning* or *imitation*. They did not want to give up this belief. Piaget's idea that they could not speed up and accelerate their child's intelligence was foreign to them. After all, the whole Headstart program was based upon this very concept. Headstart, which has been shown to be a failure when it comes to boosting IQ (Jensen, 1969), is still functioning today.

Both Freud and Piaget believed that children developed by going through stages, and they demonstrated this. Freud showed that they went through psychosexual states; Piaget that they went through intellectual stages. And, more important, both Freud and Piaget laid the groundwork for their approaches to human behavior in qualitative and not quantitative observations. That is, they made systematic and tedious observations about what was happening; Freud with his patients and Piaget with his own children. From these observations they drew conclusions, but the results of their observations were never quantified.

In Kuhn's terminology, neither Freud nor Piaget were ordinary scientists working with the established paradigm of the day. They were extraordinary scientists. They worked outside of the established frameworks and paradigms. In our opinion they made the only contributions that are worth consideration in psychology and marketing today. Freud showed that there is more in the mind than meets the eye, and most marketers and seasoned advertising executives know that. They have just not known how to get to it. Piaget showed that there are mechanisms inside of the brain that are essential for the processing of information, and vital connections that have to be made before a child can even consider certain kinds of

pendix, where we make applications to other areas outside
hology and marketing.

CRITICISM

estingly, in professional presentations and publications,
ave not been that many criticisms of the approach that is
ted here, particularly when it comes to Motigraphics. One
m that is anticipated is that although the interview process
standardized, the interview may vary from respondent to
lent. It does not vary that much, but it does vary. The ques-
main the same, but may be asked in a different sequence.
a marketing survey or an IQ test or any other interview
re, the interview varies because to a large extent the inter-
is following the lead of the respondent, responding to what
e thinks is important about the product or service that is
amined. There is a reason for this.
interviews are conducted, we know ahead of time what we
ing for. We are looking for subliminal cues. We don't know
what subliminal cues we are looking for, but we do know
s is the mission. Our experience has told us that as we do
d more interviews, the same subliminal cues will continue
yielding many duplicates. Hence, we reach a point of di-
ng returns. This means that the interviewing process is
fferent than one where the structure of the interview is
by the interviewer. In our case, the structure is at least
imposed by the respondent, who gives out subliminal cues
related to the product.
terviewer's task is to impose a laddering or circular ques-
rocedure, as illustrated in Chapter 15. In doing this, the
ver may be led down one path by one respondent and not
wn that same path by a subsequent respondent. However,
pondents were exposed to the same interview, with half in
and half in Group 2, the same proportion of subliminal
otives would arise. The interview is more correctly com-
a legal deposition or courtroom interview than it is to a
marketing interview. A deposition is a procedure, with a
ogy and a stated purpose. Its purpose is discovery.
ticipated that most of the criticisms that will arise re-
is procedure will be related to the interview and the fact
not "standardized" like most marketing interviews. But
keting interviews are simplistic and overstructured. This
compare our research procedure with a deposition and
marketing interview. When comparisons are made, this

information processing. His theories and explanations have only
recently received sound validation. For a summary of this validation, see "Fertile Minds" (Nash, 1997).

MARKETING TO THE MIND

For over twenty years, we have looked at patients and consumers using a qualitative procedure which has been fully explained in
Chapter 15. What is important here is the fact that we looked at
them in depth. If you want to find out about the steps that a child
goes through when he or she is learning to play the piano, riding a
bicycle, or keyboarding on a computer, you would not need to use
striated scientific sampling. Instead, you would look at just a few
children in depth. You would make qualitative, not quantitative
observations. If while these children were learning to play the piano you could attach electrodes to their heads you might see a very
common pattern emanating or emerging from similar brain structures. You would see that learning to play the piano involves motor
skills, auditory cues, visual cues, and interpretation. You would
see extensive involvement of the right prefrontal lobe of the brain,
and other right brain structures, since music involves emotion. But
you would also see the involvement of the left brain trying to make
sense out of all of this. You would see the involvement of some of
the different motives that we have introduced, since music—to a
large extent—involves timing, sequencing, and beat. You may recognize these as elements of the Orientation to Time Motive. Most
important, you would begin to see the emergence of a pattern, and
once you had observed eight or ten children electronically it is possible that you could construct a framework of processes that all
children go through when they learn to play the piano.

This is the process that Silent Side research took us through.
The patterns that emerged in this process have been presented in
the form of the eleven motives. These motives provide you with a
blueprint of the mind, and particularly of the unconscious mind. In
theory, there are only five Motives: Orientation, Survival, Expecta-
tion/Resolution, Adaptation, and Play. In fact, there are eleven categories within these five motives, since we recognize four categories
of Survival Motives and four categories of Orientation Motives.

ARE SILENT SIDE MOTIVES COMPREHENSIVE?

Once in a seminar I was asked about dreams that predict the
future. A lady said that she dreamed that her husband died, and
three months later it came true. Another said that she dreamed

about having a fender bender three times in the last twenty years and each time she had the dream it came true. Some might call these kinds of dreams self-fulfilling prophecies. However, Silent Side research prefers to defer on these kinds of issues, and to say, "No, we don't have all of the answers."

The factor analysis that was described in Chapter 8 accounted for 75 percent of the variation in what we have called unconscious or subconscious motives. This is more than has been accounted for in the past, but obviously falls short of 100 percent. There will be issues that we cannot describe or explain with Silent Side research, but there will be other issues that have not been explained or interpreted which now become clear and legible.

SCIENCE AND MEASUREMENT

Silent Side research started with qualitative observations. At first these observations only yielded four motives—those associated with survival. At that point we were working with patients and that was all that we needed, since a person does not become a patient, psychiatric or otherwise, unless they are engaged in a struggle for survival. But as soon as we began to apply these methods to the marketplace it was quite clear that these four motives were not sufficient and not inclusive of all consumer behavior. It was in this context that the other Motives arose: Orientation, Expectation, Adaptation, and Play.

The first claim that we made was that we have been able to establish an approach to motivation that was scientifically acceptable, since it was consistent with the Darwinian approach to evolution. It is consistent because the unconscious mind is by definition involved in activities involving survival, orientation, expectation (future), and adaptation. Freud showed us that just because we don't consciously recognize these activities is not a reason to say that they don't exist. This is true, even though there will always be people who do deny their existence because they are intangible (i.e., cannot be seen, touched, smelled, felt, etc.). The fact that unscientific or nonscientific theories and approaches to motivation are still relied upon very heavily in psychology and marketing has been dealt with extensively in this book. Nowhere is this more clearly exposed and summed up than in an article written by Soper, Milford, and Rosenthal (1995).

The second claim that is made in this book is that we can now measure motives. This means that the strength of these motives can be assessed, and this is believed to be a very important step. It is important because it makes the motives themselves more tan-

gible. Not that they can be touched, but at and seen. In addition, once we can measu their strength and their position in causi they do. With motives, we directly add people do what they do.

Motives—when we examine them dir stand other concepts such as loyalty, dislo options, inclinations, tendencies, and t indirectly at consumers in terms of their at consumers in terms of their unconsc conscious processes. This in turn gives in allowing us to predict what people w goal of science is prediction.

FROM QUALITATIVE TO Q

Not many marketers or psychologist begins with qualitative data. For many in social psychology, the qualitative/qu or phenomenon. This is unfortunate. the collection of data that were strict able to identify a basic measure of th liminal cue. When subliminal cues ar categories that have been described, gins with a simple frequency count. T one hour of introduction to the Silen subliminal cues into motives and app ment with one another (r = 0.86) add substance to this whole approach. It to other would-be interviewers.

It is unfortunate that we live in a courages a qualitative/quantitative with data or observations in a strict shortcuts where the qualitative is l oversimplification (Likert-type five tion of abstract (vs. concrete) thi thought processes to a concrete an nates the rich and profound aspect reports received by management ar flat, and ordinary.

The ability to define, identify, anc new way of looking at the custome tant, it yields recommendations th ered before. This was seen in Cha distinction should be first and foremost. Why should attorneys be the only ones who have access to the deposition as a procedure? It works very well, so why not use it?

The anticipated criticism that involves small sample sizes in one-on-one interviews is just another version of the qualitative/quantitative issue, and most of this controversy can be avoided with the use of Extended Motigraphics. In this procedure, the initial, one-on-one process is verified by incorporating the motives uncovered in the one-on-one phase into a questionnaire that is administered to a much larger sample of respondents.

ADVERTISING AND THE HUMAN BRAIN

Throughout this book references were made to the three cornerstones which provide the foundation for our approach to human motivation: advertising, the human brain, and empirical (statistical) methods.

Graduate students in psychology and marketing find out how important it is, when writing a dissertation, to achieve statistical significance. But we have often been asked, with regard to Silent Side research, why it is so important to identify brain structures when dealing with human motivation. The answer that we give is that our final goal here is to understand the processes that a consumer goes through when they interact with a piece of merchandise. Wolfe (personal conversation, 1999) has reduced this to two processes: I-values and worldview. An I-value is what he says is the most powerful influence in consumer behavior. He quotes David Ogilvy as saying, "Consumers buy products that project images of who they want to be, not who they are." In our terminology, the I-values are seen particularly in the Orientation to Person Motive. The second major determinant, according to Wolfe, is the consumer worldview. The worldview is the connection between the subjective self (orientation to person) and the objective self, which is self in the external or outside world. All that we have done in our approach is go one step beyond the subjective self and examine what goes on in the brain at the time that this subjective–objective connection is being made. We have done this in order to add more understanding to the whole process. Wolfe has demonstrated that worldview changes as people go through various stages in their lives, from adolescence to old age, and how this effects their buying habits.

In this book we have relied upon sources which show that certain parts of the human brain are intimately related to the various motives that have been defined. Just as measurement helps to make these motives more tangible, the fact that these motives are related to brain structures also makes them more tangible, concrete, and corporeal. If those brain structures are destroyed through accident, injury, or tumor compression, the whole or part of the pattern of human motivation may change. We have advanced the idea that the whole "science" of marketing rests upon the foundation of helping people to process their lives. Our interest in neuroanatomy and brain structures is simply because these structures are intimately involved in this processing.

The other part of the tripod that we have relied upon is advertising. This is because those who have worked in advertising and in marketing in the past have had an intuitive understanding of motives and motivation. They designed advertising and marketing campaigns that caught the attention of millions and did what they intended to do, and that is to sell products. In other words, advertising as an industry has brought about results, and results are what everyone is looking for in any field of endeavor. The marketplace, like the sea or like nature, is unforgiving, and when the cash register rings against untold odds, the results are most impressive.

CONCLUSION

What is amazing about the field of advertising is that results have been achieved without a paradigm or framework. Motigraphics offers a paradigm that allows us to measure things that have never been measured before.

It is believed that it won't be long before Motigraphics will take its rightful and legitimate place alongside demographics and psychographics. Both demographics and psychographics measure how the consumer responds to the worldview, or to the environment that he or she lives in, works in, and shops in. Motigraphics looks at a more powerful and important aspect of consumer behavior, and that is the customer's method of processing, assimilating, and adapting to the material that is provided by the marketer. Briefly, we need to know how our customers control their world. Even more briefly and concisely, we are what we buy.

REFERENCES

Jensen, A. R. (1969). How much can we boost IQ and scholastic achievement? *Harvard Educational Review, 39,* 1–123.

Nash, J. M. (1997, February 3). Fertile minds. *Time,* pp. 48–56.

Soper, B., Milford, G. E., & Rosenthal, G. (1995, September). Belief when evidence does not support the theory. *Psychology and Marketing,* pp. 415–22.

Appendix: Motivation Is the Missing Link

One thing I know—all of life's problems will not be solved by designer drugs or liposuction. No, sir. No matter how many new and improved liquid soaps or antacid pills they develop, life will always be filled with its booby traps, torments and nuisances. Seven hundred years ago, during a locust plague, I coined the phrase "Shit happens," and it stuck because it's true. Mothers always call at the wrong time. You can't eat a jelly donut without your hands getting sticky. And there will always be a jerk who doesn't move far enough into the intersection before making a left-hand turn. These are the annoying facts of life.
—Carl Reiner and Mel Brooks (1997)

WHY WE NEED TO KNOW WHY PEOPLE DO WHAT THEY DO

The goal of any scientific pursuit is prediction. When we know why people do what they do we will be able to predict their behavior in the future. In other words, when we know what motivates them we can make future predictions. After writing and releasing *Marketing to the Mind* (1996), it was quite clear that we had not really written a book on marketing but instead a book on motivation. We focused on marketing and advertising because marketing and advertising professionals seem to know more about motivation and why people do what they do than anyone else.

In this Appendix we will look at several applications of the motivational approach that we have advanced to other areas which rely heavily upon a knowledge of motivation. One of these fields is law enforcement, and the other is management with a focus on leadership. We will also review some contributions that this theory makes to teaching and the field of education.

THE ORIGINS AND CAUSES OF HUMAN BEHAVIOR—
GOOD AND BAD

It was stated in Chapter 12, where we reviewed the Expectation/ Resolution Motive, that we agree with Kohn (1993) that most of the control over human behavior comes not from rewards, gold stars, or bribes. For us, all human behavior originates with subliminal cues. It is in this way, among others, that human behavior is quite different from the behavior of animals, although there are some similarities. In order to give some support to this observation, we need to look not at everyday human behavior but rather at some extremes in human behavior. It is only when we look at extremes that we learn about the ordinary and the commonplace.

IMPLICATIONS FOR LAW ENFORCEMENT

Kelleher (1998) and Kelleher and Kelleher (1998) have written extensively on two extremes of human behavior: the child who kills and the female serial killer. On females who kill, the Kellehers have done extensive research on almost 100 female serial killers in the twentieth century. More than half of the crimes committed by these women were committed in America. They are a very strange breed, and because females are treated quite differently in our judicial system than males, many of these women are unknown to the general public. They have not been seen on television and have not had books written about them. Until the execution of Carla Fay Tucker on February 3, 1998, there was not much publicity or coverage of women who kill.

From my own clinical experience, I can agree with the Kellehers that most of the women who do have homicidal impulses are motivated to kill their own children, and what is called Sudden Infant Death Syndrome (SIDS) may often be a mistaken diagnosis for what is actually homicide. But the question is—and it is a question that is not answered by the Kellehers—why do women kill? Why do children kill? Or, for that matter, why does anyone kill?

Kelleher and Kelleher (1998) comment on motive in one reference in their book. On page xi in their Introduction, they indicate that the majority of male killers are motivated sexual predators, whereas female killers are rarely motivated by sex. They then go on in each capsule summary to describe the motive, method, active period, victims, and eventual disposition of each case. However, the motives that are described are cursory and descriptive, and not explanatory. Some of the motives given for women killers include money (insurance proceeds, robbery, extortion, etc.), sex, insanity, or Munchausen Syndrome by Proxy (MSBP). But again, these are really not explanations, they are descriptions. There are many women who are in dire need of money to support their families, especially if they are in the position of being a single parent. However, they don't kill to get the money. Similarly, there are many who need money badly but it would never occur to them to rob, burglarize, or plunder to get it.

MSBP is another matter. Munchausen Syndrome, discovered in 1951, is a psychiatric problem in which a woman inflicts injury or injuries upon herself so that she can demand and get the attention of medical professionals (doctors, nurses, etc.). Usually these injuries are extensive and create a medical emergency, excitement, and the need to be seen immediately. On the other hand, MSBP was not discovered until 1977, when an English pediatrician recognized the condition. In MSBP, the woman ascribes the pain and injury to her child or some other dependent person in her care and not to herself. She does this in order to get the same kind of attention and recognition that she would get if she herself were in pain. But the simple question here is, "What would cause MSBP or Munchausen Syndrome in the first place?" That brings us back to the question of why women kill.

Our response is that this behavior lies in subliminal cues as we discussed them in Chapter 3. As we saw in Chapter 15, subliminal cues are folded into motives, motives cause decisions to be made, and decisions create action. So subliminal cues, regardless of how old they are, create motives. If it works statistically, it probably works the same way mentally.

Susan Smith may be used here as an example. On July 28, 1998, she was sentenced to life in prison at the Union County Courthouse in Union, South Carolina after she left both of her children strapped into her car and pushed the car down a boat ramp into a small lake. The ostensible motive was a Dear John letter from her boyfriend. The question that we need to address is, "What made her situation unique and different?" If we can't find an answer in her present situation, then perhaps we should go to the past.

Allegedly Susan Smith was sexually molested by a stepfather. We really don't know if this is true, except for the fact that she seriously considered getting in the car with the children and driving it into the lake. When suicide is a real issue, as it was in this case, there is almost always incest or some form of sexual invasion or event in the past. And if this is the case, and if the sexual insult occurred before the age of reason (eight or nine years old), the little girl will almost always give herself the subliminal cue, "It's all my fault." She is totally incapable of seeing beyond this, and although this cue will become subliminal and not remembered consciously, she will continually blame herself for the incestuous event, even if she cannot remember the event itself. The result is what we refer to as guilt.

Women who have been through this and who have blamed themselves will often consider killing themselves or killing their children. Suicide is an escape hatch, but killing their child or children is a response to another subliminal cue; that is, "Because of what I did, I don't deserve to have these beautiful and precious children." It was this subliminal cue that eventually caused Susan Smith to push her children into the lake and drown them. We know this from our research on motives.

This is not intended to be a defense of Susan Smith, and is certainly not intended to say that she was psychotic, insane, or not in her right mind when she committed this act. The whole purpose of this discussion is to show the difference in Susan Smith (not covered in the Kellehers' book) and other women who are single, raising children, and who have received Dear John letters from their lovers but don't take such drastic measures. Very few women would even consider doing what Susan Smith did, but then thankfully most women were not violated sexually when they were young and don't feel overwhelming guilt every time they look into the eyes of their own children.

CHILDREN WHO KILL

In Kelleher's (1998) book on children who kill, the actual motives are also not clear. In Chapter 3 we showed that subliminal cues were delivered two ways; either by the self or by others. We also said that the subliminal cues were either delivered on a one-time basis under conditions of trauma, when there is a rush of adrenaline, or on a repetitive basis, when the same message is delivered over and over again, as often seen in advertising.

Children who have engineered massacres and slaughters of their teachers and classmates at schools in the last few years do not fit the typical picture of juvenile delinquents. They are middle class. For the most part they do not have juvenile arrest records. They do not come from single-parent homes. They have advantages at home that poorer children don't have, such as computers and video games. But like Susan Smith, they are different from children who don't kill, and that difference is seen in motivation. Also, just as Susan Smith was probably exposed to unwanted sexual invasion and molesting, these children have been exposed to guns—often as a methodology for settling disputes. They are also loners (not necessarily troublemakers) and are virtually ignored by their classmates, teachers, and peers, since in most schools it is the troublemakers who get the attention. Hence, they are isolated. In this area—isolation—they share a characteristic that has been seen in most of the shooters at the post office and in other office killings: isolation and disregard by peers and coworkers. Isolation is often used by management to force an unwanted worker into resignation, but as a management technique it can easily backfire and have dire consequences. In schools, students who are isolated from others because they are "different" are often found to be the ones that kill other children and teachers.

The Role of Subliminal Cues in School Shootings

The key to the mixture of environmental events described is the video game. Not any video game, but one in which the operator becomes the shooter. As a child who is isolated goes home from school each day and brings up a game on his computer, he or she is often peering over the end of a rifle and gets points for everyone that he or she shoots. Check out a video game called *Postal*, at http://www.gopostal.com. In this game, which has a disclaimer which states that it is not recommended for children, the shooter guns down fellow employees in the post office (and there are other games like this one). As the player guns them down, he or she repetitiously puts the cue into his or her unconscious mind, "Shoot, Shoot, Shoot, Shoot, Shoot." This is the second method of subliminal cue delivery that we discussed in Chapter 3: repetition. We believe that the same principles discussed in Chapter 3 would hold true in Susan Smith's case, or any case where there is violent and abnormal behavior.

One thing that is noteworthy is that some of the school shootings have been set up to mimic or emulate video games. In Jonesboro, Arkansas, the shooters arranged the scene so that they stood above a sweeping landscape where the victims stood after filing out of the classrooms in response to a false fire alarm. As the students and their teachers spread out across the landscape awaiting the "all clear," the shooters aimed down into the crowd, spraying bullets in random directions.

We know through our research with video games that for most children, video games are just what they were made to be: games.

However, any child that sits in front of a video game like *Postal* where the subliminal auto-cue is "shoot to kill," which is delivered on a repetitive basis to the unconscious mind, is a potential killer. This is because of the strength of subliminal cues and their forceful role in originating, directing, and controlling motives, and the subsequent Herculean control that motives have over behavior.

Obviously, not all children who play the shooter in video games are at risk. There are other factors. Some of these factors, such as experiencing guns as a family method of dealing with anger and resolving disputes, are essential also. For some families, guns are sacred and the whole issue of guns and firearms is a spiritual survival issue, having been elevated to this level because of the passion that is often involved in gun ownership and in shooting.

If law enforcement officials and agencies would factor subliminal cues—self-delivered and delivered by others—into their equations, it would take a lot of the guesswork out of locating and profiling potentially dangerous people and getting them into court or to jail more quickly. It also would help in defining a criminal profile and identifying people who are potentially dangerous, such as the people that the Kellehers (1998) have written about in their book. We don't know everything about subliminal cues and how they work, but we do know that they arise from the unconscious mind, and not from the conscious mind. This being the case, it would help to explain how one writer summed up the reaction of two of the young shooters as they sat in the courtroom and faced the judge: "They seemed mystified by their deeds" ("Reading, Writing, and Marksmanship," 1998).

Everyone has subliminal cues. In Chapter 12 we saw that children who have been exposed to fairy tales receive subliminal cues that tell them that things will work out. Fairy tales deliver the subliminal cue that no matter how bad the situation seems, rescue and deliverance is not that far away. This is a vital part of the Expectation/Resolution Motive. Furthermore, children who are exposed to fairy tales are told that "everyone lives happily ever after." This is perhaps the most powerful and effective subliminal cue that can ever be delivered to a child. But, of course, not all children have the advantage of having fairy tales read to them. The ones who don't are the children who end up being at great risk. We have seen this in our research.

All motives are positive. When a mother kills her baby or a gunman holds up a bank, they both believe at the time that they are taking a positive action, for one reason or another. All motives are positive, because the right hemisphere does not have an equivalent of the word "no" and does not "think" in negatives (Ornstein,

1997). This is because logical operations are assigned to the left hemisphere and not to the right and in order for there to be a negative there must be logic.

Another example of how we believe these subliminal cues work is in the supposedly benign subliminal cues associated with Santa Claus. Children learn, from the time they are very young, that at Christmas time a jolly old man with elves and reindeer comes to their home and leaves them anything that they wish for, free of charge with no obligation. No payback. No debt. Is it any wonder, then, that many grow up with an apathetic and indifferent attitude toward their jobs? They believe that they will be discovered and made famous, that they will strike it rich at the slots, or that other events will occur, as seen in Chapter 12, consistent with the 99–10–10–99 reversal theory. Is it possible that Santa Claus, through the covert and evasive work of subliminal cues, could be undermining the workforce (Maddock & Fulton, 1995)?

IMPLICATIONS FOR LEADERSHIP AND MANAGEMENT

We have authored a book (Maddock & Fulton, 1998) on management which addresses the problem of leadership in management situations and what leadership really is. We presented this book as unique, since it stated that leadership is motivation, but our editor said that this has been said many times in many different ways. But when he was reminded that leadership had been defined in many different ways but no one had defined motivation, he agreed that the book might indeed be unique. Therefore, this book takes this same approach to motivation, which has evolved out of the neurosciences and out of marketing and advertising and integrates it into a wholistic approach to leadership. No one would disagree that leaders must be motivators. On the other hand, no one has ever been exposed to a single and unitary approach to motivation.

How is motivation, as it has been defined here, applied to leadership and management? We have already seen, in Chapter 12, that the major elements that have worked in other approaches to leadership are explained by the motives and elements that have been defined by us: witness significance, membership, lawful order, and others.

The same method of Motigraphics that was detailed in Chapter 15 has been used with employees in banks, industrial organizations, and one insurance company. Twenty-five employees in the home office were interviewed using the interview procedures that were described in Chapter 15. These interviews were confined to small groups of randomly selected employees from several different departments. Silent Side research methods were applied and

234 subliminal cues were identified. The principles of Motigraphics were applied and the subliminal cues were normalized. The results of Motigraphics were then used to create a seventy-five item questionnaire that was administered to all company employees at all levels. The results consisted of a complete motivational analysis of the entire company, and these results were then used to install some major changes in personnel operations and in corporate operations. This made the workplace more worker friendly and worker compatible. Some of these changes were long overdue, and follow-up research has indicated that substantial gains have been made as a result. The results of this combined process yielded information that was much different than that seen on typical employee surveys that are done in organizations. This is because right-brain information was included for the first time in the organization's history.

This combination of small-group in-depth research followed up with motivational surveys of the whole workplace is one more example of how Motigraphics can be used in tandem with other procedures and the whole motivational structure of the entire workforce can be evaluated. It also shows how motivational research can be applied in management and leadership situations, now that motivation has been adequately defined.

MOTIVATION AND LEADERSHIP IN EDUCATION AND IN SCHOOLS

Motivation is a key issue in schools as well as in management and in marketing. One of the key issues in schools today is the management of the child who has been diagnosed with attention deficit disorder and who, as a result, is disruptive to the class and interferes with the learning process in the classroom. At a meeting of officials from the National Institutes of Mental Health and the Department of Education in February 1998, which lasted for three days, no consensus was reached on what an attention deficit disorder really was, what the symptoms were, and how to treat it effectively. This may be another example of where motivation, as it has been defined here, would make a considerable difference.

A visit to a website dedicated to ADHD indicates that there is a lot of confusion about what ADHD is and where it comes from (etiology). One Internet article said that ADHD is a "fake disease" and is nothing but an excuse for poor leadership. Another said that it is genetic. Still others said that medication was the answer and others stated that it was not the answer. Psychologists say that much of ADHD is a behavior problem and that it should be treated with behavior modification, but in most places where this has been tried it has failed. The only thing that works at this point is medication, but many parents resist having their children on medication and many children (and parents) are noncompliant when the medication is administered.

My own experience with children diagnosed with ADHD is fairly extensive, and each time I encounter one it appears to me that the most salient characteristic in that child is disorientation. Many of them are playful and will come to the office smiling and indicating that they are ready for another round of play. When they are told that there is some work to be done they are somewhat disappointed and often will revert to their old tricks to get out of whatever work is required of them.

It has occurred to me that if ADHD is a form of disorientation, then perhaps the way to treat it is with reorientation. I have had success in the past treating multiple personality disorders with a flashlight; so much success, in fact, that I kept a flashlight and spare batteries in my desk at all times. A multiple personality disorder, where a person shades off into other "personalities" who often have names and separate identities, is just another form of disorientation. While in that state they are disoriented to time, place, person, and so on. Any time a multiple personality in my office began to "shade" into a different person—which is just another way of disorienting—I would simply shine the flashlight in their eyes and reorient them back to where we were and what we were doing. In this case, medication—along with the flashlight if all else failed—was an effective treatment (but not a cure) for multiple personality disorder.

We have, in Chapter 8 and throughout this book, presented disorientation as a motive. It is possible that children who are diagnosed with ADHD may simply be wanting to check out and disconnect, since learning in general is boring and repetitious. And if disorientation is the problem in attention deficit disorder, would that not explain the propensity and disposition of children diagnosed with ADHD to not be able to concentrate more than ten minutes on a math or reading lesson but, conversely, to be able to concentrate for three hours on Nintendo? This is true of every ADHD child that I have ever seen who has a Nintendo, which most of them do. This is paradoxical and hard to explain by anything other than the motive to disorient or disconnect that has been presented in this book.

We all want to check out and disconnect. Birds do it twice a year. Bears go into hibernation. People go on vacation. Kids have recess. Even the dedicated workaholic takes a "brain break" every now and then and disconnects from his or her work—but not for long.

Could it be that ADHD is a "fake disease" and is merely a way for some stubborn children to do what we all want to do—disconnect?

THE LATERAL AND VERTICAL FIX

Several applications for Silent Side research and Motigraphics have been suggested, and some of these suggestions have already been applied. Those who are interested in education, in leadership, in management, and in law enforcement need to know more about motives and motivation, and need to be able to act on this information when they get it.

We have shown that effective counseling can be carried out in management situations by using the building blocks of human motivation as a template. We believe that the blocks in their present format and as presented in Figure 10.1 describe the ideal hierarchical sequence for motives in terms of the order of importance of things. That is, personal orientation is the most important motive and seldom ever changes position. Spiritual survival is next, then physical survival, adaptation, and on down to the bottom, where we have the least important motives. These blocks can be easily transposed from the ideal order, and it appears that when they are transposed trouble develops within the organization. The "organization" may refer to the workplace or it may refer to the family and the home. The example used in Chapter 10 was when the Sexual Survival Motive (impulse) was transposed with the Spiritual Survival Motive (Oval Office/sacred place). To fix this situation, the blocks had to be put back in their appropriate position.

The lateral fix is required when an individual gets too far out on any one of the respective blocks, either to the right or to the left. A person who was too far out on the right side of the spiritual survival block would be passionate about everything; too far out on the left side would mean passionate about nothing. The example that comes to mind here is that if you are sad and depressed all the time your relatives might take you to a mental hospital for treatment, but if you are happy and laughing all the time they might also take you to a mental hospital. The best place to be is in the middle, and when this doesn't work, counseling can shift the balance. Those who do the counseling are the leaders, and the best thing about the whole arrangement is that in doing this counseling they are not only salvaging a member of the organization but are also training a future leader.

Leadership is motivation, and motivation is leadership. A sane and emotional approach to motivation, such as the one presented here, opens up new doors for organizations, schools, police and law enforcement organizations, and groups of all kinds. Leadership is motivation, and now we know what motivation is all about.

REFERENCES

Brooks, M., & Reiner, C. (1997). *The 2000 year old man in the year 2000.* New York: HarperCollins.

Kelleher, M. D. (1998). *Why good kids kill.* Westport, CT: Praeger.

Kelleher, M. D., & Kelleher, C. L. (1998). *Murder most rare: The female serial killer.* Westport, CT: Praeger.

Kohn, A. (1993). *Punished by rewards.* Boston: Houghton Mifflin.

Maddock, R. C., & Fulton, R. L. (1995). Has Santa Claus really sabotaged the workforce? Unpublished manuscript.

Maddock, R. C., & Fulton, R. L. (1996). *Marketing to the mind: Right brain strategies in advertising and marketing.* Westport, CT: Quorum Books.

Maddock, R. C., & Fulton, R. L. (1998). *Motivation, emotions and leadership: The silent side of management.* Westport, CT: Quorum Books.

Ornstein, R. (1997). *The right mind: Making sense of the hemispheres.* Orlando, FL: Harcourt Brace.

Reading, writing and marksmanship. (1998, December 28). *U.S. News and World Report*, pp. 85–86.

Name Index

Abra, J., 4, 26, 30
Adaval, R., 143
Allen, Woody, 23, 82–83, 216, 230
Archimedes, 89
Aristotle, 89
Ashforth, B., 14–15, 19, 52, 191–192
Astin, J. A., 25, 98

Bass, Bernard, 25, 56, 98, 145
Battie, William, 91–92
Beckwith, H., 146
Bennett, Bill, 132–134, 187, 236
Bettleheim, B., 39–41, 195
Blair, M. H., 78
Blakeslee, S., 121, 140, 146–147
Boldt, D., 61
Bornstein, R. F., 4, 31
Boswell, T., 33
Bratton, William, 90
Broca, Paul, 47
Brooks, Mel, 281
Brown, A., 33
Bryan, W. J., 164
Burnett, Leo, 92–93, 95
Bush, George, 216, 229, 231

Butler, S., 160

Carstensen, L. L., 25, 130
Charles, S. T., 25, 130
Chidester, D., 33, 154
Chomsky, Noam, 26–27, 53, 143
Cipielewski, J., 227
Clinton, Bill, 69, 159–161, 170, 194, 216, 221–222, 230, 262, 269
Crain, D., 56
Crawford, Cindy, 167

Dalrymple, H., 92–93
Damasio, A. R., 44, 54, 116–117, 186
Darwin, 31, 58, 118, 274, 276
Deese, J., 26
Dichter, Ernst, 151

Einstein, Albert, 54, 78–79, 81–82, 95
Epstein, S., 31–32, 118–119

Farrell, W., 150–153
Feig, B., 96, 99, 227, 256
Ferguson, Sarah, 179

Festinger, L., 114, 184
Fialka, J., 2
Field, Syd, 43, 86–88
Fleischman, Paul, 88, 110–112,
    141, 143–145, 183, 191, 247, 253
Ford, Henry, 128, 230
Freud, Sigmund, 4, 19, 31, 45, 78,
    91, 160, 208, 273–276
Friedman, A. M., 116
Fromm, Ericka, 78
Fulton, Richard, 4, 19, 42, 57, 77,
    145, 173, 202, 214, 221, 287

Gage, Phineas, 116–117, 186, 280
Garganus, A., 88
Giuliani, Rudolph, 90
Goodman, J., 116
Goodrum, C., 92–93
Greene, "Mean" Joe, 96
Grisham, John, 88

Havercamp, S., 16
Hickey, Lynn, 135
Hinckley, John, 43
Horowitz, J., 90
Hull, C. L., 114
Humphrey, Ronald, 14, 52, 191–
    192

Iacocca, Lee, 144
Ibrahim, Anwar, 160
Inhelder, B., 194
Isaacowitz, D. M., 25, 130

Jacobsen, L., 114
Jagger, Mick, 121
Joffe, Constantin, 93
Johnson, Andrew, 159
Jordan, Michael, 94, 179–180
Jung, Carl, 19, 208

Kahn, W. A., 14
Kelleher, C. L. 282, 284, 286
Kelleher, M. D., 282, 284, 286
Kelly, G. A., 114, 184
Kelvin, Lord Baron, 96, 239
Kennedy, John F., 43, 159, 216,
    230

Kessler, B., 170
King, Martin Luther, 159
Kohlberg, L., 30, 42
Kohn, A., 3, 27, 34, 47, 282
Kuhn, Thomas, 58, 78, 88–89, 95,
    274
Kuriansky, I., 158

lang, k. d., 179
Lear, Norman, 11
LeDoux, J. E., 30–32, 43–44, 47,
    52, 62, 89, 119
Lee, R. T., 52
Lewin, K., 114, 184
Lewinsky, Monica, 216, 222, 230,
    232

MacLean, P. D., 12, 82, 107, 113,
    148, 185, 197, 199–201
Maddock, Richard, 4, 19, 42, 57,
    77, 145, 173, 202, 214, 221, 287
Malmo, John, 129, 146
Maples, Jack, 90
Masling, J. M., 4, 31
Maslow, Abraham, 18–20, 24–25,
    28, 32, 55–56, 98, 104–105, 140,
    149, 171, 208
McClelland, D. C., 10, 31
McGaugh, J. L., 43–44
McKay, M. F., 227
Mesulam, Marcel, 121
Milford, G. E., 19, 24, 32, 276

Nash, J. M., 39, 169, 275
Neale, M. D., 227
Newell, Allen, 32
Nicklaus, Jack, 183
Nixon, Richard, 216, 229

O'Brien, T. L., 134, 187, 235, 264
O'Connor, Carrol, 11
Ogilvy, David, 95, 279
Oncken, W., 52
Ornstein, R., 51, 54, 75, 79, 83,
    147, 286

Packard, V. O., 171
Pennington, Bill, 132–134, 187

Persinger, Michael, 146
Piaget, J., 30, 42, 193–194, 273–274
Portner, J., 170
Presley, Elvis, 158–159, 161
Puckett, Steve, 77, 267

Ramachandran, V. S., 121, 140, 146–147, 185–186, 201
Reagan, Ronald, 43, 159, 167
Reiner, Carl, 281
Reiss, S., 16
Robbins, Tom, 197
Rockwell, Norman, 54
Rogers, C., 67
Romero, J., 144
Rosenberg, K., 78
Rosenthal, G., 19, 24, 32, 276
Rosenthal, Robert, 114
Rothman, M., 19
RuPaul, 179
Rush, Benjamin, 91–92
Russell, Bertrand, 197

Santrock, J., 30
Sarno, Jay, 132
Schwartz, C. E., 25, 98
Seagal, Steven, 193
Seltzer, B., 116
Sexton, R. O., 42

Shapiro, D. H., 25, 98
Shields, Brooke, 158
Shorter, E., 4, 91
Simpson, O. J., 69, 161, 193, 226
Skinner, B. F., 26, 34, 53, 208
Smith, Susan, 283–285
Soper, B., 19, 24, 32, 276
Stanovich, K. E., 227
Steel, Danielle, 88
Swartz, M., 175

Thomas, Cal, 194
Thomas, Dave, 143, 191
Tolman, E. C., 114
Tomlin, Lilly, 139

Van Kampen, K., 221
Vipond, D., 31, 58
Voltaire, 183
Vroom, V. H., 114, 184

Wallace, Mike, 98
Warwick, Dionne, 179
Wass, D., 52
Watson, T. J., 24–25, 89, 98
Williams, R. N., 25
Wolfe, David, 96
Wolfe, Jack, 55
Wyer, R. S., 143
Wynn, Steve, 134

Subject Index

Abercrombie and Fitch, 158
Absurdities, 56–57, 73–78, 82–83,
  85, 93–95, 99, 129, 160
Abuse, 27, 142, 171
Adaptation, 169, 173, 176, 206;
  Motive, 13, 65, 106, 119, 149,
  182
Adaptors, 168
Addiction, 149
Addy award, 85
Adolescents, 48, 125–126, 171–
  174, 269
Adrenaline, 38, 43, 284
Advertising, 12, 29–30, 56–59, 73–
  74, 78, 82, 85–86, 90, 92–95,
  144, 171, 178, 181, 222–223,
  253, 256, 266–267, 269, 279–
  281; emotional, 57; executives,
  23, 95, 113, 274
Affirming acceptance, 115, 144
Age, 42, 130, 171, 232
Airlines, 130, 216
Alley and Gargano, 74
"All in the Family," 11, 46
Alzheimer's, 116–117, 186
American Legion, 152

American Psychiatric Association,
  161
American Psychological Associa-
  tion (APA), 25, 31, 34, 58
American Psychologist, 33
Americans with Disabilities Act,
  272
Animals, 52, 56, 97, 113–114, 119,
  148, 150, 282
Anxiety, 81, 83, 103, 115, 160, 202
Arkansas, 105, 133, 285
Athletics, 131, 153–155, 171, 179,
  244. *See also* Sports
Atlantic City, 133
Attention, 56, 121–122, 222, 283
Attention deficit hyperactivity
  disorder (ADHD), 122–123, 209,
  288–290
Attorneys, 69, 125, 213, 226
Audi, 98
Auto-cues, 38, 41–42
Automobiles, 2, 6, 14, 17, 62, 128,
  135, 177–178, 233. *See also*
  Vehicles

Banking, 136, 186, 191–193, 268

Banks, 9, 61, 65, 83, 110, 133–136, 191–192, 243, 262, 268, 287
Barnes and Noble, 65
Baseball, 33, 154
Bear, North American black, 1–3, 6
Beer, 56, 244, 271; Budweiser, 57, 94; Piel's, 29
Behaviorism, 26–28, 89
Behavior modification, 3–4, 13, 33–34, 191, 288
Belonging, 33, 115, 145, 172, 174
Benefits, 110, 124, 242
Better Homes and Gardens, 88, 150
Bhagavad Gita, 96, 143
Bible, 33, 40, 107, 117, 195
Bob and Ray, 29
Boy's Life, 152–153
"The Brady Bunch," 177
Brain damage, 118
Brand equity, 18, 96, 227, 242, 244, 256, 269
Bridgeport, Connecticut, 135
Building blocks of human motivation, 5–6, 13, 17, 29, 104–107, 109–113, 118, 127, 141–142, 149, 154, 156, 167, 197–200, 205–209, 290
Burberry, 175
Burger King, 146

Caesar's, 144
Calling, sense of, 110, 115, 144
Calvin Klein, 158–159, 162, 180–181
Career, 108, 115, 133, 155–156, 232
Casinos, 28, 131–134, 144, 187–189, 200, 234, 264–266, 271
Challenger spacecraft, 43
Chicago Bulls, 154, 180
Children, 39–42, 53, 153–154, 168–171, 193–195, 274–275, 282–286, 289
Chinatown, 176
Chris-Craft, 227–228, 242, 256
Chrysler, 10, 144, 212
Church, 33, 145, 176, 192; leaders, 37; Pentecostal, 147

Cigarettes, 19, 27, 92–93, 148–149, 164, 207
Cinderella, 40–41
Circumstantial Orientation Motive, 115, 123, 134–135
Circus Circus Casino, 132–133, 264
Civil Rights Law, 45
Clark University, 91
Clio award, 85, 212
Closed captions, 272
Clothes, 63, 125–127, 152, 163, 170, 174, 179, 198, 252–253
Cluster analysis, 5, 13, 250, 255
Coaches, 154, 221
Coca-Cola, 74, 96, 99
Cognitive–Experiential Self Theory (CEST), 31, 118–119
The [Memphis] *Commercial Appeal*, 133
Computers, 56–57, 129, 218, 268
Conflict, 40, 55, 80–82, 86, 160, 195
Construction, 151, 268
Convenience, 9, 61, 115, 130, 135, 191, 205, 254
Cooking, 14, 169, 198, 214
Cosmetics, 126–127, 152, 178–179, 250
Cosmopolitan, 152
Creativity, 56, 58, 79, 81, 86, 115, 198, 201
Crime, 90, 141–142, 170
Criminology, 27, 89–90
C-Span, 193
Cummins Engine Company, 77

Dallas Cowboys, 154
DeBeers, 57
Decade of the brain, 12, 91
Demographics, 5–6, 9, 215, 280
Dentists, 9, 181, 189
Depression, 42, 103, 127, 251
Detergents, 41–42, 222–223
Direction, in right brain research, 211, 218, 226–228
Disorientation, 28, 117–118, 128–129, 131–134, 136, 187–188, 268, 289
Displacement, vertical, 149

Doctor, 54, 109, 181, 190, 266
Dodge, 46, 135, 269
Doorknobs, dish-type, 151
Doors, marketing of, 151, 223–225, 268
Dow Jones, 156
Dreams, 96, 140, 275–276

Easter Bunny, 39
Eastman Corporation, 191
Education, 28, 30, 52, 150, 263, 288, 290; graduate, 3, 24; special, 155
Educators, 3, 19, 23–24, 27, 33, 62, 89, 114, 221, 262, 285, 289
Ego, 45
Elements, 115; of circumstantial orientation, 135, 217; of expectation, 190–192, 217, 262, 267; of personal orientation, 124, 217, 244; of physical survival, 113, 118, 140–141, 148, 217; of sexual survival, 114, 118, 140–141, 157, 160–163, 217; of spiritual survival, 80, 110–112, 141–146, 193, 217, 246, 253, 266; of territorial survival, 119, 156, 217; of time orientation, 275
Emergency medical technician (EMT), 42, 189–190
Emotion, 14–20, 52, 57, 62–63, 95–99, 191–192, 227–228, 239, 242–244, 253–256, 270
Empire State Building, 38
Empirical methods, 112, 146
Empty-nesters, 261
Endorsements, 94, 119, 179, 181
Entertainment, 10, 45, 129, 193
Epileptic seizures, 147
Escape, 115, 129, 265
Ethical Standards of Psychologists, 33
Expectation, 114, 183–184, 199, 265; Motive, 115, 185–193, 230–232, 271

Factor analysis, 109–112, 118–119, 143–145

Fairy tales, 39–41, 96, 195, 286
Family Circle, 88, 150
Family values, 80, 110–111, 115, 146, 171, 246–247, 253, 266
Fashion, 127, 134, 152, 163, 170, 178, 247, 249–250, 252–253
Features, 56, 59, 96, 110, 124, 241–242, 261
Federal Aviation Administration (FAA), 241
Federal Communication Commission (FCC), 10, 181, 266
Federal Express Corp., 74–77, 82, 85, 94, 97, 129, 191, 212, 231, 240–241
Females, 41, 92, 107, 115, 118, 150–153, 161–163, 178, 269; as killers, 282–284; magazines, 87–88, 250; research on, 169, 197–198, 214, 244; shopping, 126–127
Feminists, 41
Fetish, defined, 48
Field and Stream, 153
FileMaker Pro, 246
Focus groups, 61, 67–71, 212, 220–221, 232
Food, 115, 128, 130, 132, 148, 270
Forbes, 152, 153
Ford Motor Company, 2, 57, 227
Fragrances, 178, 270
Fraternity, 172, 175
Free will, 28–29, 186, 209
Frontal lobe, 52, 113, 116, 186
Future, 77, 115, 184–186, 230, 281

Gamblers, 134, 188, 200, 265
Gambling, 133–134, 187, 200
Gangs, 172, 175
Garage doors, 151
Gender, 40–41, 108, 157, 163, 232, 249
General Motors (GM), 227
Genetic inheritance, 39, 288
Glamour, 152
God, 117, 147
Gold Strike Casino, 264
Golf, 173–174, 197, 199–200
Graceland, 158–159

Grand Central Station, 135
Grandmother, 40, 42, 88, 124
Grand Teton National Park, 1–2
Greed, 119, 156, 217
Gucci, 175
Guilt, 160, 284
Guns, 109, 264, 285

Hairstyles, 126
Hallmark, 57, 99
Harley Davidson, 167, 177
Harvard University, 121
Hatteras Yachts, 228
Headstart, 274
Health care, 189–190, 261, 266–267
Hermes, 175
High rollers, 132
Hippies, 172–173, 177
Homicide, 142, 157, 161, 174, 282
Honda, 2, 231
Hospitals, 181, 189–190, 261, 266–267
Humanism, 25, 32
Humor, 52, 55, 74–75, 78–79, 82–83, 95, 201

IBM, 130, 174, 227
Identity, 82, 92, 96, 126–128, 170, 172, 200
Imitation, 48, 53, 115, 119, 168–169, 274
Impeachment, 92, 159–160
Impotence, 115, 157, 161–163
Impulse, 108, 114–115, 118, 157–163, 198, 217, 229–233, 249
Inhibition, 108, 114–115, 118, 140–141, 157, 161–163, 249
Inner peace, 111, 115, 144–146
Intercranial self-stimulation (ICSS), 147
Internet, 152–153, 157, 184, 288. *See also* World Wide Web
Interviews, one-on-one, 17, 67–68, 70, 210, 215, 257, 279
Iowa, 188
IQ, 51, 114, 274, 278

Jackson Hole, Wyoming, 1

Jeep, 177
Johnson administration crime report, 90
Johnson & Johnson, 98
Jokes, 55, 79–81
Jolly Green Giant, 92–93
Jonesboro, Arkansas, 285
Justifications, 62, 64, 219

Kaiser Family Foundation, 162
Kellogg, 130
Kentucky Wildcats, 154
Killers, 282
K-Mart, 65–66
Koran, 111, 143

Laddering, 222, 278
Language, 16, 26, 47, 51, 53–54, 173, 176
Las Vegas, 132–134, 264
Lateral fix, 290
Laughter, 81–83, 115, 160, 200–202
Law enforcement, 23–24, 26, 142, 209, 240, 243, 282, 286, 290
Lawful order, 110, 115, 144, 192–193, 248, 253, 287
Leaders, 37, 52, 67–70, 221
Leadership, 70, 145, 191, 221, 287–291
Left brain, 52, 55–58
Left hemisphere, 47, 51, 53–54, 75–76, 79–80, 121–122
Lifetime television, 88
Likert Scale, 241, 256–257, 277
Limbic system, 75–76, 201–202
Lincoln Town Car, 177
Little Italy, 176
Little Red Riding Hood, 40
Little Rock, Arkansas, 240–241
Long Beach, California, 170
Lottery, 107, 189
Love, 108, 111, 115, 141, 144, 164, 246
Low rollers, 132–134, 187, 188
Loyalty, 243–245, 253, 256, 277
Lynn Hickey Dodge, 135

Macintosh computers, 96

Magazines, 77, 87–88, 150–153, 247–250
Malaysia, 160
Malcolm Baldridge Award, 191
Male, 40, 46–47, 80, 87, 93, 108, 115, 118, 125–126, 150–153, 161–163, 180, 244, 282
Mammalian, 32, 197, 200
Managed care, 3–4, 26, 189–190, 266
Management, 24, 28, 135, 145, 212, 285, 287–288, 290; casino, 131–133, 264–265
Marine Corps, 96, 145
Marketers, 5–6, 9, 13, 18–19, 23, 29, 62, 74, 97–99, 127, 175, 209, 213, 240, 254
Marketing, 9, 19, 29, 62, 93, 96–97, 136, 146, 171, 181, 209, 214, 240, 253, 269, 278, 280–281
Marlboro, 48, 92–94, 96
McDonald's, 94, 146, 171
Meaningful death, 88, 111, 115, 144, 184
Measurement, 10, 52, 96, 239–240, 256, 277, 280
Medical model, 4–5
Medication, 4, 12, 42, 91, 288–289
Meditation, 147, 185
Membership, 110, 115, 144–145, 172, 174–175, 191–192, 287
Memory, 74–77, 124, 185
Memphis, Tennessee, 133, 154, 240
Men, 40, 46–47, 80, 87, 93, 108, 115, 118, 125–126, 150–153, 161–163, 180, 244, 282
Mental illness, 91
Mental state, 114, 123–124
Mental status test, 114, 116, 123
Michelin tires, 48, 57, 93–94, 159, 231
Minivan, 177–178, 212
Mirage Casino, 134
Mississippi River, 131, 133, 190
Mnemonic, 16, 25
Model-T Ford, 177
Mother, 40–42, 74, 88, 168, 285–286

Motigraphics, 5–6, 9–10, 15–17, 29, 63, 70, 83, 99, 156, 188, 206–208, 214–215, 227–228, 239–253, 264–271, 278–280, 288–290; Extended, 18, 211, 254–257, 279
Motivation, 6, 19, 24, 31, 52, 62, 92, 95–96, 104, 111, 113, 118–119, 207–209, 273, 279–281; consumer, 9, 99, 129–130, 243–244, 250; extrinsic, 47; intrinsic, 14–15, 27, 47, 100; leadership, 287–288, 290
Motivational profile, 208, 255, 288
Motives, 5–6, 10–13, 16–20, 96–99, 114–116, 133, 136, 158, 207–208, 215–217, 228, 243–247, 277
Motortrend, 153
MSNBC, 193
Munchausen Syndrome, 283
Muslim, 160

National Park Service, 1
NCAA, 154
Neonates, 168
Neural firing patterns, 44–45
Neurological research, 113, 119
Neurotransmitters, 12, 44, 91
New Balance shoes, 96
New Jersey, 10, 131
Newspaper research, 88, 183–184, 194, 226–227
New Testament, 143
New York City, 90, 135, 176
New Yorker, 175
New York Life Insurance, 83
New York Yankees, 154
NFL football, 125, 154
Nike, 48
Normalizing data, 10, 17, 250, 288
Notre Dame, 154
Nurses, 114, 267, 283
Nursing homes, 123–124
Nutri-Grain Bars, 130

Ohio, 124; River, 154
Oklahoma, 105
Old Faithful, 38
Old Testament, 111, 143

Olfactory functions, 52
Olympics, 155
Onan, 77, 82–83
Orientation, 116, 124, 127, 150, 152, 164, 246, 252; Motives, 15, 106, 113–114, 117, 121, 123, 136, 187
Orientation to Circumstances Motive, 115, 123, 134–135
Orientation to Person Motive, 106, 109–115, 125, 224, 265
Orientation to Place Motive, 106, 127, 217, 115
Orientation to Time Motive, 106, 115, 128, 217, 251, 275
Outboard Marine Corporation, 228

Pain, 27, 111, 115, 164, 181, 207, 283
Paradigms, 43, 85–96, 183, 274, 280
Passion, 32, 109, 111–112, 115, 118, 140–143, 154, 199–200, 207
Patriotism, 217, 246
Paxil, 12
Peace of mind, 112, 114, 234, 248, 253, 265
Peer pressure, 169–170
Peers, 33, 48, 95, 149, 170–173, 175, 178–179, 189, 285
Penthouse, 151–152
Pepperdine University, 263
Pepsi, 74, 99
Perception, 75, 121, 123, 130–131
Perks, 132–133, 265
Personalizations, 75–77, 85, 93–100
Person Orientation Motive, 106, 109–115, 125, 224, 265
Pessimism, 41, 109
Philadelphia Inquirer, 61, 131
Phillip Morris, 92
Physical Survival Motive, 20, 80, 106, 113–115, 118, 140, 143, 148–149, 164, 190, 217, 271
Physicians, 9, 28, 91, 114, 116, 148, 189–190, 217, 266–267
Pillsbury Doughboy, 92–94, 244

Place Orientation Motive, 106, 127, 217, 115
Playboy, 151–152
Play Motive, 13, 107, 115, 197–200
Plot points, 43–44, 86–88, 226
Politics, 12, 43, 207, 241
Pop-Tarts, 130
Pornographics, 152, 157, 162
Prayer, 107, 147, 266
Prefrontal lobe, 51–53, 185–186, 275
Procter & Gamble, 10
Product placement, 46, 269
Prozac, 4, 12, 91
Psychiatrists, 4, 24, 91, 114
Psychic, 26, 78, 82, 95, 271
Psychic Network, 179
Psychics, 24, 26, 30, 187, 240, 243, 271
Psychographics, 5–6, 9, 97, 215, 280
Psychologists, 4, 23–34, 62, 89, 213, 240, 273
Psychology, 6, 12, 14, 19, 23–26, 52, 54, 58, 62, 78, 92, 95, 98, 104, 114, 130–131, 142, 184, 206–207, 256, 263, 276–278; academic, 32, 44, 51, 207, 239–240, 279; behavioristic, 24, 28, 273; cognitive, 3–4, 20, 25, 30–31, 89, 119, 207, 273; humanistic, 25, 221
Psychotherapy, 3–4, 26, 30, 33, 67
Punch line, 79, 81
Punks, 172–175

Qualitative research, 10, 205–208, 215, 228, 246, 274–277
Quantitative research, 10, 58, 205–208, 215, 228, 246, 274, 277
Questioning, circular method, 69, 278
Questionnaire, 18, 61, 105, 112, 141, 205, 213, 255, 279, 288

Racism, 11, 45–46, 90
Railroads, 53, 116, 130, 135
Rationalizations, 62–64, 212
Razzie Awards, 193

Recall, 37–38, 78, 93
Refrigerators, 261–262
Regression, 223, 225, 232
Relaxation, 45, 211, 218–220, 225, 228, 270
Release, 78, 111, 115, 144
Religion, 32–33, 111–112, 143, 147, 176
Renewal, 111, 115, 144
Repetition, 43, 69, 221–222
Resistance, 15, 61–68, 218, 269
Resolution, 86–87, 184–190, 193–195, 198
Restaurants, 5, 79, 128, 262
Right brain, 55–59, 147, 211–215, 220, 226, 228
Right hemisphere, 47, 53–56, 75–76, 79, 121
Ritalin, 122
Rorschach ink blot, 58–59
"Roseanne," 46

Sacrifice, 111, 115, 144–145
Salespeople, 19, 65–66, 135, 146, 207, 240
Salt Lake City, 155
San Francisco, 76, 176–177
Santa Claus, 39, 287
Schizophrenic, 14, 55, 160
Science, 19, 24–26, 28–33, 58, 86, 89, 139
Scientists, 26, 34, 274
Screenplay, 86–87
SEC playoffs, 154
Segregation, 11
Self-control, 113–115, 117, 124, 212, 217, 248, 253
Senile dementia, 116–118, 123, 186
Seventeen, 152
Sewing, 198, 269
Sexual behavior, 140, 161, 172
Sexual dysfunction, 162
Sexual intercourse, 161–163
Sexuality, 118, 157, 160, 255
Sexual paraphilias, 161–162
Sexual survival, 118, 141, 201,

255; Motive, 80, 106, 115, 140, 157, 216–217, 229–232
Shoes, 40, 96, 170, 179, 244
Silent Side, 16, 103, 158, 206, 226, 273; interviewing, 232, 244, 256; research, 110, 113, 156, 261, 276
Sinbad, 40
Sitcoms, 11, 82, 125, 170
Smokey the bear, 94
Smoking, 19, 93, 107, 148–149, 164
Snow White, 41
Soccer, 153, 174, 178
Sociology, 89
Spirituality, 118
Spiritual Survival, 81–83, 111, 164, 199, 207, 246, 252–253, 261–262; Motive, 20, 80, 106, 109–110, 112–113, 115, 140–146, 154–155, 159–160, 192, 200, 217, 244, 290
Sports, 153–155, 179, 184, 193, 221. *See also* Athletics
Sports Illustrated, 152
Sprite, 178
Standard deviation, 18, 245, 251–252
Students, 24–25, 105, 114, 239–240, 263, 285
Subliminal cues, 10–11, 17–20, 37–47, 69–70, 214–228, 243–247, 282–288
Suburbs, 177, 197
Suicide, 19–20, 170, 283–284
Superbowl, 91, 106, 231
Supermarket, 68, 74, 127–128, 135–136, 192
Surprises, 70, 180, 213, 215, 219
Survival Motives, 13, 106, 118, 140, 163–164

Teachers, 3, 19, 27, 114, 122, 221, 285, 289
Teen, 152
Television, 10–11, 45–46, 73–75, 86–88, 92, 162, 270, 272
Temporal lobe, 113, 116, 147, 226
Tennessee, 105, 133
Tension, 78, 81–82, 95

Territorial Survival, 201; Motive,
80, 106–107, 115, 119, 140, 150–
156, 199, 229–232
Testimonials, 107, 115, 119, 167,
178–179, 181
Theme parks, 5, 14, 125, 134
Therapy, 25, 67; psycho, 3–4, 26,
30, 33; speech, 33
Thorazine, 4
Tickle Me Elmo, 171
Time, 179
Time Orientation Motive, 106,
115, 128, 217, 251, 275
Totes umbrellas, 84
Toyota Tercels, 2
Toys, 168–171, 227
Tracking, 244–245, 250, 253
Trauma, 38, 42, 103, 285
Trends, 10, 23, 127, 277
Triumph Spitfire, 233
Trust, 109, 115, 189–191, 217
T-scores, 17, 245, 251–252
Tunica County, Mississippi, 131,
133–134, 188, 264
Tylenol, 98

Unconscious, 16, 62, 81, 104, 161,
163, 206, 209, 239
Uniforms, school, 170, 173–174
Union, South Carolina, 283
University of Mississippi, 155
U.S. Army, 96
USA Today, 40, 130
U.S. Navy, 149

Vacations, 106, 117, 125, 128, 229,
264–265, 289

Vehicles, 42, 167, 177–178, 269.
See also Automobiles
Vermont, 116
Vertical fix, 149, 290
Viagra, 162
Video games, 284–286, 289
Vietnam, 103–104, 172
Visualization, 17, 68, 208, 218,
221, 225
Volkswagen, 177, 180
Vuitton, 175

Walgreens, 66
Walking zombies, 42
Wall Street Journal, 190, 266
Wal-Mart, 65–66
Weight Watchers, 179
Wendy's hamburgers, 143
West Memphis, Arkansas, 133
White House, 159, 201, 222, 262
Witness significance, 110, 114–
115, 143–145, 191, 266–267
Women, 41, 92, 107, 115, 118, 150–
153, 161–163, 178, 269; as killers,
282–284; magazines 87–88, 250;
research on, 169, 197–198, 214,
244; shopping, 126–127
Worldview, 115, 279–280
World Wide Web, 40, 97, 163, 288.
See also Internet

Xanax, 12, 91

Yellowstone National Park, 2, 38
Yosemite National Park, 2

z-scores, 250–251

ABOUT THE AUTHOR

Richard C. Maddock is a clinical and marketing psychologist, as well as an adjunct professor at Arkansas State University. He is founder of The Motigraphics Institute. Dr. Maddock is author of numerous articles in the professional and academic journals of his field and the coauthor of two previous Quorum books: *Marketing to the Mind: Right Brain Strategies for Advertising and Marketing* (1996, with Richard L. Fulton) and *Motivation, Emotions, and Leadership: The Silent Side of Management* (1998, with Richard L. Fulton).